# FROM THE CONGO TO SOWETO

## U.S. Foreign Policy Toward Africa Since 1960

### HENRY F. JACKSON

William Morrow and Company, Inc.

New York : 1982.

*This book is dedicated to my cousin Rebecca,*
*who has lived as a light in America,*
*and to Nelson Mandela,*
*who still suffers for the freedom of his country.*

Copyright © 1982 by Henry F. Jackson

Maps courtesy of the United Nations

Library of Congress Cataloging in Publication Data

Jackson, Henry F.
    From the Congo to Soweto.

    Includes bibliographical references and index.
    1. Africa—Foreign relations—United States.
2. United States—Foreign relations—Africa.
3. Africa—Foreign relations—1960–   . 4. United
States—Foreign relations—1945–   . I. Title.
DT38.7.J28      327.7306      81-16917
ISBN 0-688-00772-4          AACR2

Printed in the United States of America

First Edition .

1 2 3 4 5 6 7 8 9 10

# Acknowledgments

Because of their great number, it is not possible to thank all the individuals and institutions whose assistance was indispensable to my research and writing. I wish, however, to identify a few: Phil W. Petrie, who put me on the right publishing track in New York upon my arrival from the University of California, Berkeley; Professor Hollis R. Lynch of Columbia University, who was as generous with scholarly materials as with nurturing encouragement; Roger Morris, who sat with me two days in Santa Fe brainstorming on U.S. policy as he recollected it from his former service as an Africa specialist on the National Security Council; William N. Raiford of the Congressional Research Service, Library of Congress, who always responded promptly to my interminable requests for data; Monsieur Robert Cornevin of the Documentation Française (Paris), who helped to sharpen my perceptions of the Europeans' relations with Africa; Nosa-Ola Obaseki and Margaret Vogt of the Nigerian Institute of International Affairs (Lagos), who refined my interpretations of African states' responses to American policy; Professor John Waterbury of Princeton University, who queried my analysis of one chapter; Professor Herbert Weiss of Brooklyn College, who made sense of inchoate facts in another chapter; Professor Frank Roosevelt of Sarah Lawrence College, who provided timely advice and assistance; and Diane Goon and Laura Binkowski, reference librarians at Columbia's Lehman Library, who kindly countenanced my barrage of requests for sundry facts and tedious details. George Riley at Harvard University and James Dingeman, whose New York home is a library, proferred many useful sources. Jinx Roosevelt, with a grammarian's eye, scrutinized almost every page. Lester Chisholm trudged through snow and ice to deliver sections of the manuscript to Debbie McGee, who deciphered hieroglyphs of my handwriting and typed the text. The American Committee on Africa (New York) allowed me easy access to its files. I thank my editor, Robert Bender, for his intelligent probing of each chapter and his patience in waiting to receive it.

I do not forget the many individuals who enriched my research by consenting to interviews; their names are cited in the appropriate places in the notes. Nor do I omit my able research assistants, Michael A. Kamara, who worked with me on some of the early sections, and Paul D. Martin, who helped to speed my project to completion with dedication and long hours of hard work. To them is due the credit for much that is accurate and coherent in this study; any error or misinterpretation is attributable to me alone.

HENRY F. JACKSON

*New York City*
*August 27, 1981*

# Contents

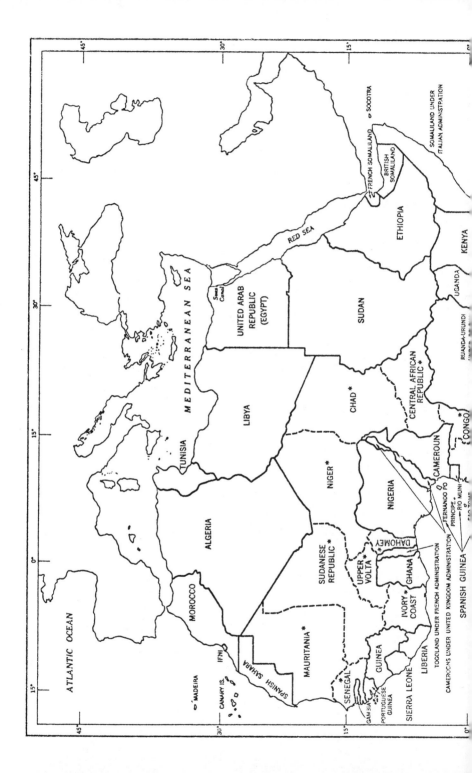

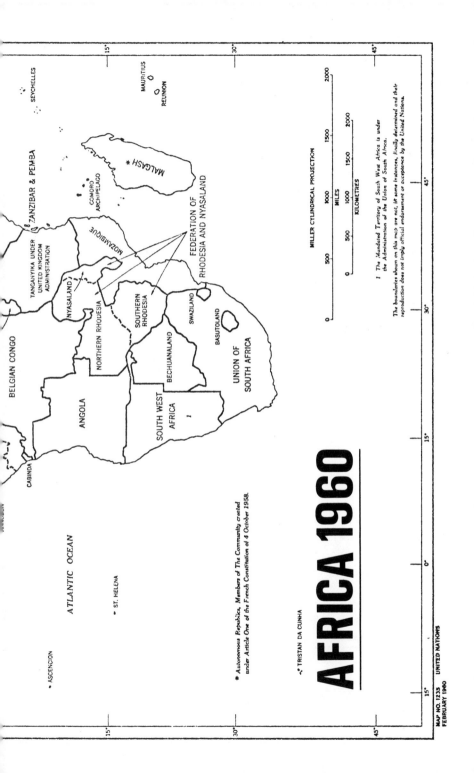

# AFRICA 1960

ATLANTIC OCEAN

BELGIAN CONGO

CABINDA

ANGOLA

SOUTH WEST AFRICA ¹

BECHUANALAND

UNION OF SOUTH AFRICA

BASUTOLAND

SWAZILAND

SOUTHERN RHODESIA

NORTHERN RHODESIA

NYASALAND

MOZAMBIQUE

FEDERATION OF RHODESIA AND NYASALAND

TANGANYIKA UNDER UNITED KINGDOM ADMINISTRATION

ZANZIBAR & PEMBA

COMORO ARCHIPELAGO

MALAGASH *

MAURITIUS

REUNION

SEYCHELLES

• ASCENCION

• ST. HELENA

-:° TRISTAN DA CUNHA

\* Autonomous Republics, Members of The Community created under Article One of the French Constitution of 4 October 1958.

MILLER CYLINDRICAL PROJECTION

MILES
0    500    1000    1500    2000

KILOMETRES
0    500    1000    1500    2000

1  The Mandated Territory of South West Africa is under the Administration of the Union of South Africa.

The boundaries shown on this map are not, in some instances, finally determined and their reproduction does not imply official endorsement or acceptance by the United Nations.

MAP NO. 1235   UNITED NATIONS
FEBRUARY 1960

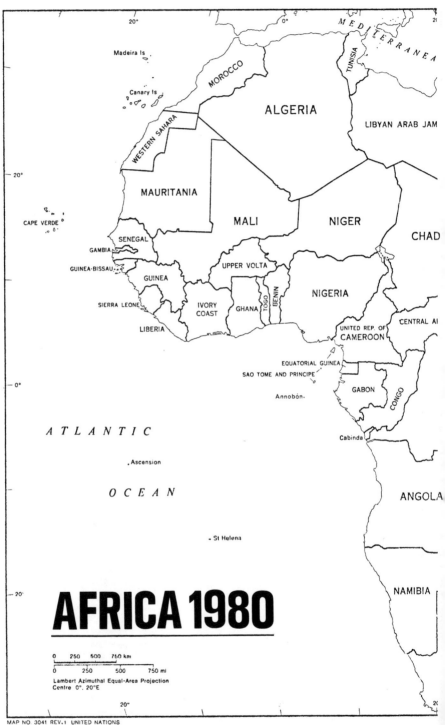

The boundaries and names on this map do not imply
official endorsement or acceptance by the United Nations.

# *List of Illustrations*

# Introduction

This work spans more than two decades of American policy toward Africa, from the end of the Eisenhower Administration to the beginning of the Reagan Administration. I have sought to clarify the economic, military, and strategic interests of the United States in contemporary Africa, and to propose reasonable options and prescriptions for change. The customary demarcation of Africa as north or south of the Sahara is not followed here; instead, my scope is continentwide. The analysis begins with the United States' emergence as a Great Power in Africa amidst civil war in the Congo and proceeds to the explosive racial situation in South Africa, where America now faces its most fateful challenge in Africa.

What is Africa and what makes it a legitimate priority of U.S. policy? Africa, now regarded as the birthplace of mankind, is a colossal continent more than three times the size of the United States. It has twice the number of inhabitants of America; for approximately 30 million Afro-Americans, Africa is the ancestral homeland. Africa's fifty independent nations represent nearly a third of United Nations membership. Africa possesses abundant natural resources, supplying major portions of U.S. oil imports and numerous nonfuel minerals indispensable to American industry. Furthermore, this vast and rich continent has emerged as a region of intense Soviet-American competition, with American strategic interests stretching from the Mediterranean Sea, where U.S. forces utilize African ports and military bases, to the Cape Coast at the southern tip of Africa, where maritime traffic passes from the Indian Ocean to the Atlantic on the way to the United States and Western Europe with cargoes crammed with commodities essential to the survival of the Western economies.

Until recently, however, the United States has typically approached Africa with singular indifference and neglect. No other continent has been so consistently ignored by our policymakers, and yet none but Europe has been so continually connected to important developments in America, from the founding of the Republic in the era of the Atlantic slave trade to the inauguration of training exercises for the new Rapid Deployment Force on African soil. The history of official lack of interest in Africa has produced widespread ignorance about the continent among Americans generally, including members of Congress, businesspeople, and even scholars, who in the past dismissed the so-called dark continent as of little or no consequence to American society.

A greater tragedy has occurred in the sphere of foreign policy, because American leaders noticed Africa only in the context of cold war competition with the Soviet Union. This approach began during the 1960s, when many African peoples sundered European colonial hegemony to rise as new and independent nations, and it subsumed the African continent under European nations of the old colonial network, such as Great Britain, France, and Portugal. African states were not recognized as autonomous societies with self-chosen goals and ambitions. Even Henry A. Kissinger, who as Secretary of State arose as the erudite pontiff of American diplomacy, failed to understand the formulation of African policy except as a reaction to Soviet activity on the continent. Anti-Sovietism, as opposed to creative and independent goals emanating from the general aspirations and ideals of the American people, thus came to dominate U.S. policy toward Africa. It has left the unfortunate but unavoidable impression in Africa that Americans are subordinate to the Soviets as actors in the shaping of contemporary international relations.

The long history of official American neglect of Africa is partly responsible for the tremendous dearth of studies on U.S. policy toward Africa—a void which this book seeks to fill. My analysis is written from the standpoint of the American policymaker and the concrete American interests in Africa which ought to shape our policies. Frequently I have searched for the origins of past policies in the primary institutions of foreign policy, the Presidency, the State Department, and the National Security Council. Ancillary institutions such as the Central Intelligence Agency have sometimes been discussed as well. By examining comprehensively American policy toward Africa, I hope to provide a service not only to Americans, but also to people beyond the shores of the United States who, for one reason or another, are interested in the contemporary role of the United States in Africa.

# 1

# THE CONGO:
# Emergence of the United
# States in Africa

John F. Kennedy disrupted the American tradition of dismissing
Africa as an appendage of colonial Europe by becoming the first
President to perceive the significance of formerly colonized societies
bursting upon the world stage as independent nations. It was not
simply that the White House had ignored Africa before Kennedy;
the Eisenhower Administration had hesitated even to designate a
separate ambassador to each of the African states reaching independence in 1960, especially the former French territories, where
Washington still deferred to France's sensibilities. The State
Department, vigilant in its attention to other areas of the world,
did not bother to create a Bureau of African Affairs until as late as
1958, and then relegated it to marginal operations. The White
House, moreover, was not alone in the American ignorance and
indifference concerning Africa; members of Congress, businessmen,
and scholars too generally viewed the so-called dark continent as a
region of little or no significance to American interests. Kennedy,
however, had a vision of Africa as a continent fraught with
intriguing possibilities in trade, defense, and ideological alignments, and it was not coincidental that he put this vision into
action during a time of war and turmoil in the Congo.

The new President acted promptly in naming U.S. ambassadors

to the individual African nations—standard diplomatic practice for Europe—and commissioned a secret panel to study the prospects for beneficial American relations with the incipient African states. Thanks to data which have only recently become declassified, the principal conclusion of that study is now known: "What we do—or fail to do—in Africa in the next year will have a profound effect for many years. . . . We see Africa as probably the greatest open field of maneuver in the worldwide competition between the [Communist] Bloc and the non-Communist world."[1] From the beginning, therefore, the American thrust toward Africa was conditioned by cold war ideology.

The outbreak of civil war in the former Belgian Congo in 1960 provided the United States with a prime opportunity for its first intervention on the African continent. With the declaration of Congolese independence just before the civil war, the Belgians abruptly relinquished their colonial hegemony of nearly a century. This produced a tremendous power vacuum in a country whose strategic and economic assets made it attractive and vulnerable to the Great Powers in the new age of cold war competition. Although American expansionism had heretofore embraced many areas of the globe, the whole African continent had appeared almost as a distant and blank spot on the map of American foreign policy. Yet, during the four years of the Congo crisis (1960–1964) the United States succeeded in establishing itself as a dominant influence in the very heartland of Africa. Through subsequent relations with the new Congolese leader, Colonel Joseph Désiré Mobutu, American policymakers also shaped the broad outlines of a policy which has since characterized American involvement with other African countries from the Mediterranean Sea to the Cape Coast.

Fundamental to the American approach to Africa was an insistence upon bilateral alliances involving the United States and the newly independent African nations. More specifically, the United States sought a mutually beneficial relationship with a pro-Western or moderate leader of an African country. Washington's approach to a new alliance ordinarily began with some form of economic association, trade and commerce representing the binding tie with the former European colony which now became an American ally. A military alliance also developed, as in the case of the Congo, wherever actual or potential strategic interests of the United States were likely to be served. Equally important, the United States waged a consistent and inflexible campaign to obtain the African nations' ideological commitment to capitalism, and more broadly to American political ideas, values, and institutions.

The strategic and economic assets of the Congo, later renamed Zaire, originally caused the United States to view it as a pivot from which to expand American influence to the other new African nations. Strategically, the Congo's location in the center of Africa offered a sweeping geopolitical range. As large as the United States east of the Mississippi, the Congo abutted the frontiers of nine other countries (Angola, the Congo-Brazzaville, the Central African Republic, Sudan, Uganda, Rwanda, Burundi, Tanzania, and Zambia). Even as the Belgians were abandoning their former colony, Africa's third largest territory, the Kennedy Administration hurried to fill the vacuum. The Soviet Union also eyed the Congo as a potential axis for Soviet strategic and ideological penetration into Black Africa. Neither Washington nor Moscow mourned the death of the Belgian empire, but both heeded Chairman Mao's reported advice to the chieftains of China: "If we can take the Congo, we can hold the whole of Africa."[2]

Economically, the Congo possessed some of the richest natural resources in the world. The Western capitalist countries obtained about 7 percent of their tin, 9 percent of their copper, 49 percent of their cobalt, and 69 percent of their industrial diamonds from the Congo in 1959.[3] The United States received nearly three fourths of its cobalt and one half of its tantalum—two minerals required in aerospace production and in scant supply in the United States— from the Congo's Katanga province. Iron, zinc, gold, manganese, and bauxite, like the other resources so crucial to the Western economies, were also found in Katanga. From Katanga's southern frontier a vast copper belt stretched into the territory then known as Northern Rhodesia (later Zambia), which provided 15 percent of the copper and 12 percent of the cobalt exports to the Western countries. The Congo contained 13 percent of the world's hydro-electrical potential. In addition, agriculture flourished on the many acres of fertile farmlands, where the Belgians had grown export crops of coffee, rubber, cotton, tea, and cocoa. Despite the Congo's rapacious exploitation by the Belgians, American policymakers reasoned that its rich and abundant resources promised the new nation a golden future.

Apart from its own national interest in the Congo, the United States had another stake in the economic and defense interests of its NATO allies. Belgium, for instance, maintained considerable investments in the Congo. Principal among the Belgian holdings was the immensely powerful corporation called the Société Générale de Belgique, which by contract had acquired exclusive control of the Katanga mining industry until 1990. The importance of Katanga's wealth was indicated by the fact that roughly half of the Congo's budgetary receipts and the majority of its foreign exchange came from revenues produced by the Katanga mines. Directly or indirectly, the Société Générale controlled about 80 percent of the Congo's national economy. This control pertained particularly to such minerals as copper and cobalt. Though willing to accede to Congolese political independence, the Belgians were determined to retain their entrenched economic position, and thereby wield significant influence on the Congo's future relations in the international market.

France, West Germany, and Italy also depended on Katanga for copper and other minerals essential to the life and productivity of an industrial economy. These traditional American allies regarded the United States as the savior of Western economic and political interests in an era of dying European colonial power in Africa, as elsewhere in the Third World. Great Britain was also anxious about the future of the Congo, not because it held important investment or other economic stakes there, but because it obtained most of its copper from the Rhodesian side of the Katanga copper belt, an area that could be destabilized by turmoil in the Congo. The United States looked on the economic viability of its partners in NATO as a vital aspect of their military capability. Thus, from deep in the heart of Africa a complex of economic and strategic interests arose to cause the United States to develop a policy orientation that was focused simultaneously on its own self-interest and on the transnational interests of the NATO partners. American intervention in the Congo therefore appeared inevitable. It responded to the opportunity provided by the sudden availability of new economic and strategic spheres of influence. This opportunity, of course, emanated from the demise of colonial Europe and the concomitant rise, in the aftermath of World War II, of the United States as the world's most powerful nation. Belgium and the other European colonizers had no desire to surrender their overseas possessions; however, having lost their much-vaunted military and economic superiority, they were now compelled to cede the field to either the United States or the Soviet Union. The former colonizers looked with envy on the unmatched American power that was rapidly replacing them in the Congo. The United States had never acquired much presence in Africa before, except in Ethiopia, which it had always accepted as an independent kingdom, and in Liberia, which had been founded in the mid-nineteenth century by freed American slaves. In the Congo the Kennedy Administration saw the chance to establish a beachhead of more or less permanent American influence.

## THE CONGO CRISIS

Civil war erupted in the Congo soon after independence on June 30, 1960, when Congolese soldiers instigated a rebellion against their Belgian officers. However, this domestic conflict spread into the international arena after Patrice Lumumba, the Prime Minister, and Joseph Kasavubu, the President, appealed to the United Nations for emergency security assistance. In the absence of these two leaders, Foreign Minister Justin Bomboko gained agreement from other cabinet members to contact Washington for direct assistance,[4] in the form of three thousand American soldiers, to restore civil order. The divisiveness of the Congolese leadership, coupled with the intensifying internal breakdown, plunged the country into one of the most brutal and disruptive episodes in modern African history. These episodes precipitated the collapse of three different governments, the disintegration of the national army, and finally the installation of an international foreign legion in the Congo—all in the first year of the new nation's independence. Most importantly, the crisis gave Kennedy's New Frontier the necessary pretext for introducing the United States as a Great Power on African soil.

The immediate background to the crisis involved members of the Force Publique, the Congolese army which the Belgians had organized to perform both army and police functions. The Belgian King Leopold II won European recognition of his imperial possession of the Congo by 1885, and three years later the Belgians organized the Force Publique with soldiers conscripted from the indigenous population. Upon Congolese independence, there were 24,000 of these Black Congolese soldiers. Commanding the soldiers were more than one thousand superior officers, who remained what they had always been—White and Belgian. The army was garrisoned mainly in three regional detachments, each under a colonel, in the cities of Leopoldville (now Kinshasa), Elisabethville (now Lubumbashi), and Stanleyville (now Kisangani). Despite the coming of independence, there continued to be a sharp dichotomy between African and European, between the colonized and the colonizers.

Native Congolese soldiers, regardless of years of service, never reached higher than the rank of noncommissioned officer, a post that had no real authority and was completely excluded from the Belgian officer corps. Furious at the terms of the independence settlement by which the Belgians were allowed to retain their positions in the army and the civil administration, the Congolese soldiers demanded an African command of the military organization. Not only did they see no sense in gaining national independence if it only meant prolonged domination, they recognized that this neocolonial settlement virtually precluded their control of their own forces.

Rebellion ensued on July 5, 1960, only five days after independence, as a few Congolese soldiers in the capital, Leopoldville, whispered the word that the time had come to stop obeying orders from their Belgian superiors. Prime Minister Lumumba encouraged the soldiers, indirectly by his speeches excoriating colonialism, and directly by insisting on a program of Africanization (the replacement of Europeans with Africans in all areas of governmental and commercial employment). Meanwhile, Lieutenant General Emile Janssens, the commander of the Force Publique, antagonized the soldiers by dramatizing his die-hard colonialist opposition through a statement he inscribed on the blackboard at Force headquarters: "Before independence = after independence."[5] This was the Belgians' ultimate outrage, for very quickly the angry soldiers set off a mutiny that spread from Leopoldville to Stanleyville and Katanga.

Lumumba rushed to mollify the rebellious soldiers by dismissing every one of the 1,135 Belgian officers then in command. His cabinet of ministers, restive and insecure in the face of the imminent crisis, approved his decision. He followed this bold action by changing the name of the military establishment from the Force Publique to the Armée nationale congolaise (ANC, National Congolese Army), a symbolic gesture to underscore the Congo's final rupture from the colonial regime. To head the new army, he appointed Victor Lundula, a civilian and a former medic in the Force Publique, whom Lumumba raised to the rank of major general. In his haste, Lumumba also designated as colonel and army Chief of Staff a young man who had become a relatively important member of the ANC in Leopoldville. The new colonel was Joseph Mobutu.

Panic then seized the European residents of the Congo. Remaining from the colonial period were 100,000 Europeans (including 30,000 Belgian settlers) amidst the Congo's native population of 18 million. The foreigners had maintained dominion over the Congolese for nearly a century through a tripartite alliance of the Belgian colonial administration, the Catholic missions, and the corporations. So monolithic was the Belgians' control that they had not even imagined the possibility of their subordination to African rule because, as political scientist Crawford Young has pointed out, "no Congolese, rural or urban, could have failed to perceive that he was being administered."[6] Furthermore, the Belgians, perhaps the most ruthless of European colonizers, had done nothing to prepare the indigenous people for eventual self-government. At independence this reality hit home most pointedly by the realization that in the entire country there were no more than a handful of Congolese college graduates and few professionals of any kind; and, of course, there were no African officers in an army that was generations old. Lumumba's instant Africanization of the army terrified the Europeans. Immediately many of them joined a Belgian exodus from the country, some retreating to the Congo-Brazzaville across the Congo River, others fleeing to Belgium. With the flight of the Europeans, the civil administration, the magistrature, and much of the army began to disintegrate.

The Congolese leaders meanwhile foundered in a state of confusion and conflict over policy as well as ideology. President Kasavubu desired a retention of Western influence in the independent Congo, and he therefore opposed Lumumba's dismissal of the Belgian officers and his alienation of the Belgian settlers in general. Joseph Ileo, President of the Senate of the Congo, shared Kasavubu's policy position and also his procapitalist orientation. Though not a national leader, Moise Tshombe wielded considerable influence with these leaders on the strength of his powerful base as President of Katanga. In opposition to the conservative wing of the Congolese leadership was a group of radical nationalists that included Antoine Gizenga, the Deputy Prime Minister, and Pierre Mulele, a militant socialist who had distinguished himself by his ideological affinity with Peking.

The undisputed champion of the latter group was Patrice Lumumba, a strong advocate of socialism, who sought to formulate a systematic program of socialist thought that was suitable to Congolese society. In foreign policy he enjoyed close relations with certain African radical leaders, such as his friend Kwame Nkrumah of Ghana, and he had been proffered assistance by the Soviet Union. Perhaps more than any other African leader at the time, Lumumba staunchly condemned attempts by the Western powers to reintroduce externally imposed servitude in Africa through the neocolonial means of economic control.

Supremely charismatic, Lumumba was a superhuman personality. He often succeeded in mobilizing people or rallying crowds through his consummate oratory and magnetic personal appeal. In political influence he strode as the giant among Congolese political elites. Lumumba indeed had the only valid claim to the title of national leader because the Mouvement national congolais, the political party he headed, was the most representative institution in the country apart from the army. Though not cohesive or firmly organized, this party was also the country's major civilian institution. Equally important, it was the political group least identified with tribal or ethnic factions. It came as no surprise therefore that Lumumba assumed the posture of the Congo's paramount chief. Given the country's wealth and resources, there was a clear possibility that a radical nationalist regime could in fact consolidate power under his leadership.[7]

Civil disorder and administrative breakdown staggered the new nation. Lumumba, like some of the other Congolese leaders, pondered the desirability of calling in foreign military assistance as Belgian troops increased their intervention in the Congo. Washington continued its general cooperation with Belgium; Lumumba, in desperation, ultimately appealed to the Soviet Union both for matériel and military advisors. Later, on July 12, 1960, he joined Kasavubu in contacting Dag Hammarskjold, Secretary-General of the United Nations, for emergency security assistance. These conflicting appeals were further complicated by the cabinet overtures stimulated by Foreign Minister Bomboko for emergency aid from the United States. One month after independence the central Congolese leadership thus split like an exploding atom, as different leaders searched in hope for an external solution to an internal crisis that was unmistakably out of their control.

Before Lumumba or his opponents had communicated their urgent appeals to the United Nations, the Brussels government further aggravated the Congo crisis when, on July 10, in violation of Lumumba's orders, it sent Belgian paratroopers to the Congolese towns of Kitona and Kamina. These foreign intervenors, not to say invaders, soon defeated the Congo's rebellious army in several different areas, including Katanga. From the standpoint of Kasavubu and his moderate allies, the Belgian unilateral action was salutary because it helped to restore order in those regions. However, their satisfaction vanished very quickly two days later—the date of Lumumba's and Kasavubu's appeal to the United Nations—when the same Belgian troops, now in the city of Matadi, pushed the country to a peak of political and psychological frenzy by inciting a battle in which they killed nearly a score of Congolese civilians.

The Congo's former corporate overlords, particularly the Belgian company Union Minière du Haut Katanga which held exclusive rights to copper mining in a large area of the province, saw the opportunity during this incident to reinforce the protection of their enterprises in Katanga and to regain control of it. Spurred by corporate interests, Moise Tshombe exploited the Matadi massacre, as Congolese nationalists termed the killings, to declare Katanga's secession from the Congo. As a result, the mineral-rich territory fell under the sway of the Union Minière, which once again assumed quasi-territorial jurisdiction over it. The Katanga secession thus afflicted the Congo with sudden balkanization, a territorial disintegration that accelerated the process of chaos and breakdown.

The Eisenhower Administration, in its last months in office, decided against direct intervention, but dispatched an attack carrier off the Congolese coast in July 1960 in an effort to block Soviet military intervention. The Republicans, like previous Democratic administrations, had been largely oblivious to Africa and African developments prior to the independence of the Congo. Not until July 1, 1958 did the Republicans obtain Congress's belated authorization for a new post of Assistant Secretary of State for African Affairs, and with it the Bureau of African Affairs also came into being. President Eisenhower, whose whole global orientation was concentrated on Europe and Great Power politics, failed to recognize the possibility of any serious American stake in Black Africa separate from the benefits it provided the NATO colonialist allies.

Black Americans, who, for reasons of heritage and race, could have been expected to present pro-African options to the Republicans, were hardly in a position to engage in pressure-group politics relative to American foreign policy. The civil rights movement had just begun to touch sensitive chords in the United States, and Black leaders such as Dr. Martin Luther King, Jr., were directing their energies toward breaking down the racist legal and political barriers to Blacks' participation at home. Furthermore, although the Eisenhower Administration had given obligatory attention to the *Brown v. the Board of Education* decision, it had not displayed any more sympathy for civil rights than for Black Africa.

Another key aspect of the Administration's political ideology concerned the policy of containment.[8] The decade beginning in 1950 was the age of massive deterrence in America's international strategy. With the advent of the cold war, the United States promised to challenge Soviet expansion anywhere in the world and to respond to Soviet military action with massive retaliation.[9] Secretary of State John Foster Dulles had threatened to "roll back the curtain" of Soviet expansion in Eastern Europe. Senator Joseph McCarthy had enshrined anticommunism as a national dogma, and McCarthyism, with its political hysteria and vicious witchhunts, destroyed the reputations and fortunes of numerous American citizens suspected of radical or communist affiliations.

From the beginning, the Republican Administration disapproved of Lumumba and actively sought his removal.[10] Washington did not regard him merely as procommunist, but also as anti-White and anti-American. CIA director Allen Dulles denounced Lumumba as another Fidel Castro who would defeat American policy in Africa. Lumumba came to the United States to address the U.N. in late August 1960; his brief visit to Washington to meet such officials as Secretary of State Christian Herter hardened their anticommunist suspicions toward him. Particular anxiety was expressed about some of the members of Lumumba's entourage. Madame Andrée Blouin, a mulatto from the former French Equatorial Africa, served as his Chief of Protocol and was depicted by Washington as a Marxist with inordinate influence upon Minister of Information Anicet Kashamura and Deputy Prime Minister Antoine Gizenga; Serge Michel, Lumumba's press secretary, another foreign Marxist, had been sent to aid the Prime Minister by the Algerian government-in-exile, which was then enmeshed in the Algerians' anticolonialist struggle against France.[11]

Soon after the Congo's declaration of independence, the Eisenhower Administration dispatched Lawrence Devlin to set up an office of the Central Intelligence Agency at the American legation in Leopoldville. This was one of the first American embassies in independent Africa. Devlin, convinced that Lumumba belonged to the communist camp, participated in an effort to overthrow the government and to assassinate some of its top leaders.[12] Presumably, Lumumba was viewed as the most prominent among them. In this way America's cold war myopia was introduced into Africa and became a new factor in international politics.

The American Ambassador, Clare Timberlake, grew increasingly suspicious of Lumumba's intentions. In a secret communication he warned the Eisenhower Administration that "if the [United Nations] does not immediately act to take the army out of Government control . . . , most of the handful of Europeans still in Leopoldville will leave and the remainder would be some foreign embassy personnel, Communist agents and carpetbaggers. We are convinced that the foregoing is the Communist plan."[13] The Ambassador characterized Lumumba, Kashamura, and Madame Blouin as communist and anti-White and Serge Michel as more anticommunist and anti-Western. In Washington the Republicans took this spurious advice to heart but did not use it to formulate a coherent American policy toward the Congo, concentrating instead on its general anticommunist and interventionist themes.

Anticommunism, however, was not the sole motivation of the incipient American policy. It was not ideology but rather economics which imposed the decisive influence. Some of the outstanding American interests in Katanga have already been identified. There were additional stakes in Katanga and other regions of the Congo; these involved a General Motors distributorship in south Katanga, Mobil Oil's $12 million investment in various service stations,[14] and private Western investments of $2.5 billion, which included American corporate ownership of about 1 percent of the total.[15]

Also provocative was the fact that the Congo's South Kasai province produced 80 percent of America's industrial diamonds at a time when there was no American domestic production of this precious commodity, used in such critical industries as mining, construction, electronics, and aircraft. Before the Congo's independence, other key American financial and corporate interests, including Morgan Guaranty Trust and American Metal Climax, had invested in the Belgian Congo.

If the Republicans in power did not recognize that internal stability was essential to the Congo's political and economic development, they surely realized its necessity for the promotion of American financial interests. Economics and ideology thus converged to give direction to American policy in the Congo.

Ultimately the Eisenhower Administration rejected the Congolese request for unilateral American assistance; instead, it supported the appeal for a United Nations Peacekeeping Force. What followed was an international security apparatus consisting of more than nineteen thousand soldiers from thirty different African, Asian, and European countries. Its basic mission was to provide the Congo with such military assistance as was necessary to restore civil order. However, throughout its four-year operation from 1960 to 1964, the United Nations Force indirectly promoted a pro-Western and primarily pro-American orientation. Washington's opposition to Lumumba intensified in August 1960 when he abruptly cut off relations with Hammarskjold, accusing the U.N. Secretary-General of collaboration with the Western powers in their refusal to stop the Belgian-supported secession of Katanga.

An unmistakable demonstration of United Nations pro-American bias was revealed in September 1960 when Andrew Cordier, an American who was the United Nations representative in the Congo, shut down Leopoldville's radio station and principal airport. Cordier's action transpired in the midst of the Congolese constitutional crisis in which President Kasavubu fired Prime Minister Lumumba, who, in retaliation, fired Kasavubu. The Cordier intervention strengthened Kasavubu and his moderate supporters in their race for power by thwarting the cause of Lumumba. Closing the airport prevented Soviet planes then in the Congo from transporting pro-Lumumba troops to his defense, and shutting down the radio station nullified Lumumba's last desperate efforts to mobilize popular support. Kasavubu, on the other hand, received full access to the radio in Brazzaville, the nearby city in the Congo-Brazzaville across the Congo River divide. Despite the role played by the Belgians in Katanga, United Nations Secretary-General Dag Hammarskjold targeted his condemnation of outside unilateral assistance at the Soviet Union only.

The United Nations Security Council established five objectives for the Peacekeeping Force at its meeting on July 14, 1960. These can be summarized as follows: (1) to restore and maintain law and order throughout the Congo; (2) to prevent civil war and curb tribal conflict; (3) to transform the ANC into a reliable internal security force; (4) to restore and maintain the territorial integrity and political independence of the Congo; and (5) to eliminate inter-ference in the Congo's internal affairs, particularly the foreign military officers and advisors assisting secessionist Katanga.[16] The first three objectives focused on the internal situation, the last two on the external. Belgium had continued to violate the Congo's territorial sovereignty by sending its troops to Katanga. Because the last objective referred directly to foreign military officers (the Belgians), it could be inferred that the United Nations meant to have a withdrawal of the Belgian invaders followed by an end to the Katanga secession.

What supports this inference is the fact that the United Nations' objectives coincided with the general goals of the United States, which took major responsibility in financing the peacekeeping mission. American policy, of course, aimed at the selection of a moderate, pro-Western leadership in the Congo and the protection and promotion of Western interests as well as the prohibition of Soviet intervention in this strategic territory. In actuality the three goals were interrelated, because a moderate Congolese leadership could be expected to align with the Western countries with vested interests in the Congo. Such a leadership, being backed by Western political and financial interests, would undoubtedly be obliged to adopt a pro-Western, anticommunist stance.

The Soviet Union, however, was not watching passively as the United States eased into the establishment of its first beachhead in Africa. Quite the contrary, Moscow had advanced the cause of Lumumba through its diplomatic representatives at the United Nations and among African and Asian independent states. The Russians had condemned Cordier's action as an effort to aid the Western corporate interests in collusion with the secessionist Tshombe. They accused the United Nations Undersecretary Ralph J. Bunche, a Black American, of serving as the middleman for Western intervention in the Congo. After Kasavubu dismissed Lumumba and replaced him with a council of ministers headed by Colonel Mobutu, the Soviets pointed to Lumumba as the only legitimate leader of the Congolese government. In August 1960 they demonstrated their support concretely by providing him with about a hundred Soviet bloc technicians together with transport aircraft, trucks, and a variety of high-powered weapons. With this military assistance Lumumba was able to rally his supporters among the ANC rebels for a projected assault on Bakwanga and Katanga.

When Soviet Chairman Nikita Khrushchev came to New York on September 23, 1960, to address the United Nations General Assembly, he reasserted Soviet diplomatic endorsement of Lumumba. He also indicated Soviet willingness to continue some form of military assistance. A few days earlier the Soviet Union had abstained on a United Nations resolution prohibiting all military assistance to the Congo except through the United Nations, evidently because Moscow had accurately perceived the peacekeeping operations there as an indirect arm of American foreign policy.

Khrushchev insisted that the foreign troops in the Congo be restricted to recruits from African and Asian countries, while concealing the reality of an ongoing Soviet intervention already in force. At that very moment, in fact, Soviet military advisors were engaged in pro-Lumumba maneuvers in Stanleyville, where Gizenga, having denounced the central government, had set up yet another regime. The Russians had channeled a certain amount of their military assistance through the United Arab Republic (Egypt) which, like the People's Republic of China, Algeria, Guinea, Ghana, Mali, and the Soviet Union, then backed Lumumba's old ally Gizenga. The combined Soviet diplomatic and military support convincingly confirmed the Soviet choice for leadership of the Congo.

The Congolese government had disintegrated into a number of autonomous and antagonistic entities, each claiming jurisdiction over its own territory if not the country as a whole. First, there was the central government in Leopoldville, still presided over by Kasavubu but newly reinforced by Mobutu and his faction of the ANC. Second, there was the rebel government in Stanleyville, friendly to the ousted Lumumba and dedicated to the overthrow of its enemies in Leopoldville. Third, Tshombe's secessionist government in Katanga claimed to represent another independent territory altogether. Finally, Lumumba was clandestinely organizing in a fierce attempt to regain direction of the country. Each of the would-be governmental group fought simultaneously to eliminate the others. The ANC, the national army, had been vitiated by fragmentation that roughly corresponded to the political divisions. Numerous ethnic divisions together with three main language groups (Lingala, Swahili, and Kikongo) further aggravated the fragmentation.[17] The Congo had in fact succumbed to total disarray, the effects of which were mitigated only by the tenuous order established here and there by the United Nations Peacekeeping Force.

Through the CIA a separate and clandestine American strategy developed in tandem with Washington's public and official policy toward the United Nations. This involved Washington's interest in reducing the influence of Lumumba. On December 1, 1960, Mobutu's soldiers apprehended Lumumba as he fled to his supporters in Stanleyville, thanks in part to CIA surveillance reports that had alerted Mobutu to the deposed Prime Minister's movements. Mobutu was henceforth entrusted with the custody of Lumumba, who remained immensely popular in the country at large and influential even among some of the troops guarding him after his unexplained transfer from a prison near Leopoldville to a location in Katanga, stronghold of Lumumba's archenemy Moise Tshombe. Because of these circumstances, Colonel Mobutu, and by extension the CIA, were implicated when Lumumba was secretly assassinated on January 17, 1961.[18]

The death of Lumumba promptly closed a fateful episode in the turbulent Congo crisis. When he gained control of the army in September 1960, Mobutu had expelled numerous politicians and had eliminated Soviet bloc military advisors and their equipment. Kasavubu and Mobutu, acting jointly, could now more easily defeat their foes in Stanleyville, and in fact Mobutu arrested Gizenga and his forces the following year. In the meantime the uprising in Katanga was quelled by the United Nations Peacekeeping Force, which, after a bloody battle with Tshombe's troops and the elimination of perhaps four hundred of them, compelled Katanga's acquiescence to the authority of the Leopoldville government. The United Nations forces finally squashed the secession when they took the town of Kolwezi in January 1963.

These developments satisfied many of the objectives of American policy by ending both the secession and much of the anti-Leopoldville rebellion. A moderate leadership, consisting of Kasavubu and Mobutu, had ascended to power, if not yet on a national scale then at least in the capital city. It remained for the United States to intervene more or less directly to shore up the position of the Congolese leader or leaders who appeared most amenable to the larger economic, strategic, and ideological interests of the United States.

## SELECTION OF THE MODERATE LEADER

When John F. Kennedy took office in January 1961, he encountered a Congo policy which, like the prevailing policy toward Cuba, was already in motion. For the first time in American history, Africa became an area of serious policy consideration. As President-elect, he had received a recommendation from his Task Force on Africa that priority be given to the immediate recruitment of personnel with expertise in African affairs. This, in the context of pervasive policy neglect toward Africa, was no easy task; during 1954 the Republicans cut back the total authorized State Department positions for Africa from 207 Americans and 361 local employees to 129 Americans and 121 locals.[19] Black Americans were virtually nonexistent in this group, and the few who did find service in the African area often worked in specialized positions; Carl T. Rowan, for instance, was Assistant Secretary of State for Public Affairs. Although Kennedy subsequently restored some of the eliminated posts, he nonetheless assumed leadership of a Congo policy that was well under way despite the inadequacy of competent personnel to execute it. Not surprisingly, the new President demanded quite early a thorough review of American policy toward Africa in general and the Congo in particular.

Kennedy's reassessment of the Congo policy was extremely significant because it fit into a broader reappraisal of American foreign policy generally. In the first place, the liberal Democrats of his Administration, younger and less marked by the cold war obsession than their conservative Republican predecessors, declared themselves ready to examine and adopt new ideas and policies, a willingness symbolized by their New Frontier appellation. Most importantly, the Kennedy Democrats aspired to replace the massive retaliation approach toward the Soviet Union with what came to be called peaceful competition—that is, a relentless and worldwide struggle with Moscow that concentrated on economic, political, and ideological challenges, but not military ones. Moreover, continuous diplomatic vigilance had to be practiced, according to this notion, so that the cold war would not become a hot war, which, in modern technological warfare, ultimately meant nuclear confrontation.

A new sensitivity and attention to Africa was also infused into the New Frontier ideology. As a senator, Kennedy had been the only major American politician to detect the historic importance of Algeria's war of independence.[20] He had similarly recognized the potential electoral appeal of Africa to Black American voters, who had given him the margin of victory over Richard M. Nixon in the Presidential election. Arthur M. Schlesinger, Jr., the Kennedy era historian, has taken the trouble to count 479 references to Africa that Kennedy uttered during his 1960 campaign. This demonstrated his keen and informed awareness of the significance to the United States of the emergent African nations.

The leader of the New Frontier surrounded himself with four key experts to shape a new policy toward Africa. In this distinguished and influential group were Adlai E. Stevenson, Ambassador to the United Nations; G. Mennen Williams, Assistant Secretary of State for African Affairs; Chester Bowles, the Undersecretary of State; and Harlan Cleveland, Assistant Secretary of State for International Organization Affairs. (It is worth noting that Williams, as Governor of Michigan, had been a strong civil rights advocate, and his appointment was in some sense a recompense to the Black voters.) These four liberal leaders contributed to the formulation of the President's new Africa strategy, whose specific direction has been pinpointed by Wayne Fredericks, a member of the State Department's African Bureau: "If we don't have a Congo policy, we don't have an African policy."[21]

Kennedy, however, did not revolutionize the traditional American approach to Africa, reversing in one stroke a long history of neglect and ignorance. It was impossible, for example, to substantially alter the cold war thrust of American foreign policy, not only because the Kennedy Democrats had not produced a fundamental alternative to it, but especially because the government and public opinion alike remained entrenched in the anticommunist, anti-Soviet animosity of the 1950s. In any case, an actual American policy toward the Congo was already in operation; it was this de facto situation which virtually ruled out a genuine redirection. What we are, and moreover what we want to be, said the conservative British philosopher Michael Oakeshott, is a creature of what we have been. Kennedy pointed the way to a fresh approach, but, in the end, the past dominated the present.

Taking office only days after Lumumba's assassination, the Kennedy Administration rushed to identify a moderate Congolese leader who could be converted into an American ally. This urgent action was provoked by a veritable flood of African and Soviet bloc hostility toward the Western powers, especially Belgium and the United States. At the United Nations the Soviet delegate decried the United Nations operation in the Congo, demanding its termination and the dismissal of Hammarskjold. The Soviets regarded the Secretary-General as an American stooge. Washington saw the specter of a radical and anti-Western regime emerging in the embattled country, as the Soviets multiplied their military assistance to Gizenga and the five thousand soldiers supporting him in Stanleyville. Sékou Touré of Guinea and Gamal Abdel Nasser of Egypt had gone so far as to give diplomatic recognition to the Gizenga regime. In frantic reaction the Pentagon prepared contingency plans for a limited war between the United States and the Congo, while studying the possibility of sending eighty thousand American soldiers to the Congo by air and sea.

Kennedy consummated the policy initiatives by ordering five United States naval vessels into the Gulf of Guinea. These so-called good will missions surfaced off the nearby Congolese coastline as embodiments of American military superiority. The struggle between the United States and the Soviet Union in the Congo had been joined in earnest; as in Cuba a year later, Kennedy left no illusion here as to America's ultimate intentions.

Acting apparently on the advice of the CIA, Kennedy decided to build his strategy around neither Kasavubu nor any of the Congolese political leaders. Instead, the President singled out the military officer whom Lumumba had appointed army Chief of Staff on the eve of independence, Colonel Mobutu. Washington recognized that the United Nations Force could not develop a modern army for him and quietly introduced its own bilateral aid to Mobutu in October 1962. The new assistance included vehicles, communications equipment, and American military advisors to train Mobutu's troops on how to use them.

Mobutu appeared to the Kennedy strategists as the only desirable choice for moderate and pro-Western leadership in the Congo. More than any of the politicians, Colonel Mobutu could claim a genuine power base by virtue of his position as commander of a faction of the ANC. Through his service in the Force Publique, he had become well acquainted with many Congolese soldiers, several of whom he had chosen as cronies and who soon emerged as his loyal subordinates among the seven thousand troops he commanded at Leopoldville and Thysville. As a journalist, Mobutu had later befriended many Congolese political and ethnic leaders. He had shown his own anti-Communist orientation by expelling the Soviet and Czech diplomats immediately after taking power in 1960. Moreover, the deputy United Nations commander, General Ben Hammou Kettani of Morocco, was supposed to assist in helping to convert the ANC into a viable internal security force—as was enjoined by the United Nations when it set up the Peacekeeping Force—but he had actually used his position during 1960 and 1961 to assist Mobutu in building his wing of the fragmented national army. It was also relevant that Mobutu maintained close and harmonious relations with CIA operatives such as Devlin. Although the Johnson Administration strongly supported Adoula, the moderate successor to Lumumba who governed from 1961 to 1964, neither he nor Kasavubu proved to be Washington's ultimate choice because they lacked both a strong civilian constituency and an effective power base. Consequently, Mobutu beckoned not simply as the man of the hour, he became the only man convenient for the needs of American policy in the Congo.

The United States' European allies reinforced Kennedy's support for Mobutu. The participation of Belgium, England, France, and the Scandinavian countries was evident in their diplomatic and material support to the United Nations operation. It became even more definite with their collaboration in an American initiative known as the Greene Plan. In July 1962 Kennedy appointed Colonel Michael J. L. Greene to head a military advisory team to the Congo for the purpose of determining the most effective means by which the United States could facilitate Mobutu's rise to power. The operating assumption was that this objective could be accomplished through bilateral assistance programs. Although the plan was later stopped by the intervention of U Thant, successor to Hammarskjold after his death in an airplane crash in Zambia, this American initiative still demonstrated a consensus among the European powers with respect to America's Congo policy.

Israel, seeking new allies in independent Africa, joined the

Western activity in the Congo by training more than two hundred Congolese paratroopers. The stellar graduate of the Israeli program was none other than Colonel Joseph Mobutu.

With the American aid he received, Mobutu developed a superior army. This preponderance of military power enabled him to dominate his political competitors and, in November 1965, to take control of the Leopoldville government through the overthrow of his colleague Kasavubu. The leadership field was now open for Mobutu as he proceeded to turn the Congo into an American client-state. By mid-1964, after the Kennedy era, the United States had delivered a total of $6.1 million in aid to Mobutu in addition to $170 million in military assistance to the United Nations Peace-keeping Force.[22] In the end, these developments enabled the United States to overshadow Belgium as the dominant foreign power in the Congo. Kennedy's vision had borne rich fruit, for the United States could now expand its world supremacy as a Great Power in postcolonial Africa.

## DEPENDENCE AND RECIPROCITY

Through U.S. intervention in the Congo, American policymakers also discovered a future strategy for their approach to certain new nations on the African continent. This can be described as the "Congo syndrome," or the practice by which the United States intervenes in an African nation, especially in its moment of internal crisis, to support a moderate or pro-Western elite struggling for power against local opponents, who may be socialists and recipients of Soviet bloc assistance. With American economic and usually military assistance, the moderate contender defeats his competitors and arises as the new paramount leader. What typically follows is the establishment of a whole series of bilateral relations between the United States government and the victorious African leader, who sets about consolidating his personal authority over the new regime. Washington thereby obtains a new ally in the dominant person-ality, as opposed to the institutionalized government, of the African nation.

After Lyndon B. Johnson assumed the Presidency, Washington did not diminish its support to Mobutu. Indeed, American involvement grew deeper and deeper. The immediate manifestation of the deepening penetration concerned American intervention in the Congo during the *Dragon rouge,* an airborne rescue mission launched by the United States and Belgium in November 1964 to send emergency assistance to perhaps three thousand foreign nationals whom Congolese insurgents held as hostages in and around Stanleyville. Evidently what propelled Washington into action was the fact that the hostages included a small number of American missionaries and consulate staff.

The insurgents, who called themselves *simbas* (Swahili for "lions"), had organized death squads in a last-ditch stand to defeat Mobutu's government. The simbas insisted that Washington prevent Mobutu from attacking Stanleyville as a precondition to releasing the foreigners. When Johnson refused, the Dragon rouge proceeded as a dozen American transport planes carried some five hundred Belgian paratroopers to forcibly rescue and evacuate the hostages. The joint American-Belgian mission succeeded, not, however, without the participation of White (mainly Belgian) mercenaries whom Mobutu had recruited. This event marked the beginning of a pattern that would become familiar in the future.

In each instance of American intervention, Mobutu learned gradually that the United States could be drawn in as a permanent underpinning of his leadership. It thus developed that Mobutu, who as an American client had become dependent on American assistance, was rapidly making the United States a captive agent in his own drive to power. One of John F. Kennedy's favorite maxims—"he who would ride the tiger's back often ends up inside"—returned with formidable irony in American policy toward the Congo.

Unwittingly, the United States facilitated the growth of its Congo entanglement through its concurrent interest in neighboring Angola. The Johnson Administration was careful not to antagonize Portugal, Angola's colonial master, because of critical American-Portuguese military ties, including the strategic air force base on

Portugal's Azores Islands. Still, Washington could sense that the winds of change in colonial Africa would eventually sweep away Portugal's colonial dominance even as they had Belgium's. Consequently, the Administration began discussions with Holden Roberto, the moderate leader of an Angolan nationalist party, whose leadership was being challenged by a pro-Soviet group led by Agostinho Neto. Mobutu, who was Roberto's brother-in-law, gave Roberto's forces modest amounts of military and monetary assistance he himself had received from the United States.

Mobutu sought meanwhile to enhance his domestic popularity by proclaiming his policy of *authenticité*, his cultural program to restore the Congo to its precolonial authenticity, at least in name. Thus the country was renamed Zaire. Zairians were required to drop their European (Christian) names for the names of their ancestors. Joseph Désiré Mobutu himself became Mobutu Sese Seko. The program of authenticity, with its implicit promise of thorough Africanization in the civil service and commerce, proved widely popular.

A most peculiar pattern of relations evolved between Mobutu and the United States. On the one hand, Zaire became economically and militarily dependent on American assistance as the United States began to replace Belgium as the country's principal foreign partner. On the other hand, the United States grew increasingly dependent on Mobutu to protect and maintain American interests in his country. These interests, as we have seen, consisted of economic, strategic, and ideological stakes. More and more, there emerged a form of reciprocity by which the United States could generally manage Mobutu according to its desires. Mobutu, in turn, extracted certain concessions, usually in the form of increased aid, as a condition of his cooperation.

In the aftermath of the Congo crisis, American assistance to Mobutu skyrocketed. Cumulative military aid jumped from the $6.1 million in 1964 to nearly $589 million in 1977.[23] In roughly the same period, economic assistance kept apace, rising from less than $76 million in 1961 to more than $468 million in 1977. The aid policy initiated under Kennedy continued unbroken through the 1970s, as indicated when President Jimmy Carter approved

$12.4 million in military sales agreements in 1977 (see Table 5, Chapter 6). This assistance did not include the even larger American private investments in Zaire. These rose from less than $20 million in 1960 to about $750 million in 1975.[24] Clearly, after Mobutu's rise to power in 1965, American dollars and military equipment fell on him like so much manna from heaven. Mobutu meanwhile remained an unshakable American ally. He welcomed Western, and especially American, investments in his country. Kinshasa (formerly Leopoldville) became a citadel of anticommunist propaganda. It also served as a base of operations for Roberto's political faction in Angola during the mid-1970s. Zaire was projected as a model of African economic development and political stability—that is, until about 1974 when official corruption began to jettison the country toward disaster. Mobutu often extended his pro-American orientation to Zaire's foreign policy; always the arch foe of China, Mobutu quickly recognized Peking after the Nixon Administration took steps toward diplomatic recognition. Mobutu persisted in his demands for additional American aid, yet he cooperated. The American-Zairian alliance thus worked to mutual advantage, if not to mutual satisfaction.

## CORRUPTION AND THE AMERICAN CLIENT

The impotence of Mobutu's military dictatorship was exposed by former Katangan insurgents who attacked Shaba (formerly Katanga) province twice from their base in northern Angola, where they had taken refuge during the civil war. The small groups of guerrillas— numbering about two thousand in the first attack, called Shaba I, during March 1977 and about four thousand in the second attack (Shaba II) during May 1978—repulsed members of the Forces armées zaïroises, Mobutu's seventy-thousand-man army. Both assaults centered in or around Kolwezi, an important mining town. Morocco rescued Mobutu with fifteen hundred soldiers during Shaba I, and French legionnaires and Belgian paratroopers parachuted in during Shaba II, as in the Dragon rouge, to rescue

Mobutu's regime as well as some twenty-five hundred foreign nationals (mainly Europeans) surrounded in Kolwezi. The United States Air Force provided the transport aircraft to airlift some of the European paracommando forces there. These episodes showed that Mobutu, in power for almost two decades, had failed to develop political and military structures capable of protecting the copper-rich province, not to mention his own regime.

Political corruption was the source of his failure. In addition to the political and military fragility, official corruption had also resulted in an annual economic growth of minus 4 percent in Zaire, a country whose fertile soil is so vast that it could have become a breadbasket for much of the continent. Under Mobutu, however, Zaire's food production had regressed essentially to subsistence farming on all but about 1 percent of the available land. Before Mobutu, by contrast, the country was self-sufficient in such foodstuffs as rice and exported cash crops of cotton, sugar, coffee, tea, and palm oil. Much of the land lay fallow as Mobutu's uncle imported vital foodstuffs under exclusive license from South Africa. While countries like the Ivory Coast prospered with far fewer natural resources, Zaire fell so low in its national growth rate that progress came to mean a return to zero growth.

Inflation reached almost 100 percent by 1978, sending deeper into poverty the masses, who now had to devote seventeen workdays to buy the sack of manioc (a staple food) that had required five workdays in 1960.[25] National unemployment spiraled to an estimated 60 percent, and perhaps to 80 percent in war-torn Shaba. Small industries were forced to shut down because of the government's failure to provide foreign exchange to purchase spare parts (usually imported from the United States or Western Europe). Poor maintenance of the roadways reduced them to wastelands where bushes sprouted. Technically bankrupt by 1980, Zaire had accumulated a foreign debt of nearly $6 billion with Western governments, international organizations, and Western banks.[26]

In contrast to the poverty and suffering of the general society was the opulence of Mobutu and the elites known as the "presidential family," his governmental and business partners. Mobutu himself accumulated a personal fortune in his rise from military chief at independence to supreme national leader afterward, ultimately becoming one of the world's grandest millionaires. By 1978 he owned property in Switzerland, Belgium, Senegal, and elsewhere that was valued at $25 million and had cash holdings of $70 million in private Swiss bank accounts. Much of this wealth, of course, derived from funds that Mobutu had skimmed from American economic assistance.

On his own authority, with no governmental restrictions of any kind, Mobutu retained personal control of 15 to 20 percent of Zaire's operating budget and 30 percent of its capital expenditures. Secretary of State Henry Kissinger tried to thwart the victory of Angola's pro-Soviet party in 1975 by funneling CIA funds to its pro-Western antagonists via Mobutu, who, to Kissinger's shock, also shortstopped a good deal of this assistance.

Mobutu's "family" has done well too. Examples abound: a regional commissioner of Shaba grossed $100,000 monthly in 1975, although his official salary amounted to only 2 percent of this amount;[27] army generals profited by selling civilians gasoline allocated for army vehicles; most incredibly, a former Minister of Culture auctioned off as his personal property treasures he had purloined from the National Museum. The absence of monitoring of the President's expenditures apparently extended to Mobutu's partners, as indicated by a 1971 budget reporting that 60 percent of governmental allocations had either been lost or diverted to purposes other than those originally designated.[28] Instead of investing in the country's productive sectors, such as agriculture, Mobutu contented himself with large expenditures on the army, which in turn maintained his domination over the fragile and corrupt political system.

To encourage a reassessment of U.S. support to Mobutu, the chief of the political section at the American embassy in Kinshasa, Robert Remole, cabled Washington in 1979 with his account of the "Zairian sickness," as the corruption under Mobutu is known. "The whole system functions on graft and corruption, but we [the United States] don't have to be locked into Mobutu's dictatorship," affirmed Remole, an African affairs specialist with a doctorate in history from Harvard University.[29] He proposed that Washington terminate assistance to Mobutu "ostentatiously" in a dramatic demonstration of U.S. disapproval of the official corruption. Remole surmised that such action would have tremendous psychological impact, inducing such Western powers as France and West Germany to stop blindly following American support to Mobutu. He also warned that many Zairians, especially young technocrats in government and commerce, were deeply alienated from the regime, and that a successor to Mobutu might be anti-American in reaction to persistent U.S. support in the past.

Even in the face of the enormous official corruption, the Carter Administration blamed outside intervention for the threat to Mobutu's regime. Walter Cutler, the Ambassador to Zaire, submitted a "bad efficiency" evaluation of Remole, prompting the conscientious diplomat's resignation. Because the ex-Katangans had crossed into Shaba from Angola, where Soviet and Cuban forces buttressed the regime, Washington suspected that Soviet bloc forces supported the attacks. This suspicion clearly ignored the fact that Mobutu's gravest dangers derived from internal political and military deficiencies. The Carter Administration soon resigned itself to continued support to Mobutu, believing that no viable alternative to his leadership existed. It was still motivated by Zaire's enticing economic and strategic assets, some of which had become indispensable to the Western economies.

Zaire not only continued to be a leading producer of copper, ranking as the seventh largest worldwide, but it was also becoming the world's major producer of industrial diamonds. Its supply of gem diamonds, though small, was expected to equal the value of the industrial diamonds (more than $600 million in 1978).[30] Revenues from gold production soared to comparable amounts with the increase in the world price of gold. Zaire possessed deposits of several other strategic minerals, including tin, columbium, and tantalum, which may be the largest deposits in the world. A single Zairian mine provided the bulk of America's (and Western Europe's) cobalt, a necessary element in the production of jet aircraft.

Despite the corruption, therefore, Western public and private interests remained well established in Zaire, especially in the Shaba copper mines, which still generated the bulk of Zaire's foreign exchange. The Belgians, with $700 million in mainly preindependence capital investments in copper, did not relinquish their economic chains after Zaire's political independence. Western banks provided Mobutu with about $800 million in loans; American banks committed $377 million of this amount, two thirds of which was owed to the Citibank of New York.[31] The French extended $110 million for the purchase of their Mirage jets and the construction of the grandiose Voice of Zaire communications complex. In exchange for $50 million annually until the year 2000, Mobutu even compromised Zaire's sovereignty by granting the West Germans concessionary rights to 38,000 square miles of northeast Shaba, allegedly for the purpose of enabling the West Germans to secretly test cruise missiles on Zairian soil. Not to be outdone by these industrial interests, Japan sank $185 million in Zairian copper.

"Notre seul espoir!" (Our only hope!) was the way the official propaganda dramatized Mobutu, who on Zairian television could be seen rising from a burst of clouds like some messiah.[32] Although American presidents never adopted this view of the dictator, still, like President Carter, they lavished millions on him on the false assumption that he represented the best hope for preserving Western interests. According to established American policy, without Mobutu, chaos and renewed civil war would result. For ideological as well as economic and strategic reasons, Washington found this scenario more plausible after the triumph of the Marxist government in Angola during 1975.

Propped up by Washington, Mobutu's government could not have survived a day without American and European support. Mobutu was not even able to defend Shaba province, which for security had to depend on 2,500 troops from other African countries after the 1978 invasion. This *Force interafricaine*, or inter-African force as it was known, included 1,500 soldiers from Morocco, 600 from Senegal, 180 from Togo, and 80 from the Ivory Coast. These outsiders saved him for the time being, but America's reliable client still presided over a regime whose chances of survival were tenuous. At this juncture, of course, American policy had become so linked to Mobutu and his dictatorship that his survival had also emerged as a vested interest of the United States. From the careful pursuit of its own objectives in 1960, the United States slipped gradually but firmly into the defense of a corrupt military dictatorship two decades later.

## PERSISTENCE OF THE NONPOLICY POSITION

Through its role in the Congo the United States asserted its presence as a world power on the African continent. Nevertheless, an American foreign policy toward Africa remained virtually nonexistent. The principal exception to this nonpolicy consisted of United States relations with the North African states of Morocco and Libya, where American military facilities were installed, and with Ethiopia, where major communications and intelligence-related operations were based. In Liberia the United States maintained air-staging and communications systems that had been constructed during World War II. South Africa, meanwhile, continued to grow in importance as America's main trade partner in Africa. Despite these exceptions the nonpolicy posture still charac-terized America's orientation toward the continent as a whole.

Economic investments can indicate American interest in a developing region or state, but military aid is equally significant. From 1950 to 1968 the United States provided $218 million in military aid (including training) to African states out of a world total of more than $3 billion. The small African component was only 0.5 percent of the total. Zaire, Ethiopia, and Liberia were the only recipients of both equipment and training. Very clearly, Africa was not on the main agenda of the makers of American foreign policy.

Given the widespread American expansionism elsewhere during the same historical period, the question may be asked, why did the United States ignore Black Africa? Why, in other words, did the State Department fail to formulate an Africa policy after it became evident that independent African states would constitute a critical force in the contemporary world?

A partial answer can be found in the absence of an influential Africa lobby within the Black American community. Like other ethnic or nationality minorities, the Black minority has traditionally pressed the American government to foster policies for the liberation or development of their ancestral homeland. However, the relative powerlessness of Blacks as a group in the American corporate system has not enabled Black demands to have a persuasive effect on the principal decision-makers of American foreign policy (see Chapter 4). In the absence of a strong domestic push for a pro-Africa policy, Washington drifted back into its traditional indifference and ignorance regarding the African continent.

What retrenched the United States in the policy of neglect, or its nonpolicy toward Africa, was the enduring American fixation on cold war struggle. Africa simply receded into obscurity on the policy planning boards as the definition of American interests in Africa from the standpoint of Europe regained sway after the Congo intervention. Eurocentrism, as this definition of U.S. interests is called, thereby surfaced as a new element in Washington's approach to postcolonial Africa throughout the 1960s. This approach was compounded by the concurrent war in Vietnam, which preoccupied Nixon's first Administration nearly as much as it had obsessed Johnson's before. The war destroyed countless human resources and produced the first great assault on American power and prestige in the post—World War II era.

Interventionism, or what has been characterized as the Congo syndrome, became another element in the formulation of U.S. policy toward Africa. Washington's alliance-oriented approach henceforth welcomed regimes of personal leadership as a viable and valid basis for the establishment of bilateral relations. The intervention in the Congo thus enabled the United States to develop the rudiments of a policy toward independent Africa. At the same time, however, the intervention also severely damaged much of America's positive prospects in Africa. As explained by Rupert

Emerson, one of the earliest critics of the emergent U.S. role in Africa, it was "the Congo, more than any other single part of Africa, which has been the scene of America's most serious fall from grace in the eyes of many Africans."[33]

The very beginning of American policy in postcolonial Africa therefore contained serious problems which leaders after Kennedy neither resolved nor, with the exception of Carter, even contemplated. Anti-Sovietism, intervention at the behest of pro-Western forces, and the failure to define U.S. policy according to autonomous American ideals or objectives became the principal benchmarks of the problems. These, of course, contributed to Zaire's transformation after 1974 into a system of egregious corruption and, consequently, into a zone of potential disaster for U.S. interests in the heart of the continent. Still, in an age when Europe and Asia consumed American policy energies, the entangling alliance with Mobutu appeared marginal in relation to the general American indifference toward most of Africa north of the Limpopo River border with South Africa.

The nonpolicy orientation prevailed even after the decolonization of such influential states as Algeria and Nigeria. Despite the African nations' severance of colonial ties with imperial Europe, the United States continued to approach the continent through the moribund colonial networks. Washington did not produce its own creative initiatives in foreign policy. Yet, as the decade of the 1970s dawned, political rumblings in the established international order could be heard as resource-rich nations of the Third World became increasingly conscious of their new capacity to seriously alter the old order that had sustained the economic dominance of the United States and Western Europe. The alteration took shape after the Arab oil boycott of 1973–1974 in which African states participated. These were potent warnings for the United States to conceive original approaches to African nations in particular and postcolonial nations in general. Washington, however, did not dissociate itself from the Europeans whom it had begun to displace. To the extent that the United States looked on the continent at all, it was once again from the vantage point of London or Paris or Lisbon.

# ANGOLA:
# Rise of the Cold War
# in Africa

Alexander M. Haig, Jr., the Army general who formerly commanded the NATO forces in Europe, launched his role as Secretary of State in 1981 by invoking the themes of a cold war American approach to Angola that had been doomed six years before: "In Angola, UNITA elements are still going strong and are functioning. Several years ago I felt that we could have done something to prevent the outcome that confronted us there."[1] He was referring to the policy developed in 1975 by Haig's predecessor and mentor in diplomacy, Henry A. Kissinger. The policy sought to prevent a socialist regime from coming to power through American support to the pro-Western factions, including UNITA (União Nacional para a Independência Total de Angola). These factions clashed with the socialist forces, which triumphed in spite of strong U.S. opposition. This was also the stupendous fiasco that put both blight and blemish into Kissinger's celebrated diplomacy.

The subsequent U.S. policy of denying diplomatic recognition to Angola, as developed by Kissinger, did not change during the Carter Administration. Well before the election of Ronald Reagan, the cold war ideology of anti-Sovietism recaptured American policy toward Angola, disposing the United States to a repetition of previous errors.

An early failure was U.S. support to the colonial rule of the Portuguese, whom Haig, at his confirmation hearings, characterized as "so-called colonialists."[2] Haig's general awareness was much improved over that of the National Security Council (NSC) of 1969, which stated about Portuguese settlers that "the whites are here to stay and the only way constructive change can come about is through them."[3] This wrongheaded advice came just six years before Angolan nationalist forces, reinforced by Cuba, destroyed White settler rule and defeated their pro-Western rivals supported by the United States and several allies, including Zaire and South Africa.

Washington's rationale for the nonrecognition of Angola was tied to the existence of several thousand Cuban soldiers on Angolan soil. The Cuban presence, however, did not prevent a large expansion of Angolan-American trade, including the operation of U.S. multinational corporations in Angola. Nor did it stop the United States from purchasing large quantities of oil for American consumers. By the time Reagan reached the White House, Angola had become a respected member of the community of nations and was recognized as such by every major Western capital except Washington.

What led the United States down the road to policy disaster in Angola was a truculent and inflexible principle that has been well articulated by Kissinger himself: "To foreclose Soviet opportunities is . . . the essence of the West's responsibility. It is up to *us* to define the limits of Soviet aims."[4] This principle, which relegated Angola to an appendage of Soviet policy as if the Angolan revolutionaries had no objectives of their own, was a modern-day equivalent of the Monroe Doctrine. However, whereas President Monroe proclaimed his ultimatum of hemispheric jurisdiction under conditions that favored unlimited American conquest and expansion all the way to the Pacific Ocean, Kissinger uttered his cold war doctrine of American world power in the face of a rising new international economic order that constricted America's influence even in the absence of Soviet challenges. This new reality not only undermined his approach from the beginning, it also exposed the irrationality of a one-dimensional policy in a new system of multipolar forces, and it revealed the fallacy of U.S. intervention in an African war of national liberation under any condition, but especially during the American debacle in Vietnam.

The U.S. strategy in Angola represented an attempt to duplicate the success of American policy in the Congo during its civil war. The Congo syndrome—or the practice by which the United States intervenes in an African nation (often in a period of crisis), identifies a local leader susceptible to a moderate or pro-Western orientation, and then provides him with enough material support to secure his victory over his opponents—was replayed. Kissinger persisted in the strategy during 1975 even after its utter failure became evident. The result was an entrenchment of U.S. hostility toward Angola that was renewed by Carter's National Security Advisor Zbigniew Brzezinski in opposition to a pro-Africa option promoted by U.N. Ambassador Andrew Young.

The resumption of the Kissinger approach by the Reagan Administration necessitates a fundamental reevaluation of U.S. cold war policy in Angola, as in the rest of Africa. Are the assumptions of this policy of nonrecognition and the ideological principle which sustains it correct? Are there creative and constructive initiatives that might enable the United States to accept and adjust to Third World realities which American power can no longer control?

## THE ANGOLAN REVOLUTION VERSUS U.S. INTERESTS

The Angolan war of independence began in 1961, fourteen years before the Ford Administration decided to inject U.S. monetary and military assistance into the conflict. It originated from the action of indigenous Angolan forces against the Portuguese colonial regime. The United States had no historic interests in Angola, except that this territory had been a supplier of slaves to the plantation South. Although President Kennedy in 1961 had supported a U.N. resolution urging Portugal to institute reforms in its colony, an American tradition of subsuming Angola under U.S. policy toward Portugal remained in effect when Gerald Ford assumed the Presidency.

Revolutionary activity in Angola began in December 1956 with the organization of the Movimento Popular de Libertação de Angola (Popular Movement for the Liberation of Angola, MPLA), which became the triumphant party at independence nineteen years later.[5] The MPLA, a clandestine guerrilla movement demanding the overthrow of Portuguese hegemony and the establishment of an independent nation-state, consisted of a congeries of nationalist forces, especially young Marxists who had previously belonged to the Angolan Communist party. Among them was the son of a Methodist pastor, Agostinho Neto, a poet and medical doctor who eventually emerged as chief of the movement. Educated, socialist, and mestiço (racially mixed) elements characterized much of the MPLA's general leadership. Its rank and file, however, frequently derived from the Mbundus, or the 1.2 million Kimbundu-speaking people in and around the capital city of Luanda who make up Angola's second largest ethno-linguistic group.[6]

Another major protagonist in the revolutionary war was the Frente National de Libertação de Angola (National Front for the Liberation of Angola, FNLA). Created in March 1961 among the Bakongo, the 650,000 Kikongo-speaking inhabitants of northern Angola, the FNLA was led by Holden Roberto, a Bakongo nationalist educated in the Belgian Congo who became a protégé and brother-in-law of General Mobutu of Zaire. The FNLA originated among Angolan exile groups who had struggled for several years before to restore the old Kongo Kingdom of northern Angola in order to separate it from Portugal as well as from the rest of Angola. For their territorial conveniences, the Europeans had imposed an arbitrary frontier between Portuguese Angola and the Belgian Congo, with the result that the Bakongos resided on both sides of the border. This factor contributed to the FNLA's affiliation with Mobutu and its evolution as an extension of Zaire's national politics. It also explained why, under the aegis of Mobutu, the FNLA established early contact with the United States.

UNITA, the União Nacional para a Independência Total de Angola (National Union for the Total Independence of Angola), was the third force in the war of liberation. It recruited its membership from Angola's predominant ethno-linguistic group, the 1.5 million Ovimbundus who dwell in the central Benguela highlands.[7] UNITA came into being in March 1966 when Roberto's chief lieutenant, Jonas Savimbi, organized his own splinter movement while condemning Roberto as a racist, a tribalist, and a tool of the United States.[8] Savimbi had earned a doctorate in political and juridical sciences at the University of Lausanne (Switzerland). As a member of the Ovimbundu people, he established the headquarters of his faction among them near the eastern town of Luso (now Luena). This was evidently done with the military connivance of the Portuguese, who hoped UNITA could be used against the MPLA.[9]

Portugal, an ancient slave trader that launched its conquest of Angola as far back as 1575, ruled the colony through the 172,529 White settlers who in 1961 dominated the indigenous Black population of 4.6 million.[10] Settler control was enforced by an estimated 55,000 Portuguese soldiers together with a special force of the secret political and security police. The Europeans enriched themselves through their absolute monopoly of the country's resources, including the cultivable land, coffee, and diamonds. The Angolans received penurious wages in agriculture or mining when they were not forced off the land and herded into increasingly restricted areas or driven to seek work in towns or even in adjacent countries.[11] The Europeans tended to spare from these harsh deprivations the small group of mulattoes, about 53,000 individuals whose origin was frequently traceable to the forcible cohabitation of Angolan women with Portuguese men. Nevertheless, a clear dichotomy prevailed between the Europeans and the rest of the population, between the colonizers and the colonized, when the founders of the nationalist parties resolved that the old order could be tolerated no more.

Anticolonial violence in which the MPLA was implicated erupted on February 4, 1961 when several hundred Angolans attacked a prison in Luanda attempting to liberate political prisoners.[12] The Portuguese police, responding with machine gun fire, aborted the Angolan insurgence. However, this defeat did not deter the Bakongo forces in the north, who unleashed a bloody assault against the settlers on March 15, 1961, the date now acknowledged as the beginning of the revolution. This uprising resulted in the death of about three hundred Europeans, precipitating colonial reprisals that eventually took the lives of nearly twenty thousand Angolans in one of Europe's most barbaric suppressions of African people. For Angolan nationalists this episode brought Portugal's supremacy of nearly five hundred years to a point of no return, and the war for independence was pursued in earnest.

President Kennedy, who as a senator had spoken in favor of Algeria's war of independence, introduced a policy critical of Portuguese colonialism as the Angolan war began. Seeking to project the image of the United States as a "friend of all oppressed people," [13] Kennedy stunned African leaders by endorsing a 1961 resolution of the U.N. General Assembly calling on Portugal to initiate measures and reforms preparatory to Angola's independence. The United States had heretofore given Portugal about $300 million for NATO defense purposes, but Kennedy reduced a planned delivery of $25 million to only $3 million. [14] Washington also banned U.S. commercial sales of arms to Portugal. To appreciate the shift in U.S. policy, it is necessary to recall that the Eisenhower Administration had abstained in December 1960 on U.N. resolutions concerning colonial independence as well as the requirement that Portugal report on the development of its overseas territories.

FNLA leader Roberto was in New York addressing the U.N. Security Council on the day of the Bakongo uprising and interpreted Washington's Security Council vote for a U.N. inquiry into the Angolan situation as unmistakable evidence of a new American policy in favor of Africa and decolonization. The FNLA obtained several million dollars of U.S. military and financial support. It appeared that the United States was aligning itself with the "rising expectations" of Africa's colonized people.

U.S. strategic interests, however, triumphed over Kennedy's good intentions as Portugal's Azores Islands air and sea bases regained importance amid renewed cold war tension provoked by the Bay of Pigs incident. The Lajes air base on Terceira Island and its back-up field on Santa Maria Island, which represented an investment of $100 million,[15] were crucial in the 1961 redeployment of U.S. troops in Europe. The air base also served as a staging point for U.S. military operations in the Middle East, especially for rearming Israel in periods of crisis.

Economic interests later constituted a significant, though not predominant, element of the U.S. policy toward Portugal. American companies acquired almost total control of oil production in Angola's Cabinda province after 1971. The Gulf Oil Corporation, for example, had invested more than $300 million by 1975, at which time the company produced 150,000 barrels a day.[16] Angola also ranked as the world's fifth largest diamond exporter. A South African corporation containing American and British interests dominated Angola's diamond industry. The Benguela railway, furthermore, conveyed copper and cobalt destined for Western markets from neighboring Zaire and Zambia to the Angolan port of Lobito. Americans and Europeans imported $321 million in Angola's prime *robusta* coffee during 1974.[17] Angola also shared a border with South-West Africa (Namibia), which raised frequent concern in Pretoria as in Washington that the revolutionary war would spill over into the mineral-rich territory under the control of South Africa, where a liberation movement—the South West African People's Organization (SWAPO)—already existed.

## KISSINGER AND "TAR BABY": DECISION OF INTERVENTION

Less than three months after Richard Nixon took office in 1969, his National Security Advisor Henry Kissinger ordered a major review of U.S. policy toward southern Africa. Kissinger had previously taught political science at Harvard University, where Africa had not been a part of his intellectual purview. To the extent that he focused on Africa at all, Kissinger viewed it in terms of its pertinence to Soviet strategy, the primary concern in his approach to world affairs. Occasionally in National Security Council (NSC) meetings Africa was even treated as comedy by Alexander Haig, then serving as a staff assistant to Kissinger. When the NSC undertook discussions on African affairs, Haig would pound his fists on the table, jungle drumbeat style.[18]

After he became Secretary of State in 1974, Kissinger approached the formulation of Africa policy in general with hesitation, partly because he lacked intellectual background in African affairs but primarily because he wanted no action until he acquired full mastery of African issues. His approach engendered confusion and instability in the office of Assistant Secretary of State for African Affairs, which had four different occupants during 1974 as a result of conflicts or disagreements with Kissinger. With respect to Angola in particular, the Secretary of State showed less hesitation, apparently because he regarded himself as a student of revolution. However, Kissinger studied revolution not as an American who could see the creative and regenerative aspects that can emanate from fundamental socioeconomic change, but as a European who, with the hindsight of centuries of social upheaval, feared revolution and therefore examined it to extract lessons that might prevent future recurrence.

Africa as an entity sui generis was clearly beyond Kissinger's policy interests. Upon assuming his functions as Secretary of State, he complained that the existence of so many different African regimes posed virtually insuperable difficulties in the shaping of American policy toward Africa. How could an African policy be formulated for fifty different countries,[19] the Secretary wondered, as he developed policy for numerous European nations, including countries as diverse as colonial Portugal and the Soviet Union.

Kissinger's indifference verged on contempt in his treatment of African ambassadors in Washington. He refused continually to receive the diplomats on individual missions and deigned to see them infrequently only en masse. (The Egyptian ambassador was the exception, for reasons discussed in the chapter on Egypt.) Still, as a learned man with vision, Kissinger could have been expected to master quickly the requirements of an effective policy toward Africa, and especially toward Angola, where no fundamental U.S. interests were involved.

Such a felicitous outcome never occurred, however, because Kissinger's globalist doctrine of cold war competition blinded him to the local realities of the Angolan revolution. This proved to be a decisive handicap in the Nixon Administration's policy toward Africa. The Administration remained relatively uninterested in Africa, while the Watergate exposés diminished Nixon's own influence at the very time that Kissinger was consolidating his position as the pontiff of American diplomacy.

Perhaps no statement of the Nixon Administration had greater policy impact than National Security Study Memorandum (NSSM) 39. Prepared by Kissinger's staff during 1969, this was a comprehensive review with policy recommendations on southern Africa. The secret study proposed four different options for U.S. policy in the region: (1) closer relations with the White-dominated states and territories, including inter alia a relaxation of the unilateral U.S. arms embargo on the Portuguese territories to permit the export of "dual purpose" equipment (machinery usable in both civilian and military operations, such as computer systems); (2) selective relaxation of America's stance toward the White minority regimes, coupled with economic assistance of about $5 million to the Black states, to encourage peaceful change; (3) an extension of present policy opposing racial and colonial policies of the White regimes while seeking to maintain correct relations with them through such means as softening criticisms of Portuguese African policy at the U.N. (in the case of Portugal); (4) disengagement from the White minority regimes, including the maintenance of the arms embargo along with political pressures on the Portuguese.[20] "Tar baby," or the second option that would cleave U.S. policy to the White supremacy regimes, became official after Kissinger recommended a "lower profile" at the U.N., reduced pressure on the Portuguese, and additional assistance of about $5 million to the Black states of the region.[21] The incipient Angola policy was nicknamed "tar baby" by a State Department critic who foresaw that it would bind the United States to the Portuguese colonialists.

Complicity with the Portuguese characterized subsequent U.S.

policy toward Angola as the Administration acted on its premise that "there is no hope for the blacks to gain the political rights they seek through violence."[22] Strategic interests prevailed as the basic determinant of U.S. policy. In addition to the Azores bases, Kissinger valued the facilities of Portugal's African territories, which U.S. naval vessels and aircraft used for refueling and space-support missions. The "tar baby" option marked the emergence in Africa of a broader cold war global doctrine. The policy applied not only to Angola but also to Mozambique, the other southern African Portuguese territory. A war of national liberation was being waged there as well. However, Neto's support from the Soviet Union and Portuguese leftists made the MPLA a target of Kissinger's opprobrium from the outset. With limited knowledge of Africa and African nationalism, Kissinger fixed on the fact of this support as his chief criterion for selecting Angola as the testing ground of America's power and will against the Soviet Union.

In conformity with the "tar baby" option, the Nixon Administration enlarged U.S. assistance to Portugal, which also retained colonial domination of São Tomé e Principe, Guinea-Bissau, and the Cape Verde Islands off the Atlantic coast of Africa. This assistance included airplanes, $400 million in credits and loans, napalm, and the training of Portuguese officers in the United States.[23] The Administration easily justified aid to Europe's major colonial survivor by pointing to Portugal's membership in NATO and America's obligation to improve Lisbon's preparedness in the mutual security pact. Yet, long before Nixon's election in 1968, there was general awareness in the United States that Portugal diverted much of the aid from its NATO suppliers to combat the anticolonial forces in its African colonies. Andrew Young testified in 1976 as a congressman before the Senate hearings on Angola: "I think the first time I heard of napalm it was being used not in Vietnam but by the Portuguese in Mozambique and Angola."[24] American-made bullets and rockets also fell on Angola. But Washington was now firmly committed to Portugal and, through this ally, to the White settlers whom NSSM 39 had anointed.

American ties to Portugal were reinforced after Egypt's secret attack on Israel in October 1973. Because the United States used the Azores to resupply Israel during the war, Portugal, which had long imposed a year-by-year contract for the base, acquired additional bargaining leverage and seized the moment to demand new weapons for direct use in Africa. Kissinger arrived in Lisbon in December 1973 from his Middle East tour and agreed to Portuguese demands in blatant violation of the U.N. embargo on such assistance. The agreement also violated the U.S. policy of embargo imposed during the Kennedy Administration.

To the Portuguese, Kissinger's secret agreement represented firm American solidarity because he then went on to serve as Secretary of State, formally playing a role he had sometimes assumed de facto while William P. Rogers held the position in Nixon's first Administration. Although Nixon and Portugal's leader Marcello Caetano had apparently broached the subject of U.S. assistance before the Secretary's arrival in Lisbon, it was Kissinger who completed the agreement providing for a range of sophisticated matériel, including transport aircraft and "red-eye" (surface-to-air) missiles. After Kissinger returned to Washington, the word was whispered among informed officials in the upper echelons of the State Department that his agreement contained a far more egregious component: Kissinger consented to Portugal's use of the weapons in Africa. Rumors spread that the few Black officials in the State Department would resign in protest. However, Portugal never had the opportunity to use the U.S. weapons because socialists in Lisbon toppled Caetano's regime in a military coup d'état on April 25, 1974, while declaring a dissolution of the colonial empire. Kissinger's arms deal was never carried out.

The coup in Portugal jolted the men in Washington struggling to preserve Nixon's Presidency. The CIA was also caught by surprise. The coup, however, transpired at a crucial juncture, permitting the United States to reverse its embrace of the White settlers whom the new Portuguese regime itself was abandoning. The domestic pressures of Watergate then consumed policymakers' energies and time. In such a climate wisdom suggested the folly of embarking on new U.S. commitments abroad, especially in

Angola, where longstanding guerrilla warfare augured clear and immediate ill for U.S. policy. Perhaps some of the U.S. leaders had even read *Portugal and the Future,* a European bestseller written by General Antonio de Spinola, a former governor and commander of Guinea-Bissau. Spinola incisively exposed Portugal's inability to win colonial wars. The book provided unassailable warning against U.S. entry into a realm where Portugal no longer dared to tread. And the author became premier of Portugal following the coup. As Nixon's fortunes began to unravel in 1974, Kissinger had all the evidence to make a decisive retreat from the "tar baby" perspective.

But no such thing happened. Instead of a retreat from "tar baby," the Ford Administration, under guidance from Kissinger, who remained Secretary of State, plunged in deeper in Angola. Instead of accepting the Angolan struggle as a war of independence, Kissinger defined it as a campaign of Soviet adventurism. Instead of assimilating the Vietnam lessons of Great Power ineffectiveness in Third World wars of national liberation, Washington intervened on the side of the presumed pro-Western and moderate forces. Each of the U.S. decisions was made, and executed, before the end of the war in Vietnam.

The fateful decision to support the FNLA in 1975 was the U.S. response to Soviet support of the MPLA. According to Kissinger, the "overthrow of the Portuguese Government in April 1974, and the growing strength of the Portuguese Communist Party apparently convinced Moscow that a revolutionary situation was developing in Angola. The Soviet Union began to exploit this situation in the fall of 1974 through the shipment of arms and equipment to the MPLA."[25] His interpretation was clearly deceptive, not only because the Lisbon coup had no causal relationship to the revolutionary situation in Angola, but especially because the Angolans had been engaged in revolution for as long as fourteen years before the coup. Kissinger's fixation on the Soviet Union prevented him from seeing the reality of the Angolan situation.

Kissinger contended that communist forces without "any historic interests" in Angola backed the MPLA.[26] Although the communist countries lacked historic interest in Angola, Kissinger's contention was still misleading because all three of the Angolan movements had obtained significant communist support at one time or another prior to Washington's intervention on the side of Roberto's FNLA and Savimbi's UNITA. Savimbi, who visited Peking during 1964 in his erstwhile capacity as FNLA Foreign Minister, later patterned UNITA after the self-reliant strategy of the Chinese.[27] Chairman Mao Tse-tung, who received Savimbi, provided a modicum of training, financial support, and publicity.

Roberto, who followed Savimbi to Peking late in 1973, also solicited Mao's assistance, and the first contingent of Chinese military instructors was dispatched to the FNLA camp of Kinkuzu (in southern Zaire) in July 1974, followed by 450 tons of arms to the guerrillas.[28] Because of the Sino-Soviet ideological conflict, Peking had its own reasons to oppose Moscow and, like Washington, decided the most effective way to undercut Soviet influence in Angola was to support the FNLA, which then appeared to be the most viable alternative to the Soviet-backed MPLA. When the Angolan movements clashed in civil war at the end of 1975, Roberto boasted that "all my troops are trained by the Chinese."[29]

The United States therefore imitated a policy of anti-MPLA support that, paradoxically, had been laid out by China. On January 22, 1975, Kissinger considered a CIA proposal for $300,000 in covert U.S. support to the FNLA at a meeting of the 40 Committee,[30] the NSC subsidiary responsible for approving clandestine activities. The meeting took place before the Angolan parties established a tripartite transitional government in Luanda at the end of January, agreeing to proceed with a regime of national reconciliation. Nathaniel Davis, one of a number of Assistant Secretaries of State for African Affairs under Kissinger, pressed the case for a diplomatic solution.[31] Kissinger nonetheless approved the CIA proposal, rejecting the diplomatic option outright and beginning a pattern of intransigence that typified his subsequent policy to confront the Soviet Union in Angola.

From the outset the Administration concealed the Angola operation from the American public and, on the whole, from Congress as well. John Stockwell, the CIA agent who headed the clandestine Angola Task Force, reports that a June 27, 1975, meeting of the NSC discussed new U.S. options, including financial support of $40 million, material, and covert action to give the FNLA and UNITA superiority over the MPLA.[32] The Africa Division of the CIA presented the 40 Committee with a plan of covert operations. President Ford promptly approved it and authorized $6 million in expenditures.[33] Another $8 million was allocated later. And on July 29, 1975, the United States airlifted the first load of arms to Kinshasa for its putative allies in Angola.

The initial decision to intervene did not include U.S. support to UNITA, but the assistance to the FNLA confirmed Washington's intention of repeating its alliance-seeking strategy which had produced such success during the Congo crisis. Roberto was then identified as the prospective American ally par excellence. Although Kissinger had the option of preventive diplomacy to muster external support for a unified Angolan government, the chance to confront the Soviet Union proved irresistible. Selection of the FNLA also extended U.S. preferences for Angolan leadership into the civil war, whose political rivalries partly reflected the existing ethno-linguistic divisions in Angolan society. Kissinger thus introduced into Africa the American equivalent of the European colonial practice of divide and rule.

Zaire's Mobutu performed a critical role in the U.S. intervention. He had provided staunch support to Roberto, whose FNLA enjoyed sanctuary on Zairian soil. For years Mobutu had singled out the socialist MPLA as an enemy of his pro-Western military dictatorship. He therefore harbored his own vested interest in the MPLA's defeat. It was Mobutu who first urged China to support the FNLA during his visit to Peking in January 1973. Mobutu's advice carried special weight in Washington, not only because of Zaire's strategic value to the United States, but because American investment in Zaire amounted to almost $800 million (or about three times more than the American investments in Angola).[34] Mobutu allowed his country to serve as a conduit of U.S. assistance to the FNLA, and later to UNITA, with the result that Zaire became a vital link in the chain of U.S. policy toward Angola.

The Soviet Union and other East European countries had been

providing exclusive assistance in arms and training to the MPLA for more than a decade before the American decision. In early 1974, however, the Soviets terminated this support, apparently on the assumption that the MPLA faced imminent demise owing to divisiveness within its ranks. A major MPLA commander, Daniel Chipenda, bolted the movement with his followers to align with the FNLA. MPLA guerrillas, who once amounted to an estimated forty-five hundred, had as few as three thousand men at the time of the coup in Portugal.[35] Neto managed to survive only by rallying new forces, particularly in Luanda and the adjacent hinterlands where the MPLA had obtained the bulk of its original recruits.

The FNLA, by contrast, had mobilized nearly fifteen hundred troops,[36] while UNITA mustered perhaps a thousand. This disparity in men and arms may have provoked the Soviets in November 1974 to resume arms shipments to the MPLA, lest Peking, through its support to the FNLA and UNITA, emerge triumphant in the global Sino-Soviet rivalry for influence among revolutionaries. By the spring of 1975, huge quantities of Soviet arms—rockets, AK-47 rifles, machine guns, and bazookas—began to reach the MPLA in Angola via the Congo-Brazzaville, a socialist ally, and directly at depots along the Angolan border.

Civil war ensued in Angola on March 23, 1975, when FNLA troops crossed the Zairian-Angolan frontier with reinforcements from Mobutu's army and gunned down scores of MPLA troops north of Luanda. The outbreak of fratricide instantly caused the two-month-old transitional government to collapse. The beleaguered MPLA managed to retain its stronghold in the region around the capital, but its prospects appeared to fade against the numerically superior FNLA. At this point the Soviet Union stepped up its delivery of weapons to the MPLA. With the new arms the MPLA put up such stiff resistance that China soon considered withdrawing its support from the battered FNLA. During the summer of 1975, as the NSC approved major increases in military aid to the FNLA and UNITA, Fidel Castro transported 260 Cuban military advisors to join the MPLA,[37] embarking on what would eventually become a massive Cuban presence in Angola.

Castro entered the fray upon Neto's urgent request. Cuba did not intervene in response to Moscow, which neither funded nor directed the Cuban operation.[38] Cuba had maintained close contacts with the MPLA since Ché Guevara initiated them in August 1965, when he fought among MPLA guerrillas in the Congo,[39] and Neto met Castro in Havana the following year. When he received the aid request from the MPLA in mid-July 1975, Castro responded in the context of relations which were both long established and consistent with his policy of assistance to revolutionary forces in the Third World. The magnitude of the Cuban military operation, however, was completely new. From the small contingent of 260, the Cuban soldiers in Angola rose to 1,000 in late September 1975, and peaked at an estimated 12,000 in January 1976, one month before the civil war ended.

U.S. entanglement in Angola also deepened. The supply of money and arms that had begun in early 1975 increased in the heat of the war. As the MPLA-Cuban forces won a series of impressive victories, Kissinger hardened in his stance of confrontation. Because he perceived the MPLA challenge strictly as an outgrowth of Soviet strategy in Angola, he persisted in his quest for an American counteraction. In the aftermath of disengagement by Portugal, Angola's old colonial overlord, the United States plunged in deeper to enforce its will in the Angolan war of independence.

## REALPOLITIK IN SEARCH OF AN ALLY

Angola's battle lines reflecting the international rivalry between the United States and the Soviet Union were drawn sharply by the summer of 1975. Arrayed against the MPLA and its Soviet bloc supporters in the internal struggle for power were the FNLA, its fractionalist ally UNITA, and the Western bloc supporting them. In addition to the United States, the Western bloc included France, which assisted the pro-Western movements with substantial assistance; Great Britain, which gave them modest material support; and West Germany and Belgium, which, like the other industrial powers, sought to secure their future interests in the mineral-rich province of southern Zaire through support to the FNLA and

UNITA. Zaire tended to function as an extension of American policy. For separate reasons, as noted, China opposed the MPLA. Thus the MPLA confronted a formidable phalanx of opposition.

The Western phalanx grew when South Africa deployed its troops inside Angola in June. South Africa evidently assumed that the disorder in Angola offered a low-risk opportunity to smash both the MPLA and SWAPO, and thus to ensure the presence of moderate regimes in Angola and Namibia.[40] The South Africans came in response to Savimbi, who begged the White supremacist regime for urgent assistance. The support of this alliance condemned the UNITA leader before the Organization of African Unity (OAU) and, fatally, among his own people.

South Africa, meanwhile, had intervened partly to protect its own interests. Its military and intelligence services were accustomed to close collaboration with those of Portugal and Rhodesia. South African soldiers had used a command post in southeastern Angola to launch assaults against both Angolan nationalists and SWAPO guerrillas before the coup in Portugal. South Africa had an additional stake in the giant Cunene River hydroelectric project in Angola, which it financed to produce energy for industry and uranium mining in Namibia, and water for irrigation in Portuguese Angola. South African soldiers engaged the MPLA in a minor skirmish early in August 1975, but when the major foreign intervention began in late October, nearly fifteen hundred White soldiers from South Africa and mercenaries from Portugal and other European countries invaded southern Angola. Crossing the border from Namibia, they aimed to inflict devastating blows on positions previously secured by MPLA and Cuban forces. Before the MPLA declared independence on November 11, South Africa had expedited four to five thousand troops to shore up Savimbi.[41]

Official U.S. policy scorned the use of American soldiers in Angola. However, mercenaries, many of them American veterans fresh from armed service in Vietnam, began to fight alongside UNITA during the fall of 1975. These adventurers numbered about four hundred and had been recruited by the CIA on five-month contracts at a cost of $172,700 per month.[42] (In the same period, there were apparently seven hundred White American mercenaries fighting on the side of Ian Smith against Black majority rule in Zimbabwe.)

Perhaps because the mercenaries were to be used in Africa, Black Americans became a special target of recruitment. Roy Innis, Chairman of the Congress of Racial Equality (CORE), based in New York City, traversed the United States actively seeking Black Vietnam veterans late in 1975. Although he denied involvement with the U.S. government, his open appeals in public speeches and the media indicated that Innis acted with the tacit consent of the Ford Administration. (Title 18 of the U.S. Code prohibits the recruitment of American citizens for service in a foreign army.) He also denied that the Black recruits would be used by the pro-Western movements, but CORE had contacted UNITA only.[43]

The White House denied that any U.S. agency had recruited or trained American mercenaries for service in Angola. In the midst of the recruitment, Press Secretary Ron Nessen declared: "There is no agency of the U.S. government using American mercenaries in Angola, nor is any U.S. government agency recruiting, hiring or training American mercenaries."[44] Belatedly the American public discovered the truth of the matter after the MPLA government paraded two of the captured Americans in Luanda and executed them.

Kissinger disclaimed U.S. complicity with South Africa at the Senate hearings on Angola early in 1976: "Some charge that we have acted in collusion with South Africa. That is not true. We had no foreknowledge of South Africa's intentions, and in no way cooperated with it militarily."[45] One of those who charged U.S. collusion was Pieter W. Botha, then South Africa's Defense Minister. He affirmed that South Africa entered Angola with the knowledge and approval of the United States.[46] (Botha argued that one aspect of the U.S. support in Angola "was that America had tried to 'out-Moscow' Moscow."[47]) The Senate Intelligence Committee issued its year-long study in mid-July 1978, documenting U.S. collusion with South Africa.[48]

A few members of Congress had maintained vigilant suspicion of Administration policy long before Kissinger warned in November 1975 that the United States could not remain "indifferent" to Soviet and Cuban military intervention in Angola.[49] Senator Dick Clark, who headed the Senate's Subcommittee on African Affairs, had traveled to Angola the preceding August for discussions with leaders of the FNLA and UNITA as well as the MPLA, and he had returned firmly opposed to U.S. intervention. Clark remained unaware that Kissinger's Angola policy had been in effect for the past six months; however, he was convinced enough of nefarious U.S. activity to propose before the Senate Foreign Relations Committee an amendment to the Defense Appropriations Bill of 1976 for a termination of all covert aid to Angola. The White House inadvertently accelerated the passage of the Clark amendment through the Senate testimony of CIA Deputy Director of Operations William Nelson, who admitted the CIA's delivery of arms to Angola. Deputy Assistant Secretary of State for African Affairs Ed Mulcahy then insisted that no arms were sent until informed that Nelson had told it all.

Two weeks later Senator John Tunney won Senate passage, 54 to 22, for his amendment to prevent the use in Angola of any funds from the Defense Appropriations Bill (of fiscal year 1976). Since this bill contained the budget of the CIA, the Senate vote was another significant sign of congressional distrust of Kissinger's policy.

Kissinger, who finally conceded to U.S. involvement in Angola after Nelson's bombshell, persisted with his policy of confrontation, still secretly, but now in defiance of the will of Congress. According to Stockwell, a CIA spokesman promised Savimbi another million dollars in arms and money on February 11, 1976,[50] two days after President Ford signed the Tunney amendment into law. A week later Kissinger instructed the American chargé in Kinshasa to inform UNITA leaders of continuing U.S. support for as long as effective resistance to the MPLA was demonstrated. It may be objected that Stockwell's account represented the embittered retrospective of a disillusioned American. But it is worth noting that William Colby, who served as CIA director during the Angola operation, has since conceded: "I wouldn't say he [Stockwell] made any of this up."[51]

The House of Representatives voted 323 to 99 in January 1976 to support the Senate bill for an embargo on covert aid to Angola. This was a month before Kissinger secreted his directive to the Kinshasa chargé. What J. William Fulbright once called the "arrogance of power" had seized Kissinger's intelligence, distorted his judgment, and finally obsessed him with a policy grossly at odds with the realities of guerrilla warfare in Angola and contrary to the majority opinion of Congress.

Kissinger, however, was not alone in his stubborn pursuit of an American resolution of the Angolan war. He maintained the support of President Ford and certain members of Congress, especially Jack Kemp, a New York representative who resurfaced in 1981 as a theoretician behind the economic program of the Reagan Administration. Kemp addressed the House on January 27, 1976:

> The United States—the people and this body—should understand clearly that getting into war in Vietnam and supplying arms to our friends in Angola are not one and the same thing. No one is asking America to send in troops, and I believe none should be sent in. However, some shipment of arms will be required if the pro-Western forces are to stand a chance at all in the field against an enemy who is being armed by the other power in today's war.[52]

Such statements ignored the advice of Tanzania's President Julius Nyerere: "At present the conflict in Angola is not a fight between Communists and anti-Communists. It is a fight for real independence, and against racialist South Africa."[53]

What eventually confirmed the broad national support of the MPLA was the failure of the extraordinary Western coalition seeking to destroy it. The United States and its NATO allies, joined by South Africa and American and European mercenaries, could not save the pro-Western movements despite their relative parity in weaponry and manpower. The MPLA had mobilized twenty thousand troops by the summer of 1975, the FNLA, fifteen thousand, and UNITA, four thousand, according to CIA estimates.[54] (If Roberto's repeated claim of thirty thousand FNLA guerrillas is given credence, then the pro-Western elements enjoyed an overwhelming superiority.) The rapid increase and mobilization of MPLA guerrillas was attributable in part to new Cuban and Soviet weapons for thousands of MPLA adherents who had been waiting hitherto without adequate arm supplies.[55] In the meantime the Western coalition and China had intervened with major external assistance to the FNLA and UNITA prior to the advent of the Cubans. The triumph of the MPLA socialist forces must therefore be seen in terms of what at the time seemed like an invincible opposition.

Although the MPLA's victory was inseparable from the support provided by Cuban soldiers and Soviet military advisors, a proper assessment of this victory must take into account the MPLA's considerable assets apart from its foreign support. It had strong leadership in Neto and his assistants, such as Lucio Lara, who became secretary of party organization and political and ideological education after independence. These leaders endowed the MPLA with a well-developed coherent ideology. They took advantage of their involuntary exile in the Congo-Brazzaville and Zambia, enforced by Portuguese military assaults in the 1960s when the movement was in its gestation period, to build a fairly autonomous organization with mass support. This was especially the case in the oil-rich enclave of Cabinda and in the wide hinterlands of eastern Angola. Luanda remained more or less an MPLA enclave during the anticolonial struggle. These advantages varied according to the ebb and flow of the MPLA's resistance to its Angolan and Portuguese opposition, but it was well-established before the arrival of the Soviet bloc forces.

UNITA and the FNLA, on the other hand, suffered from numerous deficiencies that external support failed to alleviate and even aggravated. The FNLA always operated under the shadow of Mobutu, whose support was limited to building the FNLA forces to a point just short of where they could challenge his authority. Roberto, ensconced in his Zairian refuge for thirteen years, failed to demonstrate exemplary leadership by never fighting against Portugal in Angola, whereas Neto and his subordinates penetrated settler strongholds from time to time. Savimbi meanwhile had hastily assembled his Ovimbundu legions into a regional constituency of ethnic-group solidarity, with himself as the group's, as opposed to the nation's, paramount leader. This constricted organizational base, dysfunctional and loosely formed, reduced his effectiveness. Like the FNLA, UNITA also lacked a well-defined ideology capable of inspiring a broad constituency. The MPLA program, on the other hand, did not stop at nationalist opposition to Portugal but went on to give Angolans an agenda for national economic reconstruction and development after winning the immediate objective of political independence. Savimbi himself shifted his own ideological commitments depending on the wheel of fortune; he relinquished his identity with Maoist ideology as soon as the CIA rolled in with American dollars. From the African standpoint, Savimbi was fatally compromised by his alliance with South Africa and the mercenaries.

Meanwhile Kissinger, who acknowledged that the United States had no particular stake in Angola, insisted that U.S. support to the pro-Western movements was motivated not by ideological factors but by a determination to prevent Soviet bloc forces from imposing a regime on the Angolans. At his press conference on December 23, 1975 he asserted:

> The issue is not whether the country of Angola represents a vital interest to the United States. The issue is whether the Soviet Union, backed by a Cuban expeditionary force, can impose on two-thirds of the population its own brand of government. And the issue is not whether the United States should resist it with its own military forces. . . . The President has made it clear that under no circumstances will we introduce American military forces. The issue is whether the United States will disqualify itself from giving a minimal amount of economic and military assistance to the two-thirds of the population that is resisting an expeditionary force from outside the hemisphere and a massive introduction of Soviet military equipment.[56]

The MPLA then controlled twelve of the fifteen provinces in Angola. Contrary to Kissinger's assertion, the MPLA had achieved these initial but critical strongholds in the four-month period from July to October 1975 without Cuban troops through superior organization, recruitment, and allegiance of the MPLA guerrillas. As noted, the Cuban troops did not arrive in huge numbers until late October. Although Moscow conveyed a huge supply of weapons to Angola during 1975, $200 million worth according to Kissinger's account,[57] the MPLA won its initial successes without an exceptional advantage over the FNLA in the number or quality of weapons. Furthermore, the CIA had already filtered much of the "minimal" assistance, which ultimately climbed to $31.7 million,[58] to the pro-Western factions. Kissinger thus announced policy intentions that already had been implemented. Indeed the combined American and European military aid to the FNLA and UNITA, for which there has been no final reckoning, may well have surpassed Soviet assistance to the MPLA.

Kissinger, the advocate of diplomacy as a preferred instrument of foreign policy, persisted in rejecting a diplomatic approach to the Angolan war. This continued until the eve of the decisive battlefield victories of the joint MPLA-Cuban forces that ushered the war to a quick conclusion early in 1976. The United States, according to his testimony before the Senate Foreign Relations Committee, did approach the Soviet Union the preceding October with an offer, contingent upon Soviet reciprocity, to use American influence to stop the flow of foreign military assistance into Angola.[59] Assistant Secretary of State for African Affairs Donald Easum had strongly urged the path of negotiations soon after his appointment in March 1974. In October he consulted the leaders of the FNLA in Zaire as well as UNITA and the MPLA in Angola and, during a subsequent stopover in Tanzania, had hinted at a possible U.S. diplomatic initiative vis-à-vis the Angolan war. This infuriated Kissinger, and twenty-four hours after Easum returned to Washington he was fired. During his brief tenure as Assistant Secretary Easum had successfully blocked CIA proposals to increase the small amounts of money being paid to Roberto every month for information.

When Kissinger finally did undertake diplomatic steps with overtures to the OAU in January 1976, the end of the war was already in sight. But the imminent defeat of the FNLA and UNITA was neither the exclusive nor principal reason that rendered diplomacy futile at this point. Kissinger's obsession with anti-Sovietism had foreclosed at the outset the option of diplomacy, the area where his skills might have produced salutary results.

The American fiasco in Angola set in motion a chain of other negative consequences which bedeviled U.S. foreign relations even after Kissinger left office. First of all, American intervention in Angola gravely antagonized numerous African states. The disciple of realpolitik stupefied Africans with his contention that America's "sole objective was an African solution of an African problem."[60] At this point the Angolan war of independence had been waged for fourteen years without benefit of such American concern, not to mention the much longer history of U.S. neglect and indifference toward Africa in general. Kissinger so irritated the leaders of Nigeria with pressures to oppose the MPLA (especially in the OAU) that they denied him admission to the country when he sought to go there in 1976. Nigeria was then America's second largest supplier of oil, a trade partner not to be offended.

Second, the defeat hardened American policymakers in an ideological resolve that caused them, unreasonably, to refuse diplomatic recognition to the MPLA regime. The Ford Administration pointed to the continued presence of Cuban troops in Angola as the rationale for the American refusal. Moreover, Kissinger had defined policy in such a rigid ideological dichotomy between East and West that many proponents of recognition became intimidated by the prospect of being portrayed as remiss or "soft" on communism.

The U.S. policy in Angola also began to erode détente, the successful policy of relaxation in Soviet-American tension which Kissinger himself had helped to build. Because the globalist approach necessarily conjoins discrete aspects of U.S. national interests to the totality of America's stakes in the world, Kissinger linked the Angola policy to such issues as Soviet-American negotiations at the strategic arms limitations talks (SALT). After threatening to cancel his negotiating mission to Moscow late in 1975, he declared in January 1976 that Soviet action in Angola would, if continued, impinge on SALT as well as the general relationship between the United States and the Soviet Union.[61] Cabinet-level meetings on various Soviet-American joint commissions, routine in previous years, were suspended.[62] The subsequent decline of détente can be traced to origins in the failed U.S. policy toward Angola.

For the United States, the Kissinger policy engendered a defeat of considerable proportions amid the concurrent and greater debacle in Vietnam. The establishment of a socialist regime in Mozambique during 1975 further aggravated Washington's setback in Angola. The traditional U.S. lack of policy toward Africa, America's reliance on the old European colonial balance, and the U.S. willingness to cooperate internationally with South Africa were brought to a breaking point. Dumbfounded by the rapid and revolutionary changes in Angola, the Ford Administration misunderstood the political upheavals and, in the end, succumbed to America's first major disaster in independent Africa.

## CARTER AND THE RESURGENCE OF REALPOLITIK

A neophyte to foreign policy in the Presidential campaign of 1976, candidate Jimmy Carter advanced the most trenchant observation of what was wrong with past U.S. policy toward Angola: "The United States position in Angola should be one which admits that we missed the opportunity to be a positive and creative force for good . . . during the years that we supported Portuguese colonization. We should also realize that the Russian and Cuban presence in Angola . . . need not constitute a threat to United States interests; nor does that presence mean the existence of a Communist satellite on the continent."[63] However, Carter never fulfilled the promise suggested by this early insight, for the United States not only maintained the policy of nonrecognition of Angola during the four years of his Administration, the President himself, a pioneer of foreign policy based on human rights, ultimately yielded to cold war ideology.

The Africa policy of the Carter Administration was shaped at different times and with different emphases by four key leaders: U.N. Ambassador Andrew Young, Secretary of State Cyrus R. Vance, National Security Advisor Zbigniew Brzezinski, and Carter himself. Vance, a veteran policy expert, tended to preoccupy himself with procedural rather than theoretical approaches to foreign affairs. Thus, the task of defining the philosophy as well as the strategy of an African policy devolved upon Young, who had studied African problems as a congressman from Atlanta, and Brzezinski, who had specialized in Soviet and international politics as a professor at Columbia University. Young, who advocated idealism and morality in foreign policy, proposed an all-inclusive openness toward the different African nations, whereas Brzezinski looked on Africa from a cold war perspective of resistance to Soviet expansion. Like Secretary Vance, the President was alternately instructed and persuaded by the two approaches. Between Young's regional outlook and Brzezinski's global *Weltanschauung,* policy conflict was inevitable.

Before taking office these four leaders had belonged to the Trilateral Commission. This exclusive, elite policy study group was organized in 1973 under the leadership of David Rockefeller to propose practical policy options for the Western world axis formed by the United States, Western Europe, and Japan. As the Commission's director, Brzezinski had introduced such new recruits as Carter and Young to the organization. Through this association, the Carter team presumably could have developed a consensus on Africa long before the election. But such an outcome did not happen.

"The Africa policy of the Carter administration," Young asserted in 1979, "is based on the notion that American foreign policy ought to pursue genuine, legitimate American and world interests. It ought not to be a reactionary policy simply to stop the Soviet Union."[64] As Soviet military advisors and Cuban troops maintained their positions in Ethiopia as well as in Angola, the U.N. Ambassador asserted: "I don't think the U.S. has anything to fear from the Russians militarily or in economic competition, nor do we have anything to fear of communist domination, except when it is enforced through military power." Soon after taking office Young put forth his pro-Africa orientation by declaring that the Cuban soldiers constituted a stabilizing force in Angola.

"The proper role of the United States is to deter Soviet military power,"[65] Brzezinski insisted in stating the goals of American foreign policy in 1979. Although he minimized his perceptions of the threat of Soviet domination, his previous actions betrayed him: he had linked the Africa policy to such cold war issues as SALT II; he had attempted in the previous year to prevent a Carter-approved sale of military equipment to the Soviet Union; and he had helped to shape the President's 1980 budget, which proposed the biggest military expenditures in U.S. history to that point. Born in Poland, the son of Poland's Ambassador to Canada, Brzezinski belonged to a privileged group of émigrés whose fortunes and privileges were dashed by the Soviet occupation of Poland during World War II. This background disposed him to approach American foreign policy from a manifestly anti-Soviet and Eurocentric perspective. This resulted in an ideological rigidity that defined policy in terms of a cold war bipolarity between the United States and the Soviet Union.

Brzezinski was uninterested in Africa except as it figured in Soviet strategy. Indicative of his lack of interest was the fact that the National Security Council bureau responsible for Africa remained vacant for long periods during the first two years of the Carter Administration. Brzezinski, of course, was director of the Council. Moreover, Brzezinski appeared to be less knowledgeable than Kissinger on Africa's history and development. *Africa and the Communist World,* a study Brzezinski had produced as a professor at Columbia University, offered his peculiar insight into Africa: "Today Africa is in the midst of a profound revolution, spanning in decades processes which elsewhere took centuries to mature, molding nations out of often truly primitive tribes, seeking modernity without yet, in some places, having reached even the stage of backwardness."[66]

Between them, Brzezinski and Kissinger exerted a preponderant influence on American foreign policy in the 1970s. More than other decision-makers serving the President, these two Special Assistants to the President for National Security Affairs formulated and defined the modalities of anti-Sovietism, their common ideological ground. In the assessment of Hodding Carter, III, the Assistant Secretary of State for Public Affairs during the Carter Administration, Brzezinski also "apparently saw himself as another Kissinger," although "he had neither Kissinger's intellect nor his political savvy."[67] Like Kissinger, however, Brzezinski maintained immediate access to the President, and he capitalized on this privilege to press his relentless pursuit of dominance in foreign policy.

In the meantime Andrew Young moved ahead with his pro-Africa approach, sometimes with Presidential approval and sometimes without. Not only did he see no problem in the presence of Cuban troops, he indicated that these troops might play a positive role in helping the fledgling MPLA regime to defend Gulf Oil's investments in Cabinda. From Young's standpoint, no insuperable obstacle blocked the path to U.S. recognition of Angola. For Brzezinski, on the other hand, the Soviet bloc presence was anathema to American interests in Angola as well as in the whole region of southern Africa.

Young's approach appeared to win White House favor in the first eighteen months of Carter's tenure. His popularity quickly spread to Africa, and when he traveled there in February 1977 Nigeria extended its good offices to enable him to discuss a normalization of relations with MPLA leader Neto, who had become Angola's first president. Their meeting, which took place in the Nigerian town of Kano, was a major breakthrough. Indeed, it could be argued that a meeting of such high-level officials as the U.S. Ambassador to the U.N. and Angola's Chief of State represented an implicit form of diplomatic recognition.

A significant amount of support was gathering for U.S. recognition of Angola. For instance, the consensus of a State Department conference on Angola in February 1978, which included American businesspeople, academicians and government officials, was to approve the establishment of diplomatic relations.[68] Gulf Oil Corporation also favored such an approach. Senator Paul E. Tsongas made a forceful appeal in the *New York Times:* "The outmoded outlook toward African nations as passive battlegrounds for superpowers must be replaced by a new realism. We can begin recognizing reality in Angola, and pursuing mutual interest, by immediate recognition of its Government." [69]

Never, however, did Brzezinski waver in his anti-Soviet rigidity nor in his efforts to convert President Carter to this viewpoint. In February 1977 the President hinted at a normalization of American-Angolan relations; however, this depended on the accuracy of his "indirect information" concerning Castro's promise to withdraw his soldiers. [70] Carter even declared his desire to "move toward the reestablishment [sic] of normal relationships between our own country and Angola," indicating his inclination toward Young's pro-Africa approach. But this apparent policy shift evaporated in May 1977, when Castro airlifted more soldiers to assist Neto's regime following an attempted coup by a disgruntled faction within the MPLA. This episode proved to be grist for Brzezinski's mill and the President did not return to his ostensible policy change in favor of recognition.

The policy of nonrecognition took hold in the Carter Administration during 1978. Adoption of the Brzezinski line evolved without the participation or knowledge of many Administration elites, including the chiefs of the U.N. mission. For instance, Donald F. McHenry, a Deputy Representative to the United Nations, boasted in reference to past CIA intervention in Angola: "As a matter of national policy, we simply don't engage in that kind of activity anymore." [71] This was before CIA director Stansfield Turner and David Aaron, Brzezinski's National Security Council assistant, approached Senator Dick Clark in May with a program of covert aid to UNITA. [72] The proposed program directly violated the Clark amendment's prohibition of any U.S. military assistance to Angola without congressional authorization. Carter himself declared his belief that no "responsible person in my administration would have violated the so-called Clark amendment"; however, this was before news leaks of Turner's venture forced the embarrassed President to recant. [73] According to Turner's subsequent testimony, it was not the President but a committee of the NSC which had authorized him to consult Clark. The Administration did not carry through with its evident intention to circumvent the arms prohibition to UNITA, but this episode confirmed Brzezinski's growing influence in the determination of U.S. policy toward Angola.

The subsequent hardening of the nonrecognition posture coincided with a deterioration in the influence of Andrew Young. Although the decline in his position was attributable in part to his controversial and unconventional diplomacy, it resulted primarily from larger causes. Young was credited with delivering 83 percent of the Black vote to Carter in the Presidential election, but he had failed to exploit Carter's indebtedness to him by enlarging his influence in the Administration. Thus he always remained on the fringes of executive decision-making, without major input into the policy process or decisive impact upon it. From his base at the U.N. mission in New York, the Ambassador was distant from the locus of decision-making power in Washington, where Brzezinski continually promoted his goals even in opposition to the Secretary of State. Furthermore, the U.N. ambassadorship, by definition, has traditionally been a policy-implementing rather than a policy-making position within the State Department. Young's tenuous position (discussed further in Chapter 4) declined altogether by the end of 1978 as the White House acceded to the Brzezinski school of thought.

Cold war fixation entrapped the White House anew during 1979, especially after the Soviet invasion of Afghanistan in December. Once more U.S. policy toward Angola became a hostage of anti-Sovietism. Then on June 7, 1980, South Africa invaded Angola again, with three thousand troops, killing more than three hundred Angolan civilians.[74] Pretoria rationalized the operation, which involved infantry, battalions, armored cars, and jet fighters, as a hot pursuit of SWAPO guerrillas bivouacked near Angola's southern border. The aggression was not provoked by the MPLA regime and represented South Africa's biggest attack since 1975. Regardless of the motivation, South Africa thereby confirmed that it posed a clear and continuing danger to the national security of Angola.

Angola's Ambassador to the U.N. Elisio de Figueiredo informed the U.N. Security Council that South Africa "uses our territory as its battlefield and our people as its sport."[75] Twelve of the Security Council's members voted to condemn the attack. The other three—Great Britain, France, and the United States—abstained.

As the South African invasion went forward, the Senate removed restrictions on the President's authority to provide military and covert assistance to the adversaries of the Angolan government if he determined that such aid was in the interests of the national security of the United States. As a result of opposition mounted by Stephen J. Solarz, chairman of the House subcommittee on Africa, the House rejected the measure, which recommended only that the President inform the Senate Foreign Relations Committee of his intentions in private, thus effectively eliminating the restrictions imposed by the Clark amendment in 1976. The amendment resulted from an attempt by Senator Jesse Helms, an extremist Republican conservative, to repeal the Clark amendment outright. Meanwhile Republican Presidential candidate Ronald Reagan declared that he would provide weapons to assist UNITA's Jonas Savimbi. "I don't see anything wrong with someone who wants to free themselves from the rule of an outside power, which is Cubans and East Germans."[76] Savimbi had been allowed to visit the United States during November 1979 to seek more American support for his die-hard struggle against the MPLA regime.

To appreciate the full magnitude of the resurgent anti-Sovietism in Washington, it is necessary to relate the vigorous and extensive overtures the Angolan government undertook to prepare the way for diplomatic relations with the United States. First, the Angolans reached a spectacular reconciliation with Zaire in August 1978. In exchange for Mobutu's neutralization of FNLA remnants in Zaire, and hence a demobilization of forces along the Zairian-Angolan frontier, the Neto regime agreed to neutralize the ex-Katangan militias in northern Angola, who had struck the rich Shaba region in successive attacks during 1977 and 1978. Whereas Mobutu's decision effectively eliminated the FNLA, Neto's virtually precluded a third Shaba invasion. Zaire benefited additionally by acquiring the right to ship its minerals from Shaba on the reconstructed Benguela railway, which runs from the Angolan-Zairian border in the east to the Angolan port of Lobito with its opening to the Atlantic Ocean.

Angola consummated its rapprochement with its former nemesis by agreeing to sell Zaire thirty-thousand tons of crude oil annually, beginning in December 1979.[77] Most of Zaire's Shaba exports, of course, were destined for Western markets. Notwithstanding the lack of diplomatic relations, the Neto government also received Young's associate, Donald F. McHenry, who had mediated the settlement between Mobutu and Neto during June 1978. In addition, McHenry convinced Neto to encourage SWAPO leaders to accept a U.N.-sponsored five-nation plan for a negotiated settlement of the liberation war against South African domination in Namibia. Neto was first presented with the proposal for a demilitarized zone along the Angolan-Namibian frontier by Donald Easum, who was then U.S. Ambassador to Nigeria. (South Africa, which also endorsed the resulting plan for peace in Namibia, later reneged on the agreement.)

President Neto took a second initiative to normalize relations with the United States by sending an explicit appeal to the Carter Administration: "We are prepared to establish diplomatic relations with the United States, but the Americans must accept us as we are."[78] The socialist identity of Angolans hardly represented an insurmountable impediment to American receptivity, particularly in view of the ambitious American drive begun by Kissinger and renewed by Brzezinski to establish relations with China, the largest communist state in the world. Neto made no concessions on the presence of Soviet bloc forces, which in June 1980 consisted of approximately 5,000 East Europeans and 27,000 Cubans (7,000 of them technical assistants, the rest soldiers).[79]

Third, the Angolans began in December 1978 to emphasize their desire for Western assistance to increase production in their oil fields. Gulf Oil Corporation was then producing about 135,000 barrels daily of Angola's oil, providing the government with estimated annual revenues of $600 million. Texaco retained an interest in northern Angola and in an adjacent undeveloped offshore deposit. The Arthur D. Little Company was contracted to advise Angola on oil legislation. To regulate foreign participation in its oil development, the Neto regime promulgated a law allowing foreign companies a 25 to 30 percent share of any production from new discoveries made by the companies. The law also established an exceptional premium for those companies that developed the largest number of exploratory wells and produced at the fastest output. Senator George McGovern visited Angola the same month and attested to the good relations between Luanda and the American companies.[80]

Nevertheless, U.S. policy toward Angola continued to be circumscribed by the strictures of Henry Kissinger. Despite the MPLA's effective control of Angola since 1975, the United States clung to the nonrecognition policy. On September 30, 1980, Assistant Secretary of State for African Affairs Richard M. Moose stated: "The U.S. has not established diplomatic relations with the People's Republic of Angola because of our concern about the presence of 15–21,000 Cuban troops in Angola, the role they play, and our opposition in principle to Cuban intervention in regional conflicts for purposes that serve Soviet objectives."[81] One feature of the Cubans' role concerned their participation in defending Cabinda, the Gulf Oil enclave. Another involved assistance to help the MPLA secure from attacks by surviving UNITA forces thousands of miles of frontier, the 840-mile Benguela railway, and several thousand miles of roads in the east and the central highlands. Still another Cuban responsibility was to aid in defending Angola's 1,800-mile frontier with South Africa, which remained under constant threat of attack from Pretoria.

The resurgence of anti-Sovietism in Washington grew as the advocates of recognition of Angola left the government. Young, for example, resigned as U.S. Ambassador to the U.N. in August 1979. In the meantime the overtures of the Angolan government, which were reaffirmed by President José Eduardo dos Santos after Neto's death in 1979, proved fruitless. Brzezinski's triumph was complete.

Consequently, President Carter vacated the White House with

the Kissinger policy of nonrecognition intact. From 1975 to 1980 the United States moved no closer to a normalization of relations with Angola. Indeed, the national conservative reaction that contributed to the defeat of Carter indicated that anti-Sovietism had become stronger and more deeply entrenched in the political system as a whole. Certainly it dominated the foreign policy thinking of such a cold war stalwart as Secretary of State Haig in the Reagan Administration.

The new Republican leadership has not only revealed an extreme fixation on cold war ideology but has also produced few policy-makers knowledgeable about the African continent. General Haig, a career military man with prior experience in Ethiopia, has been obsessed by an ironclad perception of the world divided sharply between the United States and the Soviet Union. He served his diplomatic apprenticeship as Kissinger's deputy in Nixon's first Administration. NSC advisor Richard V. Allen, Nixon's top foreign policy advisor until pushed aside by Kissinger in 1968, had specialized in foreign affairs as a founder of Georgetown University's Center for Strategic and International Studies but lacked a background in Africa. The Assistant Secretary of State for African Affairs, Chester A. Crocker, who had served as one of Kissinger's NSC assistants during 1970–1972, was the only official with a specialized knowledge of Africa. With no background in foreign policy himself the President was quite dependent on his advisors, including the White House staff directed by Edwin Meese, the counsel to the President, who assumed de facto decision-making power on various issues, even though he lacked foreign policy experience as well. Secretary of State Haig set the Administration's cold war approach by denouncing the Clark amendment: "I think it is self-defeating and an unnecessary restriction on the executive branch in its attempt to carry out a successful American foreign policy. I say that in the context of the highly dynamic situation in Angola."[82] Thus, five years after Kissinger's misadventure in Angola, it appeared that nothing had changed Washington's proclivity toward confrontation and failure in Angola.

## *FALLACIES OF COLD WAR IDEOLOGY:*
## *THE CASE FOR RECOGNITION*

The U.S. approach of defining its foreign policy in reaction to Soviet strategy has produced very insidious consequences. First and foremost, it arouses anti-American behavior among African nations such as Angola which ordinarily would accede to cooperative relations in the absence of the cold war fixation. Far from inducing socialist states to join the Western bloc, U.S. cold war policy in the Third World countries typically provokes them to establish even closer ties with the Eastern bloc. How else are they to defend their national security in the face of Great Power hostility from the United States? The Angolan government pursued an entente with Washington not simply because the establishment of diplomatic relations is a sensible thing in its own terms, but especially because stronger ties with the United States would alleviate, if not remove, Angola's dependence on Soviet bloc nations. The Angolans have indicated their clear preference for Western technology and trade, as well as their desire for relief from commerce with East European nations, which must be paid in precious hard currency, most of which Luanda obtains from its Gulf Oil revenues. The U.S. cold war approach, then, tends to compel Third World states into responses opposite to American interests.

Kissinger's failure to comprehend this led to disaster in Angola for the United States. In the 1960s United States support to Mobutu enhanced his predominance over his competitors. However, fifteen years later the shifts in the international order that were only nascent during the 1960s crystallized into Third World power clusters that liberated the MPLA from dependence on industrial allies for success. Cuba, not the Soviet Union, handed the coup de grâce to the anti-MPLA coalition. The blunting of American power by the joint action of Third World forces was simply inadmissible in Kissinger's anti-Soviet vision and beyond his understanding. A prince is successful when he fits his mode of proceeding to the times, said Machiavelli, and is unsuccessful when his mode of proceeding is no longer in tune with them.

American national interests can no longer be sustained by a European-oriented U.S. policy. The Organization of Petroleum-Exporting Countries (OPEC), in which African oil-producers number four of the nine member-states, and to which Angola will eventually belong, is an autonomous Third World force that now challenges Western power at its root. OPEC is not a creation of Soviet strategy, nor is it in any way connected with Soviet power. Neither will OPEC's challenge be dissipated by an old-style American show of force. That era is gone forever. President Reagan may succeed through budgetary cuts and other restrictions in setting the American house in order, but his program faces a greater challenge from a changing world system that is diminishing U.S. power and influence. Through new oil price increases, the OPEC nations could negate the gains from Reagan's economic policies. Such an impact would swiftly return Americans to the realization brought on in the 1970s; namely, that we no longer fully control our domestic fortunes, to say nothing of foreign policy.

Regionalization of conflict throughout southern Africa is another consequence of the cold war approach to Angola. At his confirmation hearing Secretary of State Haig implicitly recommended U.S. support to UNITA, which only increased the MPLA's anxiety regarding U.S. intentions. His utterance rang with a bellicosity last heard in 1975. It also provokes the regime into a deeper reliance on Soviet bloc assistance. Zaire is concerned about being drawn into another American-backed operation against the MPLA in the aftermath of the Angolan-Zairian border agreement that brought calm between the two African neighbors and led to the establishing of diplomatic relations.

More seriously, the U.S. approach encourages South Africa to resist a political settlement in Namibia, because Pretoria interprets Washington's continuing hostility toward the MPLA regime as license for its anti-SWAPO interventions into Angola. It can be said that Kissinger's policy contributed in a major way to intensifying hostilities in Angola during 1975 and 1976 by promoting Western opposition to the Cuban-MPLA coalition. The U.S. policy strengthened South Africa's resolve against Angola's independence, which Pretoria saw as the opening of a floodgate that could ultimately sweep away White minority rule not simply in Namibia, but also in South Africa itself. Kissinger seemed oblivious to the direct impact of his policy on South Africa, an astonishing oversight for a policy strategist accustomed to linking events in one sphere of the international system to those in another.

American economic interests in Angola have grown while Cuban troops increased in number and activity. Gulf Oil in Cabinda was pumping 160,000 barrels a day in early 1981, with a target of 200,000 by 1983.[83] Texaco renegotiated with Luanda on a preindependence oil agreement. Boeing Aircraft Company continues its commercial trade, and West German pilots fly the Boeing jets of Angola Airlines.[84] Two French companies, Total and Elf, maintain concessions for offshore oil explorations. Volvo and Fiat, together with an East German company, train Angolan auto mechanics. Endangerment of these interests since 1976 has resulted only from military confrontations involving UNITA remnants or invasions from South Africa.

Gulf Oil Corporation has even taken a position on the policy of nonrecognition: "It would be in the mutual interest of the United States and Angola for the United States to establish formal relations with the People's Republic of Angola," declared the company in 1978.[85]

The gravest consequence of policymakers' governance by anti-Sovietism is that such a policy precludes U.S. initiatives in the international arena. The cold war policy is a reactive policy. It does not beget creative and independent policy initiatives. It leaves the troubling impression that the United States lacks the capacity to create solutions and determine objectives deriving from the positive elements of American history and culture.

The cold war policy, finally, predisposes the United States to alliances with Third World elites who may be unrepresentative of the people they claim to lead. The approach to policy through bilateral or ideological arrangements is not viable in Africa, where nations are still in the process of political and economic consolidation, and where political instability inherited from the colonial era still plagues many societies. This explains how countries such as Somalia or Ethiopia can align with the United States or the Soviet Union today only to shift to the other power tomorrow, or how leaders such as Savimbi could shift allegiance from Peking to Washington.

The rationale of the macaronic policy by which the United States denies diplomatic recognition to Angola while retaining extensive trade relations with it is therefore pointless. More importantly, Washington's general opposition to the MPLA, as symbolized by the policy of nonrecognition, has contributed to the atmosphere of violence and confrontation in southern Africa by encouraging South Africa's resistance to peaceful settlement in Namibia. This policy is, as Senator Tsongas averred, "a testimony to the immaturity of the United States' policy on Africa."[86] America's allies Great Britain, France, West Germany, Japan, and Portugal have long since recognized Angola.

Revolution is not antithetical to the political tradition of the United States. The American Republic was born out of national revolution. The founders of the Republic understood clearly that an oppressed people would never accept their oppression, and that, as the Declaration of Independence puts it, "when a long train of abuses and usurpations, pursuing invariably the same object, evinces a design to reduce them under absolute despotism, it is their right, it is their duty, to throw off such government, and to provide new guards for their future society."[87]

Eurocentrism, on the other hand, is new to the American tradition. It now belongs to U.S. political culture after having been imported from Europe and nurtured here in the aftermath of World War II, when the United States assumed many of the economic and security interests that colonial Europe, exhausted and moribund, could no longer shoulder. Ever since George Kennan wrote the "X" article in *Foreign Affairs* in 1947, Eurocentrism has dominated the policy perspectives of American decision-makers, always confining their vision of the world to a conflictual bipolarity between the United States and the Soviet Union, between capitalism and socialism.

The new international economic order of the contemporary world has completely shattered the assumption of permanent bipolar dominance on which America's cold war ideology was founded. History is radically changing the power relationships among nations today, between North and South, industrial nations and nonindustrial, between the Western world and the Third World. United States policy toward Angola is in conflict with this history.

# 3

## EGYPT:
## Sadat and the Decline of
## U.S. Power

Egyptian President Anwar el-Sadat often amazed the world by his instinct for the *grande geste*. Examples of his grandeur included his astounding visit to Israel in 1977 and his public recommendation for direct American intervention against the Ayatollah Khomeini's Iran at the outbreak of the Iranian-Iraqi war. However, unknown to many of Sadat's admirers in Washington, his diplomacy also provoked increasingly serious opposition in Egypt. For instance, the Western orientation of his foreign and domestic policies aggravated the Islamic fundamentalists, while the failure of his economic policies prompted popular unrest. He completely isolated himself from the Arab world by signing the Camp David agreements with Israel. Despite the fact that Egypt has obtained more U.S. assistance than any other country in Africa, Sadat's problems went beyond a point where they threatened the survival of his regime. They also cast doubt on the future utility of Egypt as a staging zone for the movement of the new U.S. Rapid Deployment Force eastward into the oil-rich Persian Gulf and southward into the strategic Horn of Africa.*

* This chapter was researched and written after Spring 1980 and before October 6, 1981, the date when President Sadat was assassinated in

Egypt's internal crisis further revealed the decreasing ability of the United States to influence events in a developing country. To accelerate Egypt's economic development, Washington showered Sadat with dollars after 1975; but far from arresting the country's acute unemployment and poor productivity, the assistance intensified social instability by widening the gap between the impoverished masses and the middle-class elites, who became the prime beneficiaries of American largesse. Instead of bringing economic prosperity, the treaty with Israel tended to prolong poverty as a reward of peace.

The declining influence of the United States grew naturally from successful anti-Western challenges by emergent forces of the new international economic order that was ushered in by the Arab oil boycott of 1973–1974. It also stemmed from the fateful linkage of U.S. policy to the personal leadership of Anwar Sadat, whose domestic position was vitiated in great part by decisions that he himself had made.

U.S. intervention in the Congo in 1960 demonstrated Washington's ability to determine events in an African country, whereas its involvement in Angola displayed the opposite effect. Nevertheless, American policy in Egypt two decades after the Congo crisis and years after Angola revealed U.S. persistence in seeking to manipulate political reality according to its superpower position arising in the aftermath of World War II. In other words, the cold war Great Power approach prevailed despite the relative decline in America's power worldwide. The tradition of U.S. preponderance, daily whittled down by economic and strategic competition from abroad as well as by waning productivity at home, came under serious assault in Egypt as well. This did not occur because of Egyptians' opposition to U.S. policy, but because of economic and social forces in Egyptian society on which American power failed to exert a positive influence. The outcome was that the effectiveness of U.S.

---

Cairo. It is an expanded version of the author's article, "Sadat's Perils," which appeared in *Foreign Policy* (Spring 1981). This article became recommended reading in the U.S. Department of Defense.

policy in Africa in general was called into question. As analyzed in this chapter, U.S. policy toward Egypt under Sadat was indicative of a larger decline in American interventionist capacity in the Third World.

## EXIT THE SOVIET UNION—ENTER THE UNITED STATES

Egypt became an object of American strategic interest early in the Eisenhower era as a network of global alliances was created to halt the expansion of Soviet power in the world. The containment policy, America's ideology of combat in the cold war, dictated the strategic thinking that produced the North Atlantic Treaty Organization (NATO) in Europe and the Southeast Asia Treaty Organization (SEATO) in the Far East. However, a conspicuous gap existed between these mutual security systems, with the result that Egypt was soon eyed as a potential hub of a Middle East arrangement that would enable the United States to complete the encirclement of the Soviet Union by its opponents. The United States had already bolstered the defense of Europe by constructing Strategic Air Command bases in Morocco and Libya.

Egypt, the dominant state of North Africa, was pursued as the real prize. Thus the Eisenhower Administration proffered economic assistance to build the High Aswan Dam, a prime objective of President Gamal Abdel Nasser after he and a coterie of army officers (including Sadat) overthrew the Egyptian monarchy in the famous "Free Officers" revolt of 1952.[1] Washington subsequently reneged on the deal in reaction to Nasser's nationalization of the Suez Canal in 1956, until then the legal property of Great Britain and France. However, even this episode did not stop the American pursuit of Egypt.

Indeed U.S. policymakers proceeded under a variety of guises until Secretary of State William P. Rogers introduced the Rogers Plan, the Nixon Administration's proposal for a final and mutually binding accord between Egypt and Israel.[2] Although the plan came to naught under Nasser, it revealed an abiding American interest in Egypt and offered Sadat a convenient entry point for his ventures toward Washington. Egypt, however, had settled firmly in the Soviet sphere of influence when Sadat inherited the Presidency on the death of Nasser in 1970.

The country's appeal, and its ineluctable involvement in the cold war, derived from its numerous unique assets. The heart of the Arab world, Egypt had set the cultural, intellectual and, to a significant extent, political direction of the Arab-Islamic world for generations, thus providing either superpower with a locus of influence that could pulsate through the region. Linked physically to sub-Saharan Africa by the Nile, which Nasser characterized as "the life artery of our country,"[3] Egypt likewise penetrated the affairs of Black Africa, with which it was also associated by history and culture.[4] Certainly its most strategic attribute in the bipolar competition was the Suez Canal, maritime passage to international trade and Middle Eastern oil. This was matched at the pan-Arab level by Egypt's role since 1948 as the standard bearer in the conflict with Israel.

Nasser, who emerged as a legendary hero after he successfully stopped the combined British-French-Israeli invasions of 1956, had initiated Egypt's relationship with the Soviet Union by way of the so-called Czech arms deal.[5] This episode involved the first shipment of Soviet weapons to a North African country, shattering the political status quo in the Middle East. Not only was Soviet presence introduced into a region heretofore regarded as a Western preserve, but in particular the availability of an alternative source of assistance for both Arabs and Africans was demonstrated.

Egypt's shift from the Western to the Eastern camp shocked John Foster Dulles, the cold war lord of American foreign policy who, as Secretary of State, championed the cause of U.S. predominance in the world. The Eisenhower Administration never comprehended that Nasser and the Egyptians perceived the Soviet Union as coming to them with clean hands, devoid of any taint of an imperialist past.[6] This, of course, could not be said of the United States, with its "big stick" history in South America, its alliances with colonial Europe, and its quasi-colonial presence in Africa (Liberia) during the nineteenth century.

Thus began the buildup of a massive Soviet military and

economic presence on the African continent that remained without parallel until the Soviet buildup in Ethiopia and Angola two decades later. From a 1956 agreement on atoms for peace providing Egypt with its first nuclear reactor, Soviet assistance swelled with subsequent deliveries of such modern weapons as Tu-16 bombers and Styx ship-to-shore missiles,[7] in addition to the activity of more than thirty thousand Soviet personnel, including seventeen thousand military advisors.[8] After the die-hard colonialist attack on Suez by Britain and France, Nasser edged Egypt closer to partnership with the Kremlin. This partnership was consummated in 1967 when Nasser broke diplomatic relations with the United States because of alleged complicity with Israel in the Six-Day War.[9]

Sadat, a career military man, faced a formidable legacy upon succeeding Nasser in September 1970. Apart from the deep-rooted policy with Moscow was Nasser's personal legacy which, in the judgment of John Waterbury, was "too massive and, in a sense, too autonomous for Sadat to escape except in the most superficial manner."[10] Anxious to become a ruler in his own name, Sadat lived in the shadow of a great charismatic leader, fully cognizant that his legitimacy stemmed almost entirely from his role in the Free Officers movement and the Revolutionary Command Council, military bodies that Nasser had built and directed at will.[11] Sadat's challenge from this awesome legacy was compounded by Egyptians' widespread belief that, in view of their urgent need for strong leadership, he was not the answer, and would serve only as a caretaker of the interregnum from which a new leader might emerge.

Sadat encountered a nation in dire economic crisis. Devastated by the war of 1967, the economy still endured intolerable strains on its scarce resources. International trade necessitated a supply of hard currency, for instance, but Egypt's currency had plummeted with the closing of the Suez Canal during the 1967 war. (It was not reopened until June 1975, eight years later.) The tourist industry, a major source of revenues before the war, declined with the sharp drop in Western visitors. Israel's occupation of Sinai caused Egypt to lose nearly half of its annual oil production. The military establishment, which Nasser had sought desperately to repair, consumed almost 33 percent of national income, draining public sector development.[12] Population growth, with an annual rate of 2.8 percent, added more than a million new mouths every year, further straining Egypt's agricultural system, which could not produce adequate food supplies even for the existing population. Although Egypt's oil-rich Arab allies—Saudi Arabia, Kuwait, and Libya—provided subsidies that canceled some of the currency losses, paralysis gripped the economy in general.

An even more intense strain was the profound psychological despair pervading the whole society. Following the ignominious defeat of 1967, when perhaps ten thousand soldiers were killed in battle or perished from thirst in the desert, Egyptians succumbed to a sense of shame that sapped their energies, stymied their aspirations, and demoralized the body politic. Nasser lamented such loss by offering his resignation, only to have it instantly reversed by massive and spontaneous demonstrations of popular support. His failure to regain the right path apparently hastened his death three years later, and it also weighed upon Sadat as one more element of a formidable legacy.

This legacy, however, ultimately served as a convenient backdrop for Sadat's decision to renew hostilities with Israel. Only a few months after he took office, the new President declared that "1971 will be the Year of Decision, towards war or peace. This is the problem that cannot be postponed any longer."[13] No such decision emerged, and few in Egypt or elsewhere regarded his statement as more than the rhetorical effusion of a small man presuming to play a hero's role. The Soviets were particularly unresponsive because Nixon's policy of détente, which promised a thaw in cold war rivalry, preoccupied their interests. As an industrial European power, the Soviet Union also looked askance on Egypt's capacity to absorb new arms, especially because most of Egypt's air force, which failed to mobilize against Israel in 1967, had been easily destroyed. Despite such setbacks, as well as persistent doubts about his leadership ability, Sadat persevered and eventually conceived a strategy that would channel his leadership problem along with the economic and psychological crises into a single direction: war.

Sadat, who had sworn to continue Nasser's political policies, recognized the need to follow them in order to establish his own primacy before resort to war. Accordingly, he signed a treaty of friendship with the Soviet Union in March 1971, and reaffirmed Egypt's hostility toward the United States:

> The American broken promise was not the first neither the last to be broken, exactly as the Soviet assistance in erecting the Dam was neither the first nor the last to be extended to us. . . . In 1970 there loomed the promise of the Rogers Plan. At the same time they allocated 500 million dollars to Israel in order to encourage her arrogance and her negative attitude to a just peace settlement.
>
> Against every broken American promise, there is a Soviet promise that was already fulfilled or is now being fulfilled, in all domains: industry, land conservation, water distribution, weapons, training, and political support, unlimited and unconditional.[14]

Committing himself to liberate Egypt's territory under occupation, Sadat also reconfirmed Nasser's policies supporting pan-Arabism and the Palestinians. Simultaneously he courted the army as the main constituency to buttress his authority. The support of the Arab oil-producing states was taken for granted.

Sadat understood, however, that to establish his own form of leadership he would have to go beyond the legacy of Nasser. Notwithstanding his public anti-American pronouncements, Sadat contrived privately to reach a rapprochement with Washington, laying the foundation for a fundamental break in Egyptian foreign policy. Motivated by his search for national economic security, he perceived that realignment with the United States could make compatible his two prime objectives of economic development and war, if through warfare he could somehow enlist U.S. assistance on the side of Egypt's development. This led him to revive a plan, conceived but undeveloped late in Nasser's regime, to expand the liberalization of the economy by reintegrating Egypt into the Western world market. It was Sadat's idea, however, that the United States, not the Soviet Union, had to be involved in his designs against Israel, because he was convinced that U.S. decision-makers wielded decisive influence over the Jewish state, which, in his estimation, was "really America's stepdaughter."[15]

Consistent with this hidden agenda, Sadat purged his regime of the advocates of closer Soviet-Egyptian relations, and remonstrated against what he deemed the poor quality of Soviet arms and the paucity of Soviet economic assistance. In July 1972, he astounded the Kremlin by announcing the expulsion of the Soviet military mission in Egypt and the establishment of direct Egyptian control of all military facilities. In no time fifteen thousand Soviets were on their way out of Egypt. This action stimulated the rise in Sadat's domestic popularity, because Egyptians viewed it as a restoration of sovereignty. Moscow, on the other hand, could not mistake the clear writing on the wall.

Nor could Washington. Sadat's scheme to elicit U.S. assistance in his imminent campaign against Israel thus coincided with his slow, but definite redirection from the Kremlin to the White House.

When Sadat launched Egypt's surprise attack against Israel on October 6, 1973, he reaped instant political success. In the first place, he won the allegiance of an army anxious to regain its honor, which it achieved unequivocally by its early and astonishing victories.[16] Second, the Ramadan War, as the October campaign was called by Egyptians (or the Yom Kippur War as called by Israelis), lifted national pride to a pinnacle, atoning as it were for the shame of 1967. Third, Egypt's enemy, invincible for twenty-five years, was exposed as highly vulnerable. Also shattered was the longstanding stalemate between Egypt and Israel. Most significantly, the war triggered the oil embargo against the United States. "Even before the fighting stopped," summarized Mohamed Heikal, "oil had taken over from tanks and aircraft as the main weapon in the Arabs' armory."[17] This particular event now prompted Sadat to draw Washington directly into his quest for a rapid settlement of the Egyptian-Israeli conflict.

The opportunity came in November, immediately after the war, when Henry Kissinger arrived in Cairo, beginning his "shuttle diplomacy" with a series of U.S. proposals that, unknown to the renowned Secretary of State, fell neatly into Sadat's calculations. Working with the U.S. proposals, the two leaders took only a single day to agree on several decisive issues, including a resumption of diplomatic relations and the start of direct Egyptian-Israeli talks for a general disengagement of the two armies along the cease-fire line. Kissinger, a German-Jewish immigrant, still an outsider to the U.S. foreign policy establishment, hesitated, according to his former NSC aide Roger Morris, to "become too identified with the Middle East, for the perils of credibility it might pose in domestic politics as well as diplomacy."[18] However, Sadat, with firm belief in U.S. leverage over Israel, regarded the Secretary's ethnicity as an asset, surmising that Kissinger could be his link to U.S. assistance as well as to U.S. collaboration in settling Egypt's relations with Israel.

In Sadat's account, the meeting between the two leaders was hypnotic: "For the first time, I felt as if I was looking at the real face of the United States, the one I had always wanted to see—not the face put on by Dulles, Dean Rusk, and Rogers. Anyone seeing us after that first hour . . . would have thought we had been friends for years."[19] Sadat agreed at once to direct negotiations with Israel on disengagement with Kissinger serving as intermediary.

In the critical role of intermediary, Kissinger obtained an initial disengagement agreement and, at a midpoint in his diplomatic missions, went further to introduce the issue of territorial changes—the withdrawal of Israeli troops still west of the Suez Canal and a separation of Israeli-Egyptian forces in the Sinai by a U.N. buffer zone—as an "American" proposal.[20] This was the culmination of Sadat's most ambitious expectations. Yet, unbeknownst to the Egyptian leader, Kissinger's accepting the role of intermediary transformed him, in name as well as in fact, from interlocutor into the arbiter he had hoped to become from the beginning.[21]

Once Nasser's dubious successor, Sadat therefore skillfully reversed the entire course of Egyptian-American relations in less than four years after he took office. By methodic persistence, he succeeded in moving Egypt into the Western orbit. His incipient partnership with Kissinger, which satisfied the political ambitions of both men, sealed the outcome.

Sadat also seized upon his success in the October war to solidify his ties to Africa south of the Sahara. Nasser had predicated Egypt's foreign policy on his concept of the "three circles"—the Arab community, Africa, and the Islamic world—which led him to a continental approach, manifested particularly by his support for the anti-apartheid struggle of South Africa. Very soon after he assumed power, Nasser instructed Egyptians that they could not remain aloof from the struggle "for an important and obvious reason: we are *in* Africa."[23] Preoccupied with his grand design for rapprochement with the United States, Sadat had largely disregarded independent Africa, despite the fact that he himself, the son of an Arab father and a Sudanese mother, embodied the link between Arab Africa and Black Africa. But the 1973 war sent him rallying for African support, and the outcome was that all but three African governments registered their opposition to Israel by breaking diplomatic relations. The three which did not (Lesotho, Malawi, and Swaziland) were all linked by a vestigial colonial dependency to South Africa, which now became Israel's solitary ally on the African continent.

Arab solidarity also redounded upon Sadat because of the war. This meant considerable financial assistance from such oil-rich states as Libya and Saudi Arabia, which had generally dismissed as incredible Sadat's war threats of the preceding three years. Algeria's President Houari Boumedienne even went to Moscow to buy urgent shipments of arms for the Egyptian forces. In the one deft move to war, Sadat mobilized total African and Arab support to his cause. Thus it arose that the mantle of Nasser came to cover the shoulders of President Sadat.

However, Sadat's masterstroke was the new series of relations he struck with the United States. When Nixon visited Egypt in June 1974, Sadat took pains to offer a tumultuous welcome, aware that such publicity would ingratiate him with the American President seeking respite from Watergate. The Presidential visit thus coincided with domestic American politics that further strengthened Sadat's position.

Watergate, which diluted much of Nixon's influence in foreign policy, enhanced Kissinger's, allowing the Secretary of State a virtually free hand in diplomacy and enormously facilitating his subsequent demarches in the Egyptian-Israeli negotiations. At the same time, Kissinger's overtures toward Sadat satisfied an old and broad spectrum of pro-Arab bureaucrats in the State Department and Pentagon, if not also the CIA.[24] In Congress, pro-Arab diplomacy had long been advocated by J. William Fulbright, the powerful Chairman of the Senate Foreign Relations Committee. Sadat, therefore, insinuated himself into U.S. policy at a most propitious and critical moment.

Nixon's visit provided the chance for Sadat to complete his formal rapprochement with the United States. However, the major outcome of the Egyptian-American exchanges was the close political and personal relationship that evolved between Sadat and Kissinger. As a purely political decision to reward the Egyptian leader for a new disengagement of forces from Sinai during 1975, Kissinger ordered the Agency for International Development (AID) to dispatch $750 million as economic assistance to Egypt.[25] Another $200 million was earmarked for food supplies. The combined $1 billion package immediately reversed the eight-year U.S. policy of denying all assistance to Israel's erstwhile nemesis. Thus began a gigantic program of U.S. economic and military aid that is now exceeded in the world only by U.S. assistance to Israel.

Sadat's triumph was complete. He took advantage of the political momentum to visit Washington in 1975 seeking to obtain American arms. Despite unsatisfactory results in his negotiations with Israel, he lost no faith in his mission: "I am looking forward to my meeting with Ford. . . . I still trust Kissinger."[26] In the years before the 1973 war the Soviet Union had delivered $4 billion, and possibly as much as $7 billion, in weapons and equipment to Egypt. But Sadat searched for higher stakes from his new patron, even if this required a herculean overhaul from Soviet to American weaponry and parts. So he congratulated himself when Washington rescinded its longstanding arms embargo and agreed to sell to Egypt six C-130 military transport planes along with two nuclear reactors.

While consummating his shift to the West, Sadat refrained from complete rupture with the Kremlin, although he abrogated the Soviet-Egyptian treaty of friendship in 1976 and later terminated the Soviets' use of Egyptian ports. Shrewdness, coupled with the Soviets' desire to maintain a link to the Arab world, enabled Sadat gradually to retreat from Moscow while he appealed for new assistance. He even signed a trade agreement of about $802 million with the Soviets in April 1976, less than a year after his harvest in Washington. This preserved the Soviet Union's position as Egypt's chief trading partner.

The United States, pleased with its own new leverage on the Nile, tolerated Sadat's Soviet policies. Indeed, the Carter Administration's Secretary of the Treasury, W. Michael Blumenthal, returned from Cairo in October 1977 affirming that "we feel we are getting our money's worth in providing assistance that enables Egypt to deal not only with its immediate problems but in setting in motion longer-term development projects." [27] The billion-dollar aid program to Egypt grew so rapidly that by fiscal 1977 it surpassed U.S. assistance to the rest of Africa and Latin America combined.

At this point Sadat played his ace in the hole with his visit to Jerusalem. In his address to the Israeli Knesset on November 20, 1977, Sadat again changed history: "No one could have ever conceived that the President of the biggest Arab state, which bears the heaviest burden and the main responsibility pertaining to the cause of war and peace in the Middle East, should declare his readiness to go to the land of the adversary while we were still in a state of war." [28] In seeking a separate peace, Sadat dashed the myth of pan-Arabism—or a notion fundamental to Nasser's foreign policy of "the one Arab nation with an immortal mission" [29]—precisely because Egypt was the core of the Arab system. His journey to Jerusalem also set the future course of U.S. relations with Egypt, because it made final Sadat's break with Moscow and thus transformed him into a full-fledged American client. This development clearly suited his designs.

From the standpoint of U.S. interests, however, this curious alliance had the ultimate effect of investing the United States not primarily in Egypt, but in Sadat's personal leadership. This bond was sealed when Sadat agreed subsequently to make a separate peace with Israel at Camp David. By this act he jeopardized his African support and alienated himself utterly from the Arab world, as shown by Arab trade boycotts and cutoff of funds. The Egyptian's ensuing isolation, undoubtedly an unintended consequence of his diplomatic wizardry, solidified his material dependency on the United States just as Washington now depended on him to sustain its stake in Egypt. As a result, U.S. policy became enmeshed with Sadat's personal rule rather than allied to an institutionalized Egyptian Presidency that could safeguard American interests even through vicissitudes of leadership.

## U.S. POLICY AND EGYPT'S INTERNAL CRISIS

Beginning in 1975 U.S. policy toward Egypt sought to advance the burgeoning client relationship with Sadat by providing him with enough military and economic assistance to provide concrete evidence of American rewards for the enormous risks he took to introduce U.S. power into his country, the center of a region of vital U.S. interests. As a result of the Egyptian-Israeli peace treaty, popularly called the Camp David Accords, the United States announced a special military aid package to Egypt (with even more going to Israel). It amounted to $1.5 billion in military credits, at an annual rate of $500 million, in the fiscal years from 1979 to 1981.[30] Supplements to the basic package were also proposed, including an additional $1.1 billion after 1981. Under this program, Washington delivered thirty-five used F-4E Phantom jets at a cost of nearly $600 million, and the first fifty of eight hundred M-113 A2 armored personnel carriers and forty F-16 combat jets at a cost of $943 million.

Economic assistance, however, formed the centerpiece of the aid program, and Sadat had already prepared a fit response to the new U.S. policy, which his own designs had gone far to bring about. This was his *infitah* (open-door) policy, launched in 1974 to attract Western capital and technology to stimulate Egypt's stagnant economy, and to develop the private sector as a competitor of the public sector. Private American investment from about fifty companies, including such corporations as Union Carbide and Squibb, soon made Egypt one of the few African clients of U.S. private capital. Egypt also obtained $5.3 billion in U.S. civilian economic assistance between 1975 and 1980, providing Egyptians per capita with more assistance in real dollars than the Marshall Plan had bestowed on Europeans after World War II.[31]

Great as it was, the American assistance failed substantially to improve the lives of the majority of Egyptians because it was directed mainly toward capital-intensive operations in construction, industry, and the military infrastructure. The aid was heaped on Sadat faster than his regime could absorb it, rolling in at $100 million per month. By 1980 the regime had managed to spend only about half of the $5.3 billion received since 1975. AID committed more than $357 million on projects to increase food and agricultural production, but due to several bureaucratic and technical bottlenecks, only $61.8 million of the funds were spent. Even a U.S. government report of early 1981 conceded that the impact of the projects on Egyptian agriculture had been negligible.[32]

The emphasis on capital-intensive development, and the rush to ally with Sadat, blinded U.S. policymakers to the real needs of Egyptian development: its economic infrastructure and agricultural productivity. A review of these domains will show the reordering still necessary to correct deficiencies of past policies.

In infrastructural assistance there were several areas of long overdue development where new U.S. assistance would have produced salutary impact. First, Egypt's decrepit water and sewage system, disregarded during the years of hostility with Israel, badly needed modernization and adaptation to the needs of the rapidly expanding urban population. This was especially true in Cairo, scene of the most acute population pressure. The United States already provided $200 million to redevelop these systems for the people, but the aid was far too inadequate to finish the job.

The second critical need was low-cost housing. This emergency increased with the daily arrivals in the cities of peasants and poor dwellers from the countryside. Again, this was quite conspicuous in Cairo apartments, where twelve people resided in spaces built for two or, more tragically, in makeshift cardboard tents thrown up overnight. A U.S. program promised to construct a thousand core housing units in one region, with facilities to eventually accommodate 35,000 units. However, compared to the vast magnitude of the problem, these seemed like a Band-Aid over a gaping wound.

Third, Egypt's public transportation system was in a veritable crisis due to overcrowding and decay of equipment. It could be salvaged with new shipments of U.S. buses, or perhaps commuter-type trains, but a mere shipment of such vehicles would not meet the problem. Washington also would need to send along American technicians to train Egyptians in maintenance and local production (or substitution) of spare parts. The Suez Canal Authority, whose operations remained vital to the economy, could escape much of its operational deficiencies with new U.S. navigational systems.

U.S. assistance in Egypt's agricultural development, meanwhile, should be directed toward the production of foodstuffs. Cotton, the traditional crop, is a soil-erosive product with an insufficiently lucrative market to pay Egypt's imported food bill. The United States should therefore assist the Egyptians with crop diversification, especially grains and similar produce necessary to feed the increasing population. Vicissitudes in the world price of cotton, not to mention recent inadequacies in Egypt's domestic production, virtually assure that the country will not regain its old advantage as a major cotton exporter. This realization further underscores Egypt's need to renovate irrigation systems, and to import such commodities as fertilizer, in order to gain the capacity to feed itself. Trained American agricultural technicians could be sent to the rural areas to accelerate this task.

Because of the misdirected focus of past disbursements, many Egyptians remained in a quandary about the abundant U.S.

assistance Sadat frequently proclaimed fortissimo. A widespread though invalid suspicion held that the bulk of the assistance was consumed by corrupt deals and schemes of the infitah class, or such business and professional groups as bankers, export-import merchants, contractors and entrepreneurs in various trades. By the end of the Carter Administration, it became certain that U.S. assistance had neither enabled Washington to influence events in Egypt nor secured Sadat's domestic position.

This peculiar drama of U.S. foreign policy can be seen most instructively through its relationship to Egypt's internal stability, which was deteriorating even as Sadat masterfully executed his foreign policy initiatives. For instance, discontent among the 4,497,000 *fallahin* (peasant farmers) who made up 42 percent of Egypt's work force grew with the decline in the production of long-time staple cotton,[33] the country's main agricultural resource. This decline resulted in part from peasants who, suffering widespread unemployment and underemployment due to the unprofitability of cotton, fled to the cities looking for jobs, especially to Cairo, where an estimated thousand rural migrants arrived every day.

Food production never came close to satisfying the consumption needs of the country's rapidly multiplying population, estimated at 42 million in 1980. Whereas domestic production increased scarcely 2 percent each year, the annual birth rate increased the population by more than 100,000 people every month, giving Egypt one of the highest rates of population growth in the world.

The relative decline in agricultural productivity was not offset by annual imports of nearly half of Egypt's food supply. This included 1.5 million tons of American grain, which provided one out of every three loaves of bread available in urban bakeries.[34]

Crops of all kinds were decimated by urban sprawl. According to Egyptian agronomist Ali Abdel Wahid, this megapolization annually consumed 60,000 acres (from the country's total arable land of only 6 million acres), as home builders used the land to make mud bricks for new housing.[35] Defects from the Aswan Dam irrigation system compounded the decline in productivity. A breakdown in the system's old method of allowing the flood to come down the Nile valley each year to wash out the salt increased the soil erosion over Egypt's huge territory. Because 96 percent of the land is desert, this intensified social pressures on the inhabited area, whose density of about six persons per acre of arable land represents one of the most severe people-to-land ratios on earth.

The basic cause of agricultural decline seems to be Sadat's decision to industrialize at the expense of agriculture. After inheriting the Presidency, Sadat generally approached the rural areas with an attitude of neglect, counting on urban industrialization and trade expansion to make up the difference. His expectation did not materialize. Because of the decline in agriculture, the economic crisis penetrated the city and country alike.

Unemployment, for example, was officially recorded at 3 percent of the total work force of about 10.7 million until 1980. However, Deputy Premier for Finance and Economy Abdul Razzak Abdul-Meguid then revised the unemployment level, declaring that it was at least three times, and perhaps five times, higher than the previous figure. In view of widespread underemployment, where ten workers performed tasks that could efficiently be done by one, it is very likely that unemployment in the cities and on the land was much higher. This explains why independent economists estimated that as many as 2.5 million Egyptians, or nearly 25 percent of the work force, could properly be classified as unemployed.[36]

The unemployment crisis loomed still larger if applied to youth. Roughly half of Egypt's population was under twenty-five years old and, except for college graduates, a majority of young people belonged to the idle and unemployed. In May 1980 Sadat reinstituted a program to guarantee government jobs to all university students who had graduated in the preceding three years but had failed to obtain employment in the private sector. There were about forty thousand college graduates in 1977,[37] and comparable numbers flooded the job market each year thereafter. The declining economy augured ill for Sadat's ability to continue with the guaranteed employment program for college graduates, a Nasser creation which Sadat himself had previously abolished, deeming it financially prohibitive. Failure of this program seemed likely to provoke volatile alienation among unemployed but well-educated youth.

Inflation exacerbated the economic crisis. Generally estimated at 20 to 25 percent, inflation eroded the real purchasing power of even the upper middle class. Government bureaucrats, a huge body of about four million people, often supplemented their incomes by moonlighting. Such professionals as physicians, engineers, plumbers, and teachers emigrated to other Arab countries to obtain higher-paying jobs; there were even 337,000 Egyptians in Libya in 1977,[38] and thousands more worked in the Persian Gulf states. Although they annually sent lucrative remittances back home, $2.2 billion in 1979, their absence deprived Egypt of vital skills.

Sadat, who had sold his settlement with Israel with the promise that peace guaranteed prosperity at home, was caught offguard by the mounting internal crisis, like some thaumaturgist unable to contain the reality conjured up by his own magic.

In a policy reversal of June 1980, he tried to check public discontent over cost-of-living increases by ordering substantial rises in subsidies for consumer necessities. With a jump from $1.8 billion in 1979 to $2.21 billion a year later,[39] the subsidy increases represented a radical departure from the policies of the preceding government under Prime Minister Mustafa Khalil, who attempted to reduce the subsidies in compliance with advice from the International Monetary Fund (IMF). Although Sadat's intervention temporarily enabled Egyptians to feed themselves, it simultaneously refueled the inflation by pumping more money into the market.

Sadat no doubt recalled the mass riots that staggered such cities as Cairo in January 1977; his own budget proposal for high price increases in food and other basic necessities had provoked these "bread riots," as the uprisings were called. Seventy-nine people were killed before the riots ceased. Acutely aware of his narrow range of domestic policy options, the bold Egyptian leader was not likely to make the mistake of increasing food prices again.

The national bureaucracy, perenially inefficient, often aggravated public unrest. With thirty governmental ministries, Sadat had nearly twice the number of executive departments that the cabinet of an American President had. Nevertheless, Sadat's regime did not adequately provide such basic services as the ration cards Egyptians needed to qualify for the very consumer commodities his government subsidized. The Railways Authority, which had reported a deficit of only $4 million in 1975, lost $47 million in 1978, despite a 60 percent increase in passenger fares.[40] On any given day Cairo suffered as many as 250 power failures, despite $500 million in U.S. aid allocated to Egypt's power sector. The regime tried to reduce its budget deficit through the device of simply printing 30 percent more paper money, but it still forfeited nearly all of a $600 million loan from the IMF because of the government's failure to stay under a specified deficit ceiling. These deficiencies confirmed that much of the $2.5 billion in civilian assistance Sadat obtained annually from Western sources ($1.1 billion directly from the United States) was not only inefficiently and unproductively utilized, but also has failed to reverse Egypt's economic decline. Even Sadat himself admitted that Egypt may not begin its "economic take-off" until 1982, or five years after the original target date.

The economic crisis, and the U.S. policy intended to remedy it, contributed to the resurgence of Islamic fundamentalism in the form of a reanimated Muslim Brotherhood and a wave of neo-Islamicists inspired by the success of Iran's Ayatollah Khomeini. The Brotherhood contained perhaps three million orthodox Muslims, heirs to the political ideology of Hassan al-Banna, the charismatic schoolteacher who founded the society in 1929.[41] Although doctrinal differences separate the Iranians, who belong to the Shiite sect of Islam, from the Egyptians, who are Sunni Muslims, all fundamentalists insist on a purification of Islamic belief and practice from Western influences and on a militant defense of Islam against its perceived enemies, the promoters of Westernization among the country's leadership.

As related in his autobiography, *In Search of Identity,* Sadat was quite familiar with representatives of the Muslim Brotherhood as a result of collaborative contacts made during Egypt's nationalist period.[42] Though never trusting them, he invited them to active political participation after he became President, expecting that they would serve as an effective counterfoil against the Egyptian left, especially against the small but influential Communist party. For a time, the *Ikhwan* (Brotherhood) appeared to merge into the mainstream—that is, until the "bread riots" frightened Sadat into clamping down on all political groups except the three "legal" (government-created) parties. He thus inserted a wedge between himself and the Brotherhood.

The neo-Islamicists, denounced by Sadat as "extremists" early in 1980, sometimes associated with the Ikhwan, but differed from it in their use of violence as an instrument of policy. They embraced the concept of *jihad* (or Muslim "holy war") to challenge Sadat; this was similar to the way the Khomeini followers confronted the Shah as a matter of Islamic obligation. A dominant faction among the armed bodies was the Takfir wal-Hijra,* founded in 1971 by Shukri Ahmed Mustafa, a twenty-eight-year-old agricultural engineer;[43] it aspired to a resurrection of Islamic government in conformity with the system established by the Prophet Mohammed in the seventh century. Another was the JundAllah (Soldiers of Allah), which saw seventy-two of its members arrested for subversion in July 1977.[44] Like the fundamentalist Jihad Organization, the paramilitary factions operated autonomously, with no group or leadership coordination. Their size was not known, but each claimed branches or cells in several cities and towns of Egypt.

To preempt the spread of terrorist religious movements, Sadat introduced an antiterrorist bill in early 1977 that authorized the death sentence (or hard labor) for anyone convicted of belonging to secret army organizations.[45] He later suspended *all* societies that promoted religious fanaticism, extremism, or communal unrest. In an attempt to mollify the Islamicists, he submitted for referendum approval a constitutional amendment establishing the *Sharia,* the Islamic legal codes, as the main source of law in the political system.

The Muslim fundamentalists provided ample evidence of their anti-Sadat and anti-American resistance. First was the reappearance

---

*The government of President Hosni Mubarak, Sadat's successor, charged members of this group with his assassination.

in 1975 of *Al-Daawa* (The Call), the Brotherhood's newspaper, which quickly acquired a circulation of eighty thousand.[46] Although moderate elements of the organization favored coexistence with Sadat's regime, four years before Camp David they used the publication to vent their hostility to the United States, which they believed was imposing an American-Israeli peace on Egypt. They were intensely perturbed by a clause in the treaty that compelled Egypt to sell Israel 40,000 barrels of crude oil (from the Sinai) every day.[47]

Second, the Brotherhood attracted a large following of university students and peasant elites sympathetic to Muammar Qaddafi's theory of Islamic socialism. They probably received financial support from the Libyan leader, who then regarded Sadat as the archenemy of the Arab world.

Third, Takfir wal-Hijra kidnapped a former Minister of Religious Affairs (Dr. Mahammad Husain Al-Zahabi) in July 1977, denouncing Sadat's regime as an infidel system, and calling for Muslims' disengagement from the "heretic" society Egypt had become under him. When the government rejected the fundamentalists' ultimatum for a huge ransom and the release of sixty of its imprisoned members to free the ex-minister, they executed him. This event was particularly troublesome because Takfir wal-Hijra contained a substantial constituency of high school and university students, teachers, engineers, urban workers, peasants, and women. The fundamentalists demonstrated a remarkable capacity to attract consistently the educated and semi-educated as well as peasants.[48]

The fundamentalist resurgence was originally catalyzed by Egypt's defeat in the Six-Day War. Muslim traditionalists then began to search their society for the cause of their shame. They found it in Westernization, particularly after Sadat resumed diplomatic relations with Washington in 1974. The traditionalists took great exception to Sadat's "open-door" policy to the West. With economic security his relentless pursuit, Sadat finally aligned Egypt with Iran and Israel as one of the three defensive pillars of American policy in the Middle East. Neither Sadat nor Kissinger was aware that Ayatollah Khomeini was then culminating the movement that would destroy the tripolar alignment even as it was being formed.

## THE "BATTLE FOR PROSPERITY" AND PERSONAL POWER

"Battle for peace" was the slogan Sadat adopted after breaking with the Arab League in 1977 to make peace with Israel. In the settlement with Prime Minister Menachem Begin at Camp David two years later, Sadat approved a separate proposal to establish full autonomy for the 1.2 million Palestinian refugees of the West Bank and Gaza Strip within a five-year transitional period. After the treaty was signed, six of the dominant Arab states, including Algeria, Libya, and Syria, joined the Palestine Liberation Organization (PLO) in condemning it. The Gulf Organization for the Development of Egypt—a monetary fund composed of Saudi Arabia, Kuwait, Qatar, and the United Arab Emirates—punished Sadat by cutting off their assistance which had amounted to $2 billion in 1979.[49] The Arab League suspended Egypt.

Sadat's peace initiative so inflamed Libya's Qaddafi that he conspired to have the Egyptian's plane shot down as he flew to Washington for the treaty signing (according to a report of the CIA).[50] After first severing relations with Sadat during his rapprochement with the United States, Qaddafi subsequently manifested his contempt by announcing the construction of a $3 billion wall, a kind of *cordon sanitaire,* between Libya and Egypt.

"Battle for prosperity" became Sadat's new motto. To enforce prosperity rapidly, he announced the following in May 1980: a general increase in wages; a 10 to 20 percent reduction in the price of basic foods, textiles, and other commodities, plus supplementary subsidies for each item; a reduction or abolition of some taxes; an increase in bonuses and welfare benefits; and the extension to "all Egyptians" of social security, which already covered about 65 percent of the work force. Because the fallahin and students had been notably attracted to the Brotherhood, Sadat offered them special benefits. The peasants were made favored beneficiaries of the new wage and food subsidies; university students, as noted earlier, were guaranteed governmental jobs. Once more, as with his somersault on the cost-of-living subsidies, he tried to make another switch in time.

To stave off the domestic dangers, Sadat took what appeared to be drastic precautions. In addition to taking the Premiership himself, he designated six Deputy Prime Ministers expected to rubber-stamp his policies. (The last time he acted as his own Prime Minister had been in 1973 while preparing for the October war.) Having already appointed himself chief of the National Democratic party, the majority (government) party he created in 1978, Sadat made the provincial governors directly responsible to him, evidently to protect his authority in the countryside. He reinforced his control of the government by appointing the previous Defense Minister, Lieutenant General Kamal Hassal Ali, as the new Foreign Minister and also as Deputy Prime Minister of Defense and Information. (Sadat made another major shift at the Foreign Ministry in September 1978, after the incumbent Muhammad Ibrahim Kamel resigned to protest the Camp David Accords.) In Third World countries, especially in Africa and the Middle East, such a massive concentration of power in the hands of one or two men has occasionally presaged a military coup.

Personal rule seemed to be formalized by a new constitutional amendment of 1980, which, in article 77, abolished the previous law restricting a President's tenure to two consecutive six-year terms. Sadat would have been required to step down in 1982, but under the new law he could hope to remain indefinitely.[51] This is the kind of constitutional assurance Ahmed Ben Bella, while in power, adopted to allow his indefinite leadership of Algeria. However, Sadat even more than Ben Bella, governed his country in a virtuoso solo performance, brooking no opposition to his leadership and making major policy decisions, especially foreign policy, as a majority of one. He confided in only two assistants before expelling the Soviets, and he told no one but the Foreign Minister of his dramatic decision to go to Jerusalem.

Though his move was little noticed by the Carter Administration, Sadat revealed his evident intention to serve as President-for-Life by pushing through the constitutional amendment. For good reason Montesquieu warned that men invested with power will use it, and will push it as far as it will go.

## WESTERNIZATION AND INSTABILITY

Two powerful and well-placed groups underpinned Sadat's authority—the army and the upper middle class, which were the principal beneficiaries of U.S. assistance. With $1.5 billion in military aid from 1977 to 1980, the armed forces of 395,000 may have acquired the best-equipped arsenal in the Middle East after Israel.[52] The Carter Administration requested a supplementary $550 million military aid for fiscal 1981. The combat preparedness of these forces may still be in doubt—Egyptian military officials insist they need at least $5 billion more in U.S. weapons—but the soldiers have clearly become privileged wage earners in a nation of mass unemployment.

The upper middle class was the new infitah elites who arrived as a result of U.S. munificence. Altogether they made up a mere 5 percent of the overall population.[53] Mercedes-Benz sedans and color television sets were some of the most conspicuous symbols of these elites, who emulated European and American lifestyles.

Although Sadat managed to maintain his grip on power, internal rumblings could be detected. It is important to emphasize that the dissenters were not limited to the Islamic fundamentalists. As a case in point, the intellectuals, whom Sadat had muzzled, also dissented, and many, such as Yossef Idriss, a famous novelist, were widely acknowledged opponents of the treaty because of its failure to resolve the problem of the Palestinian refugees.

Elsewhere Sadat faced potential opposition from the Coptic Christian minority, which amounted to about 6 million, according to the Coptic church, and about 2.6 million according to the government. They not only accused the regime of religious discrimination in employment and public services but opposed the constitutional referendum recognizing the Sharia as the major source of law lest they become subjugated to a Muslim legal system. The more Sadat made concessions to pacify the Islamicists, the more he alienated the Copts.

In foreign policy, the Begin government tended to further undermine Sadat by its hard-line, inflexible postures on Palestinian autonomy and its annexation of East Jerusalem. Sadat was humiliated during June 1981 when, three days after his meeting with Begin on Palestinian autonomy, Israel bombed an Iraqi nuclear reactor in a surprise attack; a month later the Israelis bombed downtown Beirut and killed nearly 300 civilians. Needless to say, the Israeli actions did not enhance Sadat's popularity at home or in the Arab world. Hence the aggregation of his problems, not any single one, defined his internal dangers.

In consummating the U.S. alliance with Sadat at Camp David, the Carter Administration realized an objective of American foreign policy that had originated as far back as the Eisenhower epoch. Egypt now belonged to the Western bloc dominated by American power. At Camp David a further success dawned with the end of the impasse between Israel and its chief rival in the Arab world for three decades. Nevertheless, the bounty that Egypt reaped in the form of U.S. assistance did little to satisfy the needs of Egyptian development and therefore failed to substantially reinforce the regime that made the alliance possible.

Furthermore, the growing Westernization represented by American capital, weapons, and lifestyles not only provoked indigenous Egyptian forces hostile to U.S. interests but also aggravated the Islamic opposition to Sadat. The Carter Administration allowed itself to overlook these difficult signs, being determined to secure U.S. interests in a country strategically located at the northern gate of Africa and as a central corridor to the Middle East. It was not surprising that the Administration would have been willing to pay almost any price for such a prize, especially after the fall of America's longstanding ally in Iran. Still, Sadat's accumulated problems, ranging from the inadequacies of the Camp David process to Egypt's deepening economic crisis, ultimately curtailed his range of domestic policy options, threatening his survival together with that of U.S. policies in Egypt.

## THE PERSONAL CLIENT: PITFALL OF U.S. POLICY

The United States airlifted fourteen hundred soldiers into Egypt in November 1980 to launch the Rapid Deployment Force designed by the Carter Administration to reinforce the U.S. position in the Middle East.[54] The airlift also showed evidence of staunch U.S. support to America's audacious ally who had shocked the world community more than once by his grandeur in foreign policy. From his astonishing visit to Israel and his grant of asylum to the wandering Shah of Iran to his public recommendation for direct U.S. intervention against Iran at the outbreak of its war with Iraq, Sadat mesmerized Washington with his incredible displays of solidarity. His political intimacy with U.S. policymakers, begun with Kissinger, was culminated with Carter. Sadat affirmed: "I find that I am dealing with a man who understands what I want, a man impelled by the power of religious faith and lofty values—a farmer, like me."[55] In the end, he emerged as the real man of the hour because future U.S. interests in Egypt were linked to his survival as its paramount leader.

Like Zaire, Egypt showed the U.S. capacity to consolidate an extensive series of bilateral relations between the American government and the personal ruler of an African country. Unlike the U.S. role in preserving Mobutu in power, however, the policy to support Sadat was contradicted by the failure of U.S. assistance to effect a positive change in the socioeconomic conditions of most Egyptians. Little comparison existed between Mobutu's bankrupt leadership and Sadat's diplomatic brilliance, but the domestic impact of their respective policies nevertheless resulted in extremely unstable regimes. In Egypt this result occurred amidst a sea of American economic and military aid, exposing a profound decline in America's former ability to decisively influence developments in Third World countries.

All this points to the defects in U.S. policy toward Africa in the age of the new international economic order. The foremost lesson is that the old cold war formula of alliances, regional or bilateral, is not only unsuited to relations with developing nations today, but it also provokes a reflexive response by American policymakers that leads them to side with dictatorships of personal rule whose inherent instability constantly jeopardizes the U.S. policy dependent upon them. Such a policy is obviously not in the long-range interest of the United States and is likely to become counterproductive to the positive development of the country in question.

The American presence in Egypt, represented initially in goods and dollars, but more and more in weapons and military personnel, was finally expanded by an increase in diplomatic staff. At the end of his ambassadorship to Egypt in 1979, Herman F. Eilts warned Washington against this latter development. Nonetheless the embassy staff, which then amounted to 280, was joined by 28 more personnel as of mid-1980. When families are included, the U.S. embassy community reached about 800. With the inclusion of such private American residents as businesspeople and their families, the total U.S. community in Egypt rose to nearly 5,000.[56]

Unwittingly Secretary Haig worsened Sadat's position in April 1981 by extracting his consent to a U.S. plan for an international peacekeeping force in the Sinai. The Egyptian-Israeli peace treaty requires Israel to withdraw completely from this Egyptian territory by April 1982, but only on the condition that an international force has been installed to keep peace. Anticipating that the Soviet Union would veto any Security Council proposal for a U.N. force, Haig introduced an alternative plan to enlist troops from several countries, including perhaps as many as a thousand American soldiers in a total force of about four thousand. Notwithstanding the purpose of their mission, additional Americans in Egypt could rekindle Egyptian nationalist memories of the huge Soviet presence of thirty thousand. This venture, like the increasing operations of the Rapid Deployment Force, could also provoke the Islamicists into full mobilization against America's client-ally in Egypt.

What then should be the proper role of U.S. policy toward Egypt and, by extension, to independent African states in general? There are four cardinal guidelines which should become constants of a new approach. The first involves a policy of disentanglement from regimes of personal leadership. In this context, policymakers should not engage in facile distinctions between "authoritarian" regimes, qualified as acceptable partners by President Reagan, and "totalitarian" regimes, rejected on the assumption that the dictatorship of the latter is somehow more dictatorial and repressive than the former.

The second constant of U.S. policy involves the direction or objective of U.S. assistance. Instead of seeking to prop up personal rulers, U.S. aid should be concentrated on the national interests of the recipient country—on the people, the economy, and their development. Certain amounts of military aid will inevitably be requested, and ought to be provided, for defense needs. Above all, U.S. support should be *visible,* not in weapons and warfare, but in a range of technicians, equipment, and capital used to improve the country's well-being today as well as to build its material development of the future.

Third, the United States should not require African states to compromise on any aspect of their fundamental national politics as a condition of American support. At Camp David President Carter reassured Sadat of various provisions to safeguard Palestinian rights, only to see them omitted in the final draft of the treaty.[57] Given the nearly universal Arab support to the Palestinian cause, Sadat was ill advised to reach agreements on the issue in any case. However, it was American persuasion that induced him to accept the separate protocol subsequently haunting him at home and in every quarter of the Arab world. The object lesson of this experience shows clearly that although Washington may successfully impose its pressures to extract immediate benefits in negotiations with certain leaders, it does so at the expense of these leaders' political viability, not to mention the long-range interests of U.S. policy.

Finally, the cold war doctrine that demands an alliance relationship as a condition of U.S. assistance must be discarded absolutely. This Great Power ideology has conditioned the thinking of every generation since World War II, but it is no more applicable to

African realities than it is effective in containing them. Political instability is a fact of life in certain African countries because of the negative effects of their colonial heritage. As revealed over a decade ago by French analyst René Dumont in *False Start in Africa*,[58] the instability was born with independence; it has not been eradicated by Western or Soviet bloc assistance precisely because these societies are still in the process of social and political evolution, galvanizing their own national identities and forging new economic systems sometimes in the midst of penury. The occasional consequence of such realities has been the sudden switch from friend to foe, or vice versa, as in Egypt's shift from strong Soviet partner to perhaps equally strong U.S. ally.

The Reagan Administration came to power with a unique opportunity to reduce, if not break, the extreme identity of the United States with Sadat. Not only were the Republicans not associated with inadequacies of Camp David, Reagan was free of the political intimacy that evolved between Sadat and previous leaders. This policy had the additional advantage of providing a gateway out of Camp David en route to a more promising peace process. However, the Republicans persisted in the past U.S. identity with Sadat and thus continued on a course that locked U.S. interests to his personal fortunes, which in the end could lead U.S. policy into a quagmire.

# AFRO-AMERICANS AND AFRICA:
## The Unbroken Link

There has always been a significant stratum of Afro-Americans stimulated by the foreign policy of the United States because they have considered it their own country. They have identified the slave labor of their ancestors as the capital which built and enriched the Southern plantation economy that was fundamental to the later industrialization of the North,[1] and which represented their terrible investment in America's national development. It was a stake not to be surrendered at any cost. After slavery, these Americans edged their entry into the foreign policy process, seeking to extract from it what they believed should have been theirs by heritage: power in the American system.

Their pursuit of power has been indefatigable. From the American Colonization Society of the nineteenth century to Trans-Africa today, Blacks have continued in their efforts to influence American policy toward Africa, not always in unison, sometimes with contradiction, and infrequently with success. Like other Americans of foreign (though not slave) descent, Blacks have sought to use American power in the interest of their ancestral homeland. These Black Americans have also looked incredulously at the ease with which immigrants born a generation ago in Europe have risen to the commanding heights of American decision-making, while

Blacks, rooted in America for more than three centuries, have been so systematically excluded that they have never gotten closer to the levers of executive power than the long distance between the U.N. mission in New York and the White House in Washington.

Black Americans' interest in Africa clearly did not begin with Andrew Young's emergence as U.S. Ambassador to the United Nations, although Young did focus national attention on Africa to a degree unknown before in American history. He performed as a dynamic advocate of U.S. interests in Africa during the first two years of the Carter Administration, raising to priority such policy issues as the independence of Zimbabwe, and taking provocative positions designed to terminate the traditional policy of U.S. neglect in favor of a progressive embrace of the diverse African regimes. He also focused concern on apartheid in South Africa, a longstanding issue of Black opposition. As an American leader, he broke new ground, but as a Black American, he was the latest and most influential representative of Black support of the anticolonial and developmental struggles of African societies.

The historic force propelling Black interest in the policy process has been conditioned by what W. E. B. DuBois called the "two-ness" of every Black citizen of the nation—"an American, a Negro; two souls, two thoughts, two unreconciled strings; two warring ideals."[2] In every generation this impulse of divergent motivations has stimulated two distinct tendencies in the Black approach to Africa, one which demands the integration of Blacks into the process of American foreign policy to advance the goals of Africa's liberation and development, and another which insists on independent and even separatist Black institutions to achieve the same goal. The first tendency has led to integration in the American political system, whereas the latter has spawned movements of Black nationalism seeking an actual or potential unity of Americans associated by African ancestry, culture, and heritage.

The United States, which, with almost 30 million Afro-American citizens, has the third largest Black population in the world (after Nigeria and Brazil), maintains a permanent and irreducible link to Africa through these historic yearnings of Black Americans.[3] The rationale for a study of relations between Afro-

Americans and continental Africans, according to Ronald W. Walters, does not consist merely in the fact that those in the United States were "interested in Africa from an early phase in American history, but in the realization that, after all, they *were* Africans, uprooted and displaced in an alien society, under the most savage circumstances, and therefore desperate to hold on to their humanity by nurturing a vision and the experience of the land of their fathers."[4] This tenacious identity with Africa has produced an enormous and diverse spectrum of Blacks—lobbyists, governmental elites, missionaries, and Pan-Africanists—seeking to affect U.S. relations in Africa. The growing policy interests of today's Black population are not limited to any socioeconomic group; rather, they reach both the grass-roots communities and the middle class, extending, as it were, from the streets to the suites.

Blacks take umbrage at such neoconservative doctrine as that of sociologist Nathan Glazer, who contends that "compensation for the past is a dangerous principle."[5] They know that their relative lack of power in contemporary America exists precisely because of *past* suppression and exploitation; slavery and its successors from the post-Reconstruction era to the *Bakke* decision have all been decided by holders of power who were not Black. The cause of Blacks' economic, and to a considerable extent, political powerlessness must therefore be traced to another source. Legislative and judicial decisions by White governing bodies have consistently eliminated the tentative toehold some Blacks have gained during the rare episodes of their inclusion in American authority—the first Reconstruction of the nineteenth century and the second of the recent civil rights era. These realities can never be obliterated by facile theories and interpretations intended to prove the contrary. Past injustices to the Black minority are embedded in the history and mind of America as surely as Hitler's holocausts are in the present and future of Germany.

## TRANSAFRICA: NEW LOBBY ON AFRICAN AFFAIRS

To promote their historic claims on American power, Blacks in 1977 organized TransAfrica, Inc., the first mass-based Black lobby aspiring to influence U.S. policy toward Africa. Although Trans-Africa seeks to exert group pressure on American policy toward the Caribbean states as well, it has concentrated on Africa. The new lobby grew out of a 1976 meeting of 130 Blacks summoned by Charles Diggs and Andrew Young (when both were still congressmen) to challenge Secretary Kissinger's policy on Rhodesia. TransAfrica's founding members were Ronald Walters, a professor of political science at Howard University; C. Payne Lucas, chief of Africare, Inc.; Willard R. Johnson, a scholar and a member of the Council on Foreign Relations; Herschelle Challenor and Randall Robinson, who worked as aides to Diggs, who was Chairman of the House Subcommittee on Africa. This group recruited Richard Hatcher, Mayor of Gary, Indiana, to head TransAfrica's board of directors.

Randall Robinson, a graduate of Harvard Law School, was the founding member who emerged as TransAfrica's Executive Director. With an insider's knowledge of the American political process, as well as the interest-group focus of American politics, Robinson began to lobby the House of Representatives in May 1978, directing his pro-Africa appeals to legislators whose congressional districts accounted for a substantial portion of the Black electorate. Using political contacts and a small team of volunteers, he set out "to have a systematic capacity in each congressional district where we have more than ten percent of the population to move opinion from the population to the congressperson, or to the president or to the secretary of state."[6] With roots deep in the American political system, TransAfrica sought to influence U.S. policy toward Africa from within the system.

This Black interest group was also distinguished by the size of its constituency. With a membership of ten thousand in 1979, the successful lobby presented clear evidence of Black Americans' enduring interest in Africa and their contemporary opposition to apartheid. When Young was removed as U.N. Ambassador, for instance, Robinson took the opportunity to remind President Carter that "we have been all too alone in our protests of growing intimacy between Israel and the state of South Africa."[7] On a signal from Robinson, the lobby's membership flooded the White House with letters, telegrams, and telephone calls protesting the circumstances of Young's resignation.

Three years after its formation, TransAfrica had also established itself among African nations. The Organization of African Unity (OAU) elevated the Black American lobby to a functional status in its council of ministers, and it received Robinson as a quasi-plenipotentiary without portfolio at the 1980 OAU meeting in Sierra Leone. The TransAfrica leader participated in drafting an OAU declaration that vilified Western investments in South Africa and the Sullivan Principles (fair employment guidelines for U.S. corporations in South Africa) as detrimental to South Africa's Black majority. At the annual TransAfrica fundraising benefit earlier, Tanzania's Ambassador to the U.N. Salim A. Salim, who then served as President of the General Assembly, keynoted the occasion, providing further witness to TransAfrica's kindred links to the African continent.

In the political system TransAfrica proved extraordinarily effective in mobilizing governmental and Black leadership in foreign affairs. It developed a close working relationship with such civil rights organizations as the National Association for the Advancement of Colored People (NAACP) and People United to Save Humanity (PUSH). Robinson consulted regularly with such members of the Carter Administration as Assistant Secretary of State for African Affairs Richard Moose, and with congressional leaders such as Stephen J. Solarz, who had replaced Diggs at the House Subcommittee on Africa. Major results of TransAfrica's lobbying appeared late in 1979:

> Without our work, the United States would have lifted the economic sanctions on trade with Rhodesia long before this year, and the London conference [which prepared the way for Black majority rule in Zimbabwe] would not have happened. When he was Prime Minister, Muzorewa tried to get Washington to lift the sanctions as a step toward recognizing his regime; we were able to stop that from happening.[8]

Besides helping to prolong the U.S. embargo on chromium imports from Rhodesia, Robinson counted TransAfrica's pressures for increased U.S. foreign assistance to African and Caribbean countries among the major accomplishments of his burgeoning organization.

## THE AMERICAN COLONIZATION SOCIETY

The roots of current Black involvement in U.S. policy toward Africa can be traced almost to the beginning of the American Republic, when, on January 1, 1817, the American Society for the Colonization of Free People of Color of the United States, or the American Colonization Society as it became known generally, was founded to transport certain categories of Blacks to their ancestral homeland. Freedmen, consisting of Blacks born free and those who had purchased their freedom, were designated as the first of a group to build an American colony on the west coast of Africa. In 1847 this colony became the independent state of Liberia, the first republic on the African continent.

Colonization, or the establishment of an American empire, surfaced as a national objective with the founding of the American Republic. The United States then lacked the economic and military capacity to fulfill such an ambition, but the concept of *imperium* was well ingrained; George Washington had referred to the new nation as a "rising empire" as early as March 1783. Richard Van Alstyne points out in his book that America's subsequent "evolution from a group of small, disunited English colonies strung out on a long coastline to a world power with commitments on every sea and in every continent, has been a characteristically imperial type of growth."[9] The colonization of Liberia therefore belonged to a larger, preconceived national agenda. What made American colonization unique was the fact that it evolved out of slavery and used Black people as the colonizing constituency.

Historians have commonly portrayed the American Colonization Society as a venture of private persons and groups; actually, for all intents and purposes, it represented the second major policy of U.S. government toward Africa, following the original involvement with the Barbary States of North Africa (discussed in Chapter 6). Anxiety was caused among the nation's leaders by the growing number of Africans, and their descendants, in the United States, especially free Blacks, who made up 10 percent of the total Black population of around 2 million in 1808.[10] As early as 1794 Congress enacted a law prohibiting Americans from further participation in the Atlantic slave trade, but it persisted as slave traders in the American colonies obtained slaves from their counterparts in the British West Indies and elsewhere. This increased the size of the Black population in the United States and, consequently, the likelihood of friction from free Blacks and revolt from the slaves. The alarm of Whites was exemplified by the Virginia legislature's decision to have Governor James Monroe query President Jefferson on the possibility of purchasing a tract of land outside of Virginia, where "persons obnoxious to the laws or dangerous to the peace of society" could be relocated.[11] Jefferson, a slave owner, never acted, but on March 3, 1819, Congress enacted legislation giving President James Monroe broad powers to remove slaves captured at sea to Africa and appropriated $100,000 for the purpose.

The Society itself was founded with George Washington's nephew Bushrod Washington as President, and Robert Finley and Francis Scott Key as Vice-Presidents. Soon it attracted the support of Jefferson and Senator Henry Clay of Kentucky. Though Congress did not provide the Society with a subvention or charter, as desired by its founders, the organization clearly owed much of its existence to the sponsorship of the U.S. government.

The Society was maintained by a paradoxical mixture of three different groups: Black nationalists, who longed for a homeland free of slavery; White abolitionists, who regarded slavery as inherently evil and saw African repatriation as an expedient relief from it; and slaveholders, who welcomed African colonization as a convenient way to expel slaves who had become too aged or enfeebled to work, not to mention those slaves whose smoldering hatred of oppression made them a permanent threat to White society. In the American Colonization Society these disparate elements found common ground, with the result that Bushrod Washington and slaveholders deliberated with such free Black leaders as Alexander Crummell, an

Episcopal clergyman educated in England at Cambridge University, and Paul Cuffee, a wealthy Massachusetts shipowner who, at his own expense, sent thirty-eight freedmen to the British colony of Sierra Leone in 1815.[12] Through their joint efforts, the Society purchased a strip of land three miles wide and thirty-six miles long on Africa's western coast, named it "Liberia" for freedmen, and called its capital "Monrovia" in honor of the incumbent President Monroe. More land was acquired by the time Liberia became a republic, ostensibly for the new Black settlers. In reality, however, Liberia was Whites' answer to the race problem in the United States.

Not all Black nationalists supported the Society. For example, Martin R. Delany, a Harvard-trained physician, now regarded by Black Americans as the father of Afro-American nationalism, condemned the Black settlement in Liberia as a colony controlled by Southern slaveholders; he believed the Society was determined to deposit free Blacks there in order to protect the institution of American slavery. At a meeting of the Negro Convention Movement, a well-organized group of free Blacks similarly hostile to the Society, Delany made an impassioned plea for a Black nation-state, fully convinced that the Society was an insidious guise for slaveholders to dump their unwanted slaves in Africa: "We look upon the American Colonization Society as one of the most arrant enemies of the colored man . . . , anti-Christian in character, and misanthropic in its pretended sympathies."[13] Insisting on "Africa for Africans," he proposed the creation of a powerful Black state independent of the White control of Liberia. This staunch African nationalist position put him at loggerheads with such abolitionists as William Lloyd Garrison, whom he knew personally, as well as with Black nationalists committed to the colonization scheme.

Surely the lasting disgrace of American policy toward Liberia was the fact that the United States was the last among the Western nations to recognize this republic which official U.S. efforts created and later maintained as an informal protectorate. With the Society's approval, the Black settlers proclaimed their small terrain the independent and sovereign nation of Liberia in 1847; Great Britain,

France, and several other European nations recognized it at once. The U.S. delay increased Delany's suspicion that Southern slave-holding interests dominated the leadership in Washington, which trembled at the prospect that Liberian diplomats, some of them former slaves, would arrive in the American capital to hobnob with slavemasters. In fact, the White aristocracy built upon slavery prevented the United States from recognizing the modern world's first Black republic, Haiti, which, like Liberia, was not finally recognized until June 1862.

The repatriation of U.S. Blacks to Liberia, which proceeded at a trickle, sped up after Nat Turner's revolt in 1831 slew scores of White Virginians. By the outbreak of the Civil War the Society had conveyed some thirteen thousand Blacks to the new Afro-American colony.[14] The state of Maryland reacted to the bloodshed in Virginia by passing an "Act Relating to Free Negros and Slaves" that prohibited anyone of African descent from settling in their state. The Maryland legislature also carried its fear a step further by appropriating $200,000 for the Maryland Colonization Society for the export of additional Blacks to Liberia.[15] Maryland's desperation, however, was not unique among the American states, even the nonslave states, for anxiety about what to do with the slaves had by now become a national crisis. The official frustration culminated in 1857 when the Supreme Court, under Chief Justice Roger B. Taney, ruled in the *Dred Scott* case that no Black person, not even a free Black, could be a citizen of the United States.

The Americo-Liberians, as the Black settlers in Liberia became known, imposed a uniquely American image on the new country and its institutions. They established a system of government patterned after the American model—with a presidency, bicameral legislature, and a judiciary in a nominal system of checks and balances—and eventually built a "White House" for Joseph Jenkins Roberts, the Americo-Liberian who was the country's first President. The Americo-Liberians created a system of authority that was so discriminatory and repressive toward the indigenous peoples that it recalled the American slave system from which they had fled. Not only did they assume an absolute monopoly of political power, they also succeeded, with American support, in wresting control of most of the land from the indigenous Africans who had been corraled into this new entity called Liberia.

It must be emphasized that the Black settlers in Liberia did not represent an "in-gathering" of Africa's lost children, as the state of Israel represented to Jews a century later, because, as Liberia specialist J. Gus Liebenow discovered, "these were Americans, and their views of Africa and Africans were essentially those of nineteenth-century Whites in the United States." [16] Arriving with a pledge to civilize and govern what they regarded as backward Africans, the Americo-Liberians finished by erecting an antinative oligarchy that prevailed for the next 133 years, until April 1980 when dissidents of indigenous ancestry in the Liberian army overturned the regime of President William Tolbert.

## THE MISSIONARIES

Generally invisible in mainstream studies of American history, Afro-American missionaries made a significant and indelible impression on the United States cultural penetration, not only in Liberia and the other Black-settler colony of Sierra Leone, but ultimately in much of sub-Saharan Africa. Certain characteristics of the Black missionaries associated them with White American missionaries, who first introduced the Blacks into Africa to Christianize it early in the nineteenth century, then began to exclude them from the White mission boards at the beginning of this century. Blacks often shared Whites' bigoted presumptions of African cultural inferiority together with an unquestioned belief in American and European superiority. They therefore perceived Africans as "heathens" and "uncivilized," despite the fact that Africans, such as the Ashanti of the Gold Coast, [17] often flourished under traditional authorities or governments, and objectively were not less fortunate than the Americans just emancipated from chattel slavery. The American missionaries, Black and White, were also overwhelmingly Protestant and female. But the Black missionaries parted company with their White colleagues on the matter of their

Pan-Africanist sentiments, or on ideas based on race, which identified them with the African people and consequently with Africans' anticolonial aspirations.

Lott Carey, a former Virginia slave who had purchased his emancipation, arrived in Sierra Leone in 1821 with a large delegation of ex-slaves, with funds provided by the American Colonization Society and the Whites' Baptist Board of Foreign Missions. Soon Carey led his group to Cape Mesurado, or Liberia as the region would be renamed years later, rallying the settlers to resist the legitimacy and domination of Whites running the Society. In June 1824, for example, Carey and his followers staged a rebellion against a Society agent accused of enforcing an arbitrary apportionment of land sites. The self-educated Richmond missionary had already established himself in Liberia by serving as a colonial inspector and health officer; but at the hour of his successful revolt, the Society acceded to his appointment as vice regent of the colony. In this capacity he warred against slave traders for the Atlantic market, and attacked Africans who raided the colonists as invaders.

Not surprisingly, the Baptist board reconsidered using freedmen as African missionaries after Carey's rebellion. The memory of his success at converting Africans, however, stimulated the formation of an independent Black mission board in 1897 at Shiloh Baptist Church of Washington, D.C., under the name of the Lott Carey Baptist Foreign Missions Convention. It was the first and only Afro-American organization devoted exclusively to foreign mission work. Starting out as a protest against the general absence of Black Americans in foreign missions, particularly among the Northern Baptists, the Lott Carey convention expanded its activities from Liberia, reaching the Congo by 1901 and as far as South Africa by 1925.

Even as the Lott Carey missions took shape, White mission boards in the United States were adopting policies that drastically reduced Blacks' participation. Though an important consideration, Whites' fear of rebellious alliances between Africans and Afro-Americans was not the principal cause of the new exclusionary policies. Instead, the advent of European colonial expansion in the late nineteenth century decisively polarized the interracial American missionaries, as Afro-Americans tended to advocate African independence, and Whites to condone European domination of the African societies. According to historian Lillie M. Johnson, an exemplary case of the exclusionary policies was provided by the Presbyterians, who had made extensive use of Black missionaries during the nineteenth century. A mission board official of the Presbyterian Church explained in 1928, when the church sent only two Blacks to the Cameroon, that "one of the African Missions was for some years staffed entirely by colored missionaries and in its entire history has had three times as many colored missionaries as white." [18] Indeed the board had actually decided to send only Black missionaries in 1842, because they were regarded as immune to the tropical diseases that had killed their White predecessors. By 1928, however, the church went on record as opposed to using Afro-American missionaries until the attitudes of the colonial governments could be ascertained. Thus the Presbyterian mission board, like the U.S. government on most African issues, deferred the question to European colonial authorities.

In southern Africa the European imperialists intensified the racial divisions among missionaries by providing White Protestants with free grants of land seized from the indigenous people. For example, American Methodists obtained land at old Umtali in Southern Rhodesia (now Zimbabwe) during 1898. Cecil Rhodes, who gave Americans additional land along the border of Portuguese East Africa, had conceived the land grants to British and White American missions exclusively as part of his scheme for Anglo-Saxons to rule the world. [19]

Meager financial resources hampered development of the Black missions from the beginning. Nevertheless, the Black missionaries forged ahead—making Liberia and South Africa their mission fields—and surely none was more impressive than the leader of African Methodist Episcopal Church (AME), Bishop Henry McNeal Turner. The AME was founded in the same year as the American Colonization Society, as Blacks seceded from the White-dominated Methodist congregations. Turner, elected Bishop in 1880, ambitiously launched a dual campaign of missionary expansion and Black American repatriation in Africa, infusing the AME mission with a singular Pan-Africanist orientation. As a supporter of colonization, he had endorsed the unsuccessful bill of South Carolina Senator Matthew Butler for $5 million in transportation funds for Afro-Americans who wished to leave the South to become citizens of another country. As Vice-President of the Society, he was assigned to oversee the AME churches that originated in West Africa in 1885. The Black nationalist Bishop increased the AME mission to Liberia in 1891, then to Pretoria and Cape Town in 1898. Today the AME is still the largest Black American religious group in Africa, with a church membership of 250,000 from West to South Africa. The majority of these, or 180,000, reside in southern Africa.

The Black missionaries contributed to the spread not only of Christianity in Africa but of African nationalism as well. They melded political ideas into their religious dogma to evolve a rationale for their work in Africa. The church work in Liberia—the earliest and most intensive ever carried out on the continent—ultimately provided an organized church for the Christian expatriates from America. As freedmen imbued with ideas borrowed from such American ideology as found in the Declaration of Independence, they arrived in Africa with potent moral and political weaponry against the racism of White American missionaries and the domination of European colonizers.

As confreres of the Africans they converted, the Black Americans also helped to maintain a Pan-Africanist vision among the colonized people. This influence was powerfully illustrated in the British Protectorate of Nyasaland (now Malawi) in 1915, when the Zulu revolutionary John Chilembwe led his small army against the colonial order, killing three Whites, wounding others, and, for at least a brief time, threatening to stem the growth of settler power.[20] The British Colonial Office later reported Black American complicity in the rebellion:

In 1900, Mr. Cheek and Miss Delany, American Negros, came to Nyasaland. Cheek married Chilembwe's niece and was a preacher in his church. . . . Cheek . . . and Chilembwe planned to send for more

American Negro missionaries to settle in countries and influence tribes to drive Europeans out.[21]

The missionary with Pan-Africanist convictions identified with Africans' desire for political independence and consequently contributed, here and there, to the political radicalization of African converts.

The radical tradition in Black Christendom has been preserved in the contemporary era by the Progressive National Baptists Convention, a group of 1.4 million Black Americans who broke away from the conservative parent body, the National Black Baptists organization, because of the latter's refusal to support Martin Luther King's leadership during the civil rights movement. Headed by Reverend William A. Jones, Jr., the Progressive Baptists have paralleled the activity of Black political groups by concentrating their pro-Africa efforts on fierce opposition to apartheid. Reverend Jones has even introduced a theological justification for armed struggle:

> Genocide, on a massive scale, is being practiced in South Africa. To be non-violent in the context of genocide is to affirm violence and is tantamount to alliance with the adversary. To resist, by whatever means necessary, is the only sane and spiritual response of one who calls himself a Christian.[22]

The Black Christians thus added a revolutionary perspective to Afro-Americans' historic defense of African liberation.

On the other hand, Black missionaries have failed to equal their White counterparts in resolving the problem of leadership in the African churches. A basic concern of all missionaries was whether the new African Christians should be allowed to form their own leadership or continue under the tutelage of the foreigners. Reacting to their own sense of guilt, as well as the practical need to make some concessions to counteract the expansion of African nationalism, White missionaries laid the groundwork for the emergence of a whole class of African church leaders, including Bishop Abel Muzorewa of Rhodesia's Methodist Church, Bishop Eduardo de Cavalho of the Angola Methodists, and John Gatu, who became executive secretary of the Presbyterian church of East Africa.

By contrast, the Black American missions have not produced one major church or political leader. (Kwame Nkrumah, whose education included a degree in theology, studied at Lincoln University, a Black college in Pennsylvania, not at the missionary schools in Ghana.) Nowhere in Africa did indigenous church members rise to the rank of bishop, or other adjudicatory position, under the Black missionaries. As the victims rather than the progenitors of slavery and colonialism, Blacks felt no guilt in maintaining control of the churches they inspired. The AME in particular has taken this conservatism to an extreme form in South Africa, where the church manifestly refuses to appoint African bishops. Not only have the AME missionaries played no significant role in combating apartheid, but they have abstained from involvement in domestic politics.

Black Americans nonetheless surpassed all missionary groups in indigenizing, or adapting, Christian worship to Africa. Culturally more secure than racial outsiders like the Presbyterians or the Anglicans, the Afro-Americans identified with African traditions; accordingly, they approved the use of drums and native dress to make their imported theology more authentic in the African culture. The eclecticism has accelerated the emergence of indigenous churches in African society and has multiplied the number of converts. There are approximately 130 million Christians in Africa today,[23] due in part to the Blacks adapting Christian worship to African culture. Thus, from colonization to Christianization, Black missionaries have stayed in the forefront of change in Africa. Their continental influence, through conversions, has far exceeded their comparatively small numbers, although in political impact they have been surpassed only by the Pan-Africanists.

## THE PAN-AFRICANISTS

At the turn of this century there emerged the largest and most successful Black mass movement in American history. It sought both to "return to Africa" and to completely overwhelm official U.S. relations in Africa. This was Marcus Garvey's Universal Negro Improvement Association (UNIA), a Black nationalist organization dedicated to "uniting all the Negro peoples of the world into one great body to establish a country and Government absolutely their own." [24] It is important to note that Garvey, born in Jamaica, was not a native American, and his movement, organized in Jamaica in July 1914, eschewed involvement with U.S. policy toward Africa. Nevertheless, Garvey and the UNIA belong in this discussion because, once transplanted in New York City in 1916, they surpassed all other Afro-American groups in promoting Blacks' goals relative to Africa. Indeed, Garvey achieved his greatest success in the United States, as native Black Americans not only swelled the ranks of his organization, but also served, even until the present day, as the main purveyors of his ideology and program.

The emergence of the UNIA coincided with three key developments that were shaping the destiny of Black Americans on the one hand and Africans on the other. In America the Great Migration—the movement of huge numbers of Blacks from the rural South into urban areas of the industrial North—unfolded as Blacks in the North searched desperately for the "promised land" of political freedom and economic opportunity denied them in the South. [25] With the tacit approval of the federal government, Southern Whites had disfranchised the newly emancipated Blacks after 1876. They also brought about political conditions akin to those under slavery as White terrorism resurfaced in the form of the Ku Klux Klan, organized in Pulaski, Tennessee, in April 1867, before Reconstruction had taken hold.

This was a shameful period in American history; race relations here showed remarkable similarities to the apartheid society of South Africa. As revealed in *White Supremacy,* George M. Fredrickson's comparative history of South African and American race relations, President Theodore Roosevelt "and other turn-of-the-century northern progressives found the rationale for condoning new forms of southern discrimination primarily in an extension of the same logic that supported imperialist adventures abroad leading to the forced incorporation of nonwhites into a new American empire. If the United States was justified in exercising protective and educational trusteeship over 'our brown brothers' in the Philippines, then the segregated southern blacks of 1900 could be viewed as undergoing an analogous and equally salutary tutelage." [26] The legalized segregation and disfranchisement in the South after Reconstruction was thus sanctioned by the federal government.

Black soldiers, who had comprised 13 percent of the U.S. forces in World War I (when Blacks constituted only 10 percent of the general population), also faced renewed segregation and White violence. President Wilson sent Booker T. Washington's successor at Tuskegee Institute, Robert R. Moton, to lecture the Black soldiers of the U.S. Army in France and to warn them not to expect freedom and equality upon their return. (Black men were accepted only as messboys and servants by the Navy, and not at all by the Marine Corps.) [27] Having just served to "make the world safe for democracy," these veterans, 380,000 in all, now demanded rights to jobs and votes. What they got instead was a bloody White reaction in such cities as Washington and Chicago. The violence climaxed with the lynching of seventy-seven Blacks in 1919, including several war veterans still in uniform. [28] Like the migrants bound for the North, many of the Black veterans looked for political and emotional succor in the Garvey movement.

The few Black diplomats in Africa meanwhile encountered increasing hostility from the colonial powers. This is best illustrated by the case of John L. Waller, a prominent Black Republican from Kansas whom President Benjamin Harrison appointed as U.S. Consul to Madagascar in 1891. Waller remained there after he retired in 1894 to start trade between the United States and Madagascar. The French, who were then entrenching their dominion over the island, were suspicious of him, in part because native rulers had granted the enterprising American a large land concession to develop rubber and timber resources. [29] French troops arrested Waller, and a military tribunal sentenced him to twenty years in prison. Waller stayed in jail for nearly a year until the combined efforts of Harrison and several U.S. diplomats secured his release.

The Europeans were then consolidating their imperial conquest of the continent. Although Africa is characteristically represented as having an ancient history under European colonialism, most Africans remained under the authority of indigenous leaders until as late as 1885. However, after the dominant European powers—Great Britain, France, Italy, Portugal, and Germany—agreed at the Congress of Berlin to partition the continent into their individual spheres of influence, Africa was rapidly subjugated to European armies and traders. From being a continent overwhelmingly under Black leadership at the start of the nineteenth century, Africa by that century's end was ruled by White men everywhere except Liberia and Ethiopia, the ancient kingdom where native leaders retained their authority.

Garvey thus arose on the world scene when both Black Americans and Africans were losing power and hope. Financed and led exclusively by Blacks, the UNIA promised to unify Black people everywhere, including Africa, as a first step toward their liberation from racial and colonial oppression. Harlem, which was then a burgeoning Black community in an area that had only recently been an aristocratic White suburb,[30] provided the majority of Garvey's following in New York City. He claimed to have recruited two thousand members within a single week after he transferred the UNIA to its New York headquarters. Soon the UNIA reported nine hundred chapters in a worldwide membership of 6 million (most of whom were Black Americans). As explained by Garvey critic Tony Martin, this membership made Garvey the leader of the largest organization of its type in the history of the Black race.[31] As an autonomous movement, the UNIA neither sought nor obtained support from the U.S. government, and singlehandedly it amassed multimillion-dollar revenues through its manifold business enterprises, including restaurants, hotels, and a newspaper.

The Black Star Line, a shipping company, was established to generate international commerce among peoples of African heritage and to transport expatriates to Africa. Garvey made extensive preparations to send American Blacks to Africa to help build what he dreamed would some day become a powerful and independent empire. To accommodate his colonization movement, he negotiated with the Liberian government for a grant of land, and he recruited twenty to thirty thousand Black American families for repatriation, each of them holding a worth of $1,500, with another $2 million provided by the UNIA to finance the operation.[32] Such grand designs soon aroused the suspicion of the Americo-Liberians, who had already usurped territorial authority from the native-born Africans, and who were now unwilling to share it with Garvey nationalists. It also appeared likely that neighboring colonial powers had warned the Liberians they would not tolerate an organization dedicated to the overthrow of European authority. Consequently, the Black Star Line never sailed to the African continent nor did Garvey settle a single expatriate there.

In the United States, however, Garvey realized enormous success, especially through his convocation in 1920 of the first International Convention of the Negro Peoples of the World. This month-long assembly in New York brought the UNIA together with 25,000 delegates from 25 countries of Africa, the Caribbean, Central and South America, and Canada, where the Black population of Nova Scotia included a faction of Garveyites. The biggest international Black assembly America had ever seen, the convention elected Garvey Provisional President of Africa. The convention also issued the *Declaration of the Rights of the Negro People of the World,* a lengthy document that exposed the injustices inflicted on Blacks by European colonization in Africa and White brutality in America. Despite the UNIA's collapse after the U.S. government convicted Garvey on dubious mail fraud charges in 1925 and later deported him, his ideology left an indelible mark on the thinking of a whole generation of Black Americans. It redefined their relationship and sense of duty to Africa, and it raised racial pride and identity with Africa's destiny to a new pinnacle.

W. E. B. DuBois, one of the major American intellectuals of the early twentieth century though often ignored by White scholars, sought very deliberately to mitigate the colonial hegemony over Africa through the instrument of American policy. Known popularly as the "father of Pan-Africanism" because of his leadership in the first six Pan-African congresses, he either organized or played a dominant role in each of them. With fifty-seven delegates from fifteen countries of the West Indies and Africa, as well as from the United States, he arrived in Paris in 1919 to lead the Second Pan-African Conference, scheduled to coincide with the Versailles Peace Conference, and to demonstrate international Black solidarity before the assembled delegates of Europe. DuBois seized the opportunity to demand that the United States and its European allies establish laws to protect Africans' racial, economic, and political interests, and that these laws be enforced through the League of Nations. Specifically, he requested that the German colonies of Tanganyika and Cameroon be turned over to an international body, rather than returned to defeated Germany or put under the rule of any other colonial authority. He also stunned the Europeans by proposing to link the German colonies to the Belgian Congo and to the Portuguese territories of Mozambique and Angola, which DuBois believed Portugal was economically too weak to support. In essence DuBois was recommending an intermediate solution between colonialism and independence.

The European imperialists scoffed at the Pan-Africanists' demands, but in his proposals DuBois planted the seed of what came to be the mandate commission of the League of Nations. After the United Nations was created in 1945, this seed evolved into the U.N.'s trusteeship system.

Undeterred by the European intransigence and United States indifference, DuBois persevered in his anticolonial protest during the interwar years. He welcomed the collapse of Europe in World War II as the herald of the new age of African decolonization. He was the first Black American leader to internationalize the racial problems of American Blacks and to connect them politically to African nationalism. As a scholar he documented U.S. involvement in African history, beginning in 1896 with *The Suppression of the African Slave-Trade to the United States,* and he recorded Africa's rich cultural heritage in numerous publications. As a Pan-Africanist he influenced the ideological positions of many young African nationalists, notably the future ruler of Ghana, Kwame Nkrumah, who referred to DuBois as "my father."[33] The Pan-African conferences that he promoted have been widely recognized by contemporary African leaders as the genesis of today's Organization of African Unity (OAU).

By the 1950s DuBois had become convinced that future world power belonged to people of color. This belief motivated him to criticize Black Americans for waning in their identity with African nationalism in the postwar era: "When we think of the help which Irish Americans have given Ireland, and how Scandinavia, Italy, Germany, Poland and China have been aided by their emigrants in the United States, it is tragic that American Negroes today are . . . doing little to help Africa in its hour of supreme need."[34] As a founder of the NAACP in 1909, DuBois was originally a radical pioneer for racial integration. However, by the time of *Brown* v. *The Board of Education,* while the domestic civil rights struggle consumed the energies of Black Americans and perforce diminished their support to African liberation, he swung completely behind the cause of African independence. Ultimately, he agonized so much at American society, especially U.S. collaboration with the Europeans, that he repudiated the United States, first by declaring his membership in the Communist party and finally by accepting Nkrumah's offer of citizenship in independent Ghana. In accepting the citizenship DuBois said: "I have returned that my dust shall mingle with the dust of my forefathers."[35] In 1963 he died in Ghana, at age ninety-five, a Pan-Africanist to the end.

The path of African expatriation was also followed by Stokely Carmichael who, as leader of the Black Power movement during the 1960s, spearheaded the cultural revival of African identity and heritage. As an ideologist he viewed America's Black minority as a "colony" dominated by the larger White society.[36] Consequently, he never aspired to influence U.S. relations toward Africa through American foreign policy. Instead, he exiled himself as a guest of President Sékou Touré in Guinea, where Kwame Nkrumah (in exile after the army coup that removed him from power in Ghana in 1966) then lived. In Guinea Carmichael renamed himself Kwame

Touré, after his African fathers, and laid the framework for his All African Peoples Revolutionary Party, which is a Pan-Africanist movement now functioning in the United States among radical factions of the Black college population.

## THE RADICALS AND THE INTEGRATIONISTS

The Council on African Affairs was a major exception to DuBois's complaint about Blacks' poor support for Africa's decolonization. It was the very first organization that Blacks created for the express purpose of influencing U.S. policy toward Africa. Interracial but under Black leadership, the Council was founded in New York during January 1937, less than a year after Italy's invasion of Ethiopia, which for Black Americans had been the worldwide symbol of Black dignity and power. Among the Council's original twelve members were Max Yergan, a YMCA official with seventeen years of service in African countries and the first Black faculty member of the City University of New York; Mordecai W. Johnson, president of Howard University, the nation's leading Black institution; Paul Robeson, the world-renowned actor and concert singer; and Ralph J. Bunche, a professor of political science at Howard University who later became the Assistant Secretary-General of the United Nations. An important White member was Raymond Leslie Buell of Harvard University, a political scientist with a specialization in African affairs and a member of the prestigious Foreign Policy Association. It was not until William Alphaeus Hunton, a brilliant Black scholar and a Marxist, joined in August 1943 that the Council developed a radical ideological defense of African liberation.

Radical and liberal intellectuals dominated the Council. Johnson, Bunche, Buell, and Hunton all had Ph.D.s, and Robeson had been educated at Rutgers University. This elite group was later joined by Adam Clayton Powell, Jr., the Harlem congressman. This membership guaranteed the Council a high degree of access to American institutions and policymakers. Council Chairman Paul Robeson, who was then perhaps the most famous and controversial

Black in the world,[37] attracted significant national and international attention. The Council also produced definite objectives: (1) to provide concrete assistance to African nationalist struggles; (2) to disseminate accurate information on Africa and African peoples; (3) most significantly, to influence the U.S. government to adopt policies favorable to African independence. It also endeavored to swing public opinion behind these goals through press releases, radio programs, mass meetings, and *New Africa,* the organization's monthly publication. Membership rose to two thousand, and the Council's budget jumped to about $11,000 by 1942 to a peak of nearly $40,000 four years later.[38]

From the beginning, the Council devoted intense interest to South Africa, partly because, through Yergan, Council members acquired extensive contacts with progressive South Africans, especially with the African National Congress (ANC), the oldest and biggest nationalist organization in Black Africa. Modest but regular donations from the Council's budget went to assist African nationalists and labor groups in Kenya, Nigeria, and South Africa. This assistance increased in the summer of 1949, when the Council appointed DuBois Chairman of its new African Aid Committee, with a hundred prominent Americans as sponsors. In 1950 the Council made an unprecedented demand for South Africa's expulsion from the United Nations.

To influence American policy, Council members maintained assiduous correspondence and consultation with both the State Department and the White House. On January 15, 1944, the State Department created a separate Division of African Affairs under Henry S. Villard, a former Assistant Chief of the Near Eastern Division, under which Africa had incomprehensibly been included until this time. In a meeting with officials of the new division, a council delegation including Yergan and Hunton demanded an aggressive pro-Africa policy. Perhaps because of Council appeals, that year the State Department dispatched its first Black American experts to Africa, mainly to Liberia and Ethiopia.

At this time the Council, aware of the Allies' plan for the establishment of the United Nations, sent a letter to President

Franklin D. Roosevelt and Secretary of State Edward R. Stettinius, Jr., advising them that "the promotion of the welfare of the millions of Africans and other dependent peoples of the world must be an integral part of the projected international organization's program and functions."[39] As World War II approached an end in March 1945, Yergan and Hunton urged Assistant Secretary of State Archibald MacLeish to pressure the European Allies either to relinquish their African colonies or to put them under the international supervision of an effective trusteeship. Council members were waiting in hope of a favorable U.S. response when Roosevelt, whom many Blacks regarded as a champion of the oppressed, died, just two weeks before the United Nations organizational conference at San Francisco.

The subsequent Truman Administration looked on the radical Council members with contempt. This view was scarcely abated by the presence in the State Department of former Council leader Ralph Bunche, then the Associate Chief of the State Department's Division of Dependent Affairs. The White House's contempt for the Council spread to all major Black organizations in July 1945, when Truman appointed South Carolina's James F. Byrnes, a powerful and openly racist politician, as Secretary of State.[40]

After World War II the militant Council on African Affairs, which historian Hollis R. Lynch describes as the "longest-lived and most influential American organization of its kind,"[41] encountered fateful blows from three different sources. First, there was Washington's hostility, which intensified after the Council denounced the Marshall Plan, the North Atlantic Treaty, and the establishment of NATO as mechanisms "to guarantee that colonial people under . . . (European) rule shall not win their destiny of freedom and independence."[42] Hunton, before the Senate Foreign Relations Committee, and DuBois before the House Committee on Foreign Relations, testified against the treaty in 1949. Second, there was an internal leadership rift pitting Max Yergan against Robeson and his partisans. Originally a radical, Yergan now switched to the side of ideological conservatism, thereby precipitating his expulsion from the Council late in 1948. Finally, there came vicious, red-baiting attacks from Senator Joseph McCarthy, who smeared the Council in his anticommunist witchhunts and destroyed its credibility. The Council managed to survive until 1955, but McCarthyism had struck it a deathblow.

Malcolm X, who became renowned as the militant spokesman of Black Muslims in the United States during the 1960s, revived certain objectives of Garveyism and the Council when he created the Organization of Afro-American Unity in 1964 to "include all people of African descent in the Western Hemisphere, as well as our brothers and sisters of the African continent."[43] This was his small but vocal constituency fighting for domestic political rights as the Black Power movement took full course. Malcolm fashioned it after the OAU in terms of its Pan-Africanist orientation to international politics. Washington had despised him during his previous leadership of the Nation of Islam, the Black Muslim movement, and continued to ostracize him after his separation from it. Two years before his assassination in 1965, he proposed discussions on Africa policy with Secretary of State Dean Rusk and U.N. Ambassador Adlai Stevenson, both of whom shunned him. Yet Malcolm's decision to approach the American leaders, a gesture that would have been unimaginable in his earlier role as a radical Muslim representative, indicated clearly that he was moving in the direction of the Council insofar as a dialogue with Washington was concerned. However, his death terminated this hopeful departure.

Black moderates did not fare much better than Malcolm X, as is evident from the experience of the American Negro Leadership Conference on Africa (ANLCA), which was organized in 1962 to promote the awesome and simultaneous tasks of seeking civil rights in the United States and national independence in Africa. Roy Wilkins, leader of the NAACP, recognized the potential political power of this new lobby:

> The not inconsiderable abilities we American Negro citizens possess should be harnessed in an effective fashion to the task of persuading our Government to aid the emerging peoples of Africa toward their place in the world of nations.

In developing this activity we should not relax our prime efforts to achieve our proper place in our own country since progress toward that end will enhance our own influence in behalf of Africa.[44]

Wilkins participated in the ANLCA with a hundred of the top Black leaders in America, including Reverend Martin Luther King, Jr., who was running the civil rights movement at the head of the Southern Christian Leadership Conference (SCLC); Whitney Young, who directed the National Urban League; Dorothy Height of the National Council of Negro Women; and trade-union pioneer A. Philip Randolph of the AFL-CIO's Brotherhood of Sleeping Car Porters. Together, these leaders spoke for almost eight million Black Americans.

King and the other ANLCA leaders appealed to the Johnson Administration in 1964 to take a firm stand against South Africa, prohibit future American investments there, and endorse a U.N.-sponsored oil embargo against the apartheid state. The influential Black leaders further demanded a quick termination of the traditional practices of excluding Black Americans from U.S. missions to South Africa. Yet, despite the domestic importance of its members, Johnson turned a deaf ear to the ANLCA. After its failure to win approval as a mediator in the Nigerian civil war, this moderate party also sank into oblivion.

## THE AID PROGRAMS

In contrast to the pressure-group appeals of the Council on African Affairs and the ANLCA, Reverend James H. Robinson, a Presbyterian minister, used the power of example to pull Washington's interest toward his Operation Crossroads Africa, the oldest and best known of Black aid programs in Africa. Interracial in composition, Crossroads began in 1957 with a "pick and shovel" contingent of sixty volunteers to five African countries.[45] The volunteer and youth-oriented approach of Reverend Robinson's brainchild later became a model for the U.S. Peace Corps, which President Kennedy developed in 1961.

Robinson's influence, though crucial to the conceptualization of the Peace Corps, fell short of the strictly political aspects of Black

Americans' interest in African independence. Nonetheless it represented a milestone, coming, as it did, after nearly two centuries of official neglect of Africa.

Africare, Inc., was created in 1971 as another private Black aid program. It enlarged on the goal of private support to African development and also attracted U.S. governmental assistance. Africare was created under the leadership of C. Payne Lucas, a former Peace Corps director. Its inspiration was an idea of President Hamani Diori of Niger, who had suggested that Black Americans ought to become organized around the cause of African development. It has promoted self-development as the guiding principle of African development, which recalls Julius Nyerere's ideology of self-reliance.[46] Africare volunteers helped to stop mass famine in the drought-stricken Sahel during the late 1970s. They also contributed to agricultural productivity and the development of land resources in such countries as Upper Volta, Chad, Mali, and Ethiopia. In September 1978 the organization established a permanent office in Lusaka to coordinate its expanding programs in southern Africa.

In seeking U.S. governmental support for African development, Lucas frequently solicited support from the White House and the State Department. Although the bulk of Africare's operational funds derived from the Agency for International Development (AID), important supplements came from foundations and corporations, Black churches, fraternities, and sororities. AID subsidized Africare operations with $6 million in 1979, but Blacks themselves provided both the basic professional skills and additional money. C. Payne Lucas stated: "We have demonstrated our ability as a predominantly Black institution to attract skilled and competent Black Americans. Blacks are now prepared, in talent and money, to support African development."[47] Africare, which started "without a nickel," has since become a multimillion-dollar program with a host of projects in such areas as reforestation, animal husbandry, and rural development. Its prestige on the African continent was indicated in 1979 when Zambia's President Kenneth Kaunda was named as Africare's international chairman.

## LOBBY AND TRADE

The Congressional Black Caucus expected to exert political influence on Washington after the sixteen Blacks in the U.S. House of Representatives organized their own forum in 1969. What favored this prospect was the group's supervision by Charles Diggs, Jr., the seven-term Detroit Democrat who held the important chairmanship of the Subcommittee on Africa in the House Committee on International Affairs.

At Howard University in May 1972, the Caucus sponsored an ANLCA meeting which, among several provocative measures, proposed the establishment of a national Black strategy on Africa and a nationwide program of support for African liberation struggles. Four years later the Caucus produced the Afro-American Manifesto on Southern Africa, a document that allied Black Americans to the goals of African liberation in that region, while upbraiding the Ford Administration for opposition to Angolan and Mozambican nationalists. Evidently impressed by the endorsement of the Manifesto by such civil rights organizations as the NAACP and the National Urban League, Kissinger summoned the Black leaders to listen to their demands in October 1976. Nothing concrete emanated from the meeting, and the Caucus never attained decisive impact on U.S. policy in Africa. The Caucus's fledgling position was weakened further when Congress censured Diggs because of his 1978 conviction on charges of mail fraud and falsifying staff payrolls. The censure terminated his career.

Together with their efforts to affect U.S. government policy, Blacks in the 1970s also tackled the more difficult task of trying to influence the obdurate policies of U.S. multinational corporations in South Africa. Reverend Leon H. Sullivan, who had founded the Opportunities Industrialization Corporation, a Black self-help group based in Philadelphia, was the first and only Black on the General Motors board of directors and the formulator of the Sullivan Principles (six fair-employment guidelines for U.S. corporations in South Africa discussed in Chapter 7). Secretary of State Cyrus R. Vance was so impressed by the Sullivan Principles that in March

1979 the State Department welcomed them "as a potentially major force for change in South Africa."[48] Thus Sullivan's guidelines obtained Washington's "strong support." Black Americans, on the other hand, generally denounced them. For example, a group of two hundred Black church leaders rejected the Principles overwhelmingly at their summit meeting in New York in 1979. Reverend William Jones of the Progressive Baptists decried the Sullivan guidelines as "well-intentioned but no longer sufficient," emphasizing that "the very presence of United States corporations in South Africa serves to legitimize the apartheid system of White supremacy."[49] The ministers demanded total corporate disengagement.

The International Freedom Mobilization Against Apartheid, a Black religious leaders' lobby, was subsequently organized to seal their unequivocal opposition to Sullivan. The incipient protest movement was headed by Reverend Wyatt Tee Walker, the secretary general, who had worked during the civil rights era as chief of staff to Martin Luther King. The ministers, who came from thirty-eight states and fifty-two cities, did not limit their protest to a moral condemnation of apartheid. They took the additional political step of declaring support for the African National Congress (ANC), the anti-apartheid movement of South Africa.

It was the Reverend Andrew Young who, as U.S. Ambassador to the U.N., galvanized large segments of the Black middle class into a greater awareness of U.S. policy toward Africa. The middle class, which E. Franklin Frazier once dubbed the Black bourgeoisie,[50] has frequently been content with incremental advances into the socioeconomic mainstream of America, but Young interested it in foreign policy. When, for example, the moderate NAACP issued its *NAACP Task Force on Africa Report* in 1978, it produced perhaps its strongest statement in the sixty years that had elapsed since DuBois and other NAACP founders infused the original organization with a radical image and program.[51] The NAACP, according to the report, "should encourage Black Americans to seek entry into various branches of our foreign service and to use their best efforts in such careers to shape U.S. policies toward Africa."[52] Most significantly, the civil rights organization proposed economic sanctions against the South African government and U.S. corporations with business operations in the apartheid state. The largest Black organization thus moved toward the progressive orientation of TransAfrica.

Afro-American trade with certain African states also ensued during Young's U.N. stewardship, when a small number of Black businesses expanded their commercial links to Africa. For instance, Johnson Products Company, a Chicago-based manufacturer of cosmetics and hair-care goods, established operations in Nigeria with a direct investment of $4 million.[53] The Afro-International Corporation of New York exported such commodities as grains and cement to a number of countries. H. F. Henderson Industries of New Jersey, a manufacturer of automatic weighing equipment and control panels, traded with Egypt, Liberia, Nigeria, and even South Africa. The Black businesses were encouraged by the Interracial Council for Business Opportunity, a minority-support organization whose board of directors included David Rockefeller, Chairman of the Chase Manhattan Bank. The Carter Administration assisted through such agencies as the Small Business Administration; a special staff of the Department of Commerce rendered useful advice and information. To be sure, the lack of giant Black corporations in the United States meant that there were no large operations of Black businesses in Africa, most consisting of export-import traders, building contractors, and brokers of various kinds. The viability of some of the Black operations was threatened by the subsequent withdrawal of governmental support under the Reagan Administration.

## BLACKS IN GOVERNMENT: THE "THURSDAY GROUP"

Blacks in foreign policy positions of the U.S. government have never reached positions of pivotal influence on U.S. relations toward Africa. Even with Andrew Young in the Carter Administration, Blacks were excluded from high policy-making positions in the

White House, the State Department, and the National Security Council—that is, from the decision-making nucleus of foreign policy. Never have the few Blacks intermittently employed on the White House staff acquired responsibility for formulating Africa policies.

A 1976 State Department survey showed that no Black had ever held the post of Assistant Secretary of State for any of the geographic bureaus, including Africa.[54] Four Black appointees have served as Deputy Assistant Secretary of State for African Affairs, beginning in 1964 when Johnson appointed Samuel Westerfield. Black involvement in State Department affairs reached an apex with Young at the United Nations. During the Carter Administration, Henry Richardson sat briefly and without impact on the National Security Council (NSC), in charge of its Africa desk, until NSC director Brzezinski eased him out. The denial of definitive policy-making authority is what led Jake C. Miller, the professor who conducted the survey, to conclude that few Blacks "could be said to have held positions with major decision-making power" not only in the State Department and not only in the context of U.S.-Africa relations, but in the whole field of American foreign policy.[55]

There is, of course, a long tradition of appointing Black Americans as ambassadors to Black nations of Africa or to Haiti. In 1871, nine years after Washington recognized Liberia and as long as twenty-four years after its independence, J. Milton Turner became the first Black minister to this territorial offspring of U.S. policy. Numerous Black Americans have since been designated ambassadors to African nations, partly because of Blacks' preference for diplomatic assignments in the land of their ancestors, but mainly because of a racist tradition by which American Presidents have confined Black ambassadors to posts in Black Africa or Haiti. The first ambassadorial appointment of a Black American outside of the traditional locations did not occur until President Kennedy sent Clifford R. Wharton to Norway in 1961. However, like American diplomats generally, the Black ambassadors were not policymakers, and served only as representatives of the President in the countries assigned.

In policy implementation, whether in missions abroad or in the State Department bureaucracy at home, Black input has been marginal. Comprising about 15 percent of the American population in 1978, Black Americans accounted for 1.5 percent of senior foreign service officers (15 out of the total personnel of 1,032), and 4.0 percent of middle-level officers (144 out of a total of 3,576). Even in Africa, Blacks held only 6.6 percent of the foreign service posts (50 out of 752).[56]

Notable exceptions to this gross underrepresentation of Blacks in the policy process include the few key positions held by such Carter appointees as Goler T. Butcher, who headed the Africa Division of AID, and John Reinhardt, chief administrator of the new International Communication Agency. The Peace Corps has traditionally accepted Blacks in large numbers, perhaps in recognition of the Black role in the creation of the agency. Since it was launched in 1961 as a semi-independent arm of the State Department, Blacks have held many leadership positions in the Peace Corps, beginning in 1963 with Franklin H. Williams, who was named director of its African regional office. The Carter Administration named Carolyn Patton the first woman to head the Peace Corps, then summarily ousted her over conflicts on policy. Though denied a policy-making role, these Blacks did exercise important authority within the policy guidelines decided by State Department executives.

The "Thursday Group," a gathering of the few Blacks who were employed by the top foreign affairs agencies under the Nixon Administration, was organized in 1969 by C. Clyde Ferguson after he returned from serving as chief coordinator of U.S. relief assistance to civilian victims of the Nigerian civil war. The group urgently sought an increase of Blacks in foreign service, and demanded an end to what he termed the "ghetto-ization" of Black ambassadors—the tradition by which the President assigned Black ambassadors to Haiti or African countries only.[57] With Ferguson were Reinhardt and W. Beverly Carter, two officers of the United States Information Agency (USIA), and David B. Bolen, a Foreign Service career officer. Thanks to the Thursday Group's pressures, the State Department assigned Terence A. Todman to Costa Rica in 1975, making him the first Black in U.S. history to be appointed to a South American country. The group made no headway in breaking another insidious tradition—the practice of not appointing Blacks to Asian countries. With humor, the Black men selected "Thursday" to identify their group of civil servants because it is traditionally a day of rest for Black domestics in White American households. Like other Blacks in government service, none of the members of this group achieved a decisive role in the making of foreign policy.

Finally, Blacks in the armed services continued to increase during the Carter Administration, a process that had begun during the Vietnam war. The Secretary of the Army, Clifford Alexander, was an influential advocate of Black integration into the armed services. Young Black recruits flocked to military service in disproportionately higher numbers than the percentage of Blacks in the overall U.S. population. In the Army, for example, Black enlistments accounted for 34.9 percent of male recruits during fiscal year 1978.[58] By the first quarter of fiscal 1979, they had already reached 36.7 percent, or almost three times the percentage of Blacks in the nation as a whole.

The smallest representation of Blacks in any of the services was in the Navy, but even there they supplied 9.4 percent of personnel in 1979,[59] or roughly the equivalent percentage of Blacks in the total American population. In the Army, however, Blacks retained high representation, or 34.7 percent as recently as June 1980.[60] This unprecedented development in which 15 percent of the population provided the manpower for more than a third of the U.S. Army meant that Black soldiers would bear a dominant responsibility in future U.S. military operations. It also posed the delicate question of how the "two-ness" of the Black soldier would cause him to behave if ordered to take up arms against Africans in some hypothetical conflict in southern Africa.

## THE RISE AND FALL OF ANDREW YOUNG

After he became Ambassador to the U.N. in 1977, Andrew Young catalyzed national attention on Africa as no American official, regardless of race or position, had done before. For the first time also, here was a Black leader who enjoyed close proximity to decision-making power, though not the power itself. Formally tied to the State Department, the U.N. Ambassadorship belonged to the President's Cabinet, and the U.N. Ambassador has traditionally spoken as the voice of the President at the world body. What gave Young stronger influence was his personal friendship with President Carter, who had already declared his political indebtedness to Young for mobilizing Black voters to provide the margin of votes responsible for his narrow victory in the 1976 Presidential election. In reaction to Young's initiatives the new Carter Administration began to give unprecedented priority to its Africa policy.

Carter's personal ambitions in 1976 seemed to be limited to winning the Presidency, and he reached the White House as a neophyte to foreign policy, with no program or vision for the future foreign relations of his Administration. This void at the zenith of political leadership was soon filled not by the Secretary of State, who is formally charged with proposing foreign policy to the President, but by the NSC director, Brzezinski, who seized the opportunity to initiate his own policy preferences based upon cold war struggle between the United States and the Soviet Union. Young's unconventional pro-Africa orientation therefore encountered opposition from the beginning.

Because of unresolved policy and ideological conflicts within the Presidential Cabinet, Young's proposals were increasingly called into question, if not rejected outright. After twenty months in office this trailblazer of U.S. policy toward Africa and the Third World was out of office because of a controversy he ignited over American policy in the Middle East. At the level of policy implementation, Young's assistant, Donald F. McHenry, joined in challenging the White settler dictatorship of southern Africa. In the end, however, it was Young's diplomacy that provoked strong interest in Africa and triggered an explosive confrontation between American Blacks and Jews. Not since Woodrow Wilson came back from the Versailles Peace Conference had the diplomatic behavior of an American leader aroused so much controversy abroad and inflamed so many passions at home.

Almost singlehandedly Young stressed the significance of Africa's rise to prominence in world affairs, and hence America's need for a new and progressive approach to foreign policy, particularly as it related to the developing and resource-rich nations of Africa, Asia, and South America. He articulated his mission at the U.N. as aligning the United States on the right side of moral issues in the world. Accordingly, he took the lead in encouraging U.S. consultations with leaders of African liberation movements, such as Robert Mugabe and Joshua Nkomo, who then headed the Patriotic Front, the guerrilla insurgents fighting for independence against the Whites who ruled Rhodesia. Breaking a well-established U.S. practice, Young expressed a ready willingness to confer with African leaders suspected of Marxist or communist leanings. At the same time he proclaimed unequivocal opposition to racist domination in South Africa. In contrast to Kissinger's realpolitik approach, which confined policy considerations to concrete issues of American national interest, Young, the Congregationalist preacher and former aide to Reverend Martin Luther King, Jr., believed that morality could serve as the handmaiden of political action. To Africans committed to wars of national liberation, Young recommended nonviolent resistance in the mold of the U.S. civil rights movement. Political idealism thus arose in the Administration's approach to Africa.

In his first year at the United Nations, Young frequently declared U.S. support for Black majority rule in Rhodesia by criticizing the vestigial colonial leadership of Ian Smith, Rhodesia's Prime Minister. The Ambassador followed his U.N. speeches with friendly overtures to the Patriotic Front leaders, including a meeting with Nkomo, when he and Mugabe came to address the U.N. Security Council in March 1978. Young also intensified his efforts to win international approval of the Anglo-American proposal which sought joint consultations between the Patriotic Front and the Smith regime as a means to a peaceful resolution of their ongoing struggle. Though Kissinger had initiated the proposal in the last days of the Ford Administration, Young promoted it as policy. The proposal called for free elections, an impartial administration during the electoral period, and a national constitution to protect the rights of all citizens in a country where 6.7 million Africans were dominated by 280,000 White settlers.

Young also insisted on free elections for South-West Africa, or Namibia, as African nationalists called the diamond-rich territory, where the South West African People's Organization (SWAPO) was fighting for the national self-determination of 723,000 Africans under the foot of a White minority of 99,000. South Africa had gained control of the former German territory in 1920, had transplanted apartheid there, and was now enforcing it strictly. As in Rhodesia, free elections in Namibia would have had the de facto effect of guaranteeing a nonviolent victory of the Black majority. Sometimes carrying out instructions from Washington, sometimes acting on his own intuition, Young advocated the cause of African independence in the name of the United States.

McHenry, the United States Deputy Representative to the U.N. Security Council, assisted Young with the new Africa policy. A career Foreign Service officer with experience at the Brookings Institution and the Carnegie Endowment for International Peace, McHenry was already associated with the Carter Presidency as a member of the transition team that had prepared papers and recommendations for the President-elect. Young, however, was responsible for bringing McHenry to the U.N., where he acquired an important role in the Administration's policy toward Namibia. For example, he helped to negotiate a 1978 agreement that promised Namibian independence. Supported by five Western powers (the United States, Great Britain, Canada, France, and West Germany), the complicated pact provided for U.N.-controlled elections, the withdrawal of South Africa's armed forces prior to independence, and a U.N. Peacekeeping Force to guarantee the country a proper transition to independence after nearly sixty years under South African hegemony. Not only was the agreement originally accepted by South Africa, but also by SWAPO leader Sam Nujoma. Yet despite McHenry's impressive work, and SWAPO's recognition by the U.N. and the OAU as the only legitimate representative of Namibia, the agreement collapsed in

December 1978 when South Africa reneged by proceeding with its own unilateral elections, rigged to retain Namibia as a puppet of Pretoria.

Unlike Young, McHenry, a trained diplomat, avoided controversy. Still, like Young, he agreed that "government should do more to make the business community an ally."[61] The premier Black representatives of American policy in Africa thus welcomed American corporate interests seeking trade and commerce with African nations. For example, Young defended the continuation of Gulf Oil's investments in Angola. Neither man favored a withdrawal of the U.S. companies in South Africa, both believing that the multinationals offered Washington a leverage to stimulate peaceful reforms in the apartheid system. Young went so far as to suggest that neocolonialism—or the economic domination of former colonial territories by industrial powers—would be a good thing if this phenomenon, which contradicted Africa's independent development, could somehow be made to support it.

Until mid-1978 Young's provocative role seemed to be producing significant, if not fundamental changes, especially in winning friendly responses from such African nations as Nigeria and such African leaders as President Nyerere of Tanzania, powers that heretofore were either lukewarm or hostile to the U.S. presence in Africa. To see the change in African opinion of America, it was enough to recall that the government of Nigeria denied an entry visa to Henry Kissinger when he attempted to go there after his visit to Lusaka in 1976. McHenry, meanwhile, was trying to alter the Carter Administration's refusal to recognize Angola's Marxist government. He had also started discussions to settle a border conflict between Angola and Zaire that had erupted when ex-Katangan forces exiled in Angola struck at points inside Zaire's Shaba province.

As enunciated by Young, the new policy was apparently exemplified by the Administration's sponsorship of the 1977 congressional defeat of the Byrd amendment, which annually had allowed American companies to import Rhodesian chromium in violation of a U.N. embargo on trade with Rhodesia. The success of the pro-Africa policy, however, was merely apparent, never real, and it was soon eclipsed by the contrary influences of Brzezinski. With no interest in Africa apart from its relationship to the cold war, Brzezinski early in 1978 pressed President Carter to immediately decelerate Young's motions concerning the Africa policy. His success was first indicated by Washington's decision to permit Ian Smith and his three Black collaborators, including Bishop Muzorewa, to visit the United States in October to plead what turned out to be a virtual White supremacist apologia against the Patriotic Front. The most striking aspect of Washington's attitude was not that twenty-seven senators had requested approval of the Smith visit, but rather the alacrity with which the Administration responded to a request so contradictory to its previous positions as represented by Young.

Smith took advantage of his official visit to privately lobby several members of Congress for a repeal of the existing U.N. embargo on imports of Rhodesian chromium. To persuade them, he not only bemoaned the breakdown of Rhodesia's economy resulting from fourteen years of White resistance to African nationalism, but he also insisted that the Soviet Union backed fifteen thousand guerrillas of the Patriotic Front.

Stronger indications of the Administration's retreat from the Young position appeared in October 1978 when Secretary Vance returned from South Africa declaring U.S. acceptance of the bogus elections that the apartheid regime had arbitrarily decided to undertake in Namibia. The recent international agreement signed by South Africa, SWAPO, and five Western powers (including the United States) was now nullified by Washington's toleration of Pretoria's unilateral action in an internal affair. With one blow, McHenry's negotiating efforts of several months came to naught.

The clearest evidence of the Administration's retreat was Young's sudden withdrawal from the diplomatic forefront. His speeches on the Africa policy, even his evocations of Carter's human rights policy vis-à-vis South Africa, ceased. "I haven't said a thing about Africa in six months because everything is going right,"[62] offered the U.N. Ambassador in January 1979. "If things are not going well in Africa," he continued, "it is not because we are not doing what we are supposed to do." It was true that South Africa had renewed its agreements to the old plan for Namibian independence under U.N. supervision. However, any arrangement fixed beforehand by Pretoria, as was this case, automatically predetermined the results, whether the U.N. was involved or not. Young unwittingly strengthened the impression of his decline by uttering such an implausible defense so soon after the White House's rejection of his own initiatives.

These developments combined to signal the victory of the Brzezinski school of thought in the Carter White House. Brzezinski's globalist approach gained additional support during the later buildup of Soviet bloc forces in Ethiopia, where Russian military officers and eighteen thousand Cuban soldiers were reinforcing the Marxist government of Addis Ababa. Washington focused anew on the strategic value of South Africa's Cape Coast sea route in January 1979 upon the downfall of the Shah of Iran. With other policymakers, Brzezinski drew attention to the possibility that Soviet penetration into the Persian Gulf could precipitate a stoppage of Iranian oil exports to Israel, Western Europe, and South Africa. It was not long before the Ayatollah Khomeini vetoed future Iranian exports to Israel and South Africa, adding grist to the cold warrior's speculation. In Washington, such economic and strategic realities resumed their dominance over political idealism.

Elliott Skinner, a former Ambassador to Upper Volta and a colleague of Brzezinski at Columbia University, put the problem simply: the United States "is not yet willing to make the hard decisions for dealing with the explosive situation in South Africa. We should be biting the bullet in that area—moving South Africa toward permitting Blacks a more significant role in the economic and political life of that society, leading ultimately to one man one vote. Anything else flies in the face of history."[63] Under Brzezinski's influence, the Carter Administration was rapidly revising its own history with respect to a progressive policy, and it seemed undeniable that the age of hard decisions had been postponed indefinitely. When Congress repealed the ban on imports of

Rhodesia's chromium early in 1980, Washington rejected Young's approach once and for all.

What finally brought Young's downfall was not Africa, but his own venture into Middle East policy. Apparently on his own volition, the Ambassador secretly consulted the U.N. representative of the Palestine Liberation Organization (PLO) on July 26, 1979, in violation of established U.S. policy forbidding recognition of the PLO. Through undisclosed means, Israel learned of Young's action and promptly dispatched a formal complaint to Secretary Vance. As soon as the public got wind of the diplomat's indiscretion in mid-August, various groups, U.S. Jews in particular, deluged the White House with an avalanche of bitter protest. The protest quickly overwhelmed President Carter and, in less than a day, Young was forced to resign.

Apart from the obvious diplomatic complications from Young's illicit discussions with Zedhi Labib Terzi, the PLO representative, a major cause of the subsequent public antagonism stemmed from an inveterate belief of White Americans that Blacks exceeded their proper limits when they took positions on U.S. foreign policy, especially in relation to regions outside of Africa or the Caribbean. According to this racist notion, foreign policy was the exclusive domain of a White power elite. Traditionally, the practitioners of American foreign policy have been overwhelmingly Anglo-Saxon, Protestant, male, and middle-to-upper class. No senior foreign policy advisor of the last six Administrations has been non-White or come from a genuinely underprivileged economic background. This tradition of excluding Blacks kindled the attacks upon Young.

## POLICY INFLUENCE: BLACKS VERSUS JEWS

Because of the force of racism in American foreign policy, Whites who had supported Martin Luther King on civil rights suddenly regarded him as a traitor to national interests when, in the last year of his life, he condemned America's role in the Vietnam war. The same reflex motivated the general outcry against several of Young's controversial positions—for example, his judgment that Cuban soldiers in Angola functioned as a stabilizing influence in a society that had reached political independence in the throes of civil war. Whites therefore excoriated Blacks who intruded on the domain presumed to be a reserve of White elites.

For their part, Black Americans reacted with massive and spontaneous solidarity against Young's removal, which they almost universally perceived as the result of pressures from Jews. The American Jewish Committee and other organizations that collectively made up the influential Jewish lobby insisted that Jews had not demanded his resignation. However, the Black mobilization in Young's defense drove a final wedge into latent antagonisms between Blacks and Jews, who, during the leadership of King, had constituted some of the strongest allies of the civil rights movement.[64]

The national Black solidarity in Young's defense climaxed in the Black American Leadership Summit, an urgent convocation of two hundred spokesmen at the NAACP's headquarters in New York on August 22, 1979. Speaking for his 400,000-member organization, NAACP director Benjamin L. Hooks expressed the general viewpoint that Young had "contributed immeasurably to elevating U.S. foreign relations with Third World countries, and, with regard to the incidents leading to his resignation, we are convinced that he acted in the best interest of this nation."[65] The meeting was attended by diverse Black representatives, including Congressmen Charles Diggs and William Gray, PUSH leader Reverend Jesse Jackson, California Assemblyman Willie L. Brown, Georgia State Senator Julian Bond, and Vernon Jordan, President of the National Urban League. These leaders claimed to represent twenty-five states, including several (such as New York and Illinois) with large Black constituencies. To combat the White mindset against Black participation in foreign policy, they rejected "the implication that anyone other than Blacks themselves can determine their proper role in helping to shape and mold American foreign policies which directly affect their lives."[66]

Preston Greene, a specialist in international law who upbraided Carter for allowing "one of our own" to be "removed from office

. . . upon the whim and caprice of a foreign power,"[67] had already described Blacks' perspective on their stake in U.S. policy: "The point . . . is not that American foreign policy must or should be formulated or conducted by certain ethnic groups. Rather, it is that the multi-ethnic character of America can be a tremendous asset when positively or constructively utilized."[68] Blacks thus insisted that their goals and demands be incorporated into American foreign policy.

A general conviction among Blacks was that their relative lack of power had lately been exacerbated by Jewish opposition to Black socioeconomic advancement in American society. Specifically, they criticized Jewish positions in the *DeFunis* and *Bakke* cases,[69] two court decisions that emasculated special admission programs for Black access to professional schools. Jews, who had enjoyed phenomenal economic success after the mass migration of East European Jews to the United States near the beginning of this century, were comfortably settled in the mainstream of middle-class America when the civil rights movement began. Many were in such fields as real estate, garment manufacturing, building, and entertainment and some had garnered multimillion-dollar fortunes.[70]

Although they comprised only 3 percent of the American population, or 5.7 million people, Jews usually pressured the United States to take a pro-Israeli posture.[71] George W. Ball, the Under Secretary of State from 1961 to 1966 and Young's predecessor at the U.N., has characterized the impact of the highly successful pro-Israel lobbyists:

> They exert a strong and continuing influence on [United States relations with Israel], contributing in a major way to the constrictions imposed on American freedom of diplomatic action toward Israel. Not only do Israel's American supporters have powerful influence with many members of the Congress, but practically no actions touching Israel's interests can be taken, or even discussed, within the executive branch without it being quickly known to the Israeli government.[72]

Blacks, on the other hand, with 15 percent of the population, had failed to significantly influence American policy toward Africa until

Young's short-lived and inconclusive tenure. The lack of economic clout by Blacks was the cause of this failure.

U.S. economic and military assistance to Israel and African states can be taken as a measure of the relative interest-group influence of American Jews and Blacks. Israel, a quasi-industrial nation with a population of 3 million, received $790 million U.S. economic assistance in fiscal 1979, whereas Nigeria, a developing nation of 90 million people, received nothing. Israel alone received nearly two thirds of total U.S. military assistance (or $4 billion out of $6.6 billion) to all countries in the world.[73] The Nixon Administration closed the AID office in Lagos, Nigeria, in 1975, offering a graphic gesture of U.S. denial of assistance to African states. Such evidence indicates clearly that the pro-Africa interests have not gained significant impact on the policy process.

## POLICY GOALS AND THE QUESTION OF POWER

Amid the dispute over Young's resignation Blacks rediscovered a lesson taught by Harold Cruse more than a decade before: the "relationships between groups in America, and on the international plane, are actuated by the power principle, not by morality and compassion for the underdog classes."[74] Blacks today maintain the pro-Africa goals that they have always fostered—namely, Africa's political liberation and its economic development—although the emphasis has shifted to the latter since nearly all the African countries, except those under apartheid domination, have acquired independence. Blacks' frustration in foreign policy is therefore not due to lack of objectives, but to a lack of power to advance them in the American system.

Indeed, the power position of Blacks has declined absolutely since the Nixon Administration began to dismantle what can be termed the "second Reconstruction," namely, federal assistance supporting various socioeconomic programs, such as urban renewal projects, that had begun under the Great Society legislation of President Johnson. Although Black businesses brought in aggregate receipts of $8.6 billion in 1977,[75] from Motown Industries' leading position with $58 million down to the small incomes from mom and pop stores, the accumulated wealth of all Black businesses combined was only about one tenth of 1 percent of U.S. giant corporate wealth. In the political arena, there was an increase of Black officeholders in national, state, and local positions from 1,185 in 1969 to 4,912 in 1980.[76] However, Blacks still held only 1 percent of all elective offices in the United States. This represented little progress, especially when it is remembered that fourteen Blacks served in the House of Representatives between 1869 and 1877, but in 1981, more than a hundred years later, there were just sixteen Black representatives who could vote.[77] Two Black men held the office of U.S. senator during Reconstruction, but today's Senate contains no person of African descent.

A special report commissioned by President Johnson after the urban riots of 1967 underscored the economic poverty of Black Americans with the dire warning that "our nation is moving toward two societies, one black, one white—separate and unequal."[78] In the next decade there were few, if any, improvements in the Black minority's material deficits—low income, high unemployment, and meager access to higher education—notwithstanding modest numerical increases in the middle class. This failure of the American system explains why a Bureau of the Census report of 1978 concluded that the "25.4 million Blacks in this country remained far behind Whites in almost every social and economic area."[79]

Stark as this reality is, it is not nearly as disturbing as a 1979 Harris poll, which showed that Black Americans believe large and small corporations, banks, labor unions, White Protestant churches, professional schools, local real estate agencies, and government from the federal to the local levels are indifferent to Black's quest for greater equality or are downright opposed to it.[80] The poll presents clear-cut evidence that jobs constitute the singular area where Blacks feel most frustrated and most left out in the cold, and where Black desperation could erupt into confrontation and trouble in the near future.

This vicious reality explains why economist Robert S. Browne, whom the Carter Administration appointed as U.S. representative to the Africa Fund of the African Bank for Development (Ivory Coast), has spoken about Black powerlessness in the American political and economic system.[81] It also resurrects the question once posed by Martin Weil in *Foreign Policy*.[82] That is, can Blacks do for Africa what Jews have done for Israel? TransAfrica's response to the question was unequivocal:

> We do not seek to do what they have done. We do not seek to hold American policy or action to ransom in the interest of this or that policy or ambition of any foreign country. We can help lead our country to overcome past inequities and images, and help it to live in harmony and peace, and mutual respect, with the new nations and with those still struggling to be born.[83]

The dominant Black foreign policy lobby of America's dominant minority thus found its rationale in the historic mission of Blacks regarding U.S. relations toward Africa.

TransAfrica's position, which represented the orientation of a majority of Black Americans, was consistent with the interest-group basis of American politics. However, in light of the powerlessness of Blacks, the real question is whether the growing economic and military power of independent African states will someday redound to the group power of Black Americans. After all, it was not the monetary donations of American Jews, but Israel's enormous human capital—the skilled and well-educated Jews from Europe who arrived in Israel as already trained professionals—that was mainly responsible for transforming the Zionist territory into a military and economic force. Israel's national power, especially after its victory over Egypt in 1967, enhanced the prestige and influence of Jews in the United States. The international power of such states as Nigeria and Zimbabwe can be expected to produce similar benefits for Blacks in American society. Historically, Black Americans have persevered in their support for African liberation and development precisely because they sensed that strong and independent African nations would magnify the influence and power of Blacks in America.

The force of ethnicity in American group politics has been

impressively illustrated by the case of the Japanese-Americans of California, who were herded into concentration camps in the aftermath of Japan's attack on Pearl Harbor.[84] However, a generation later, after Japan's return to world power, Californians sent S. I. Hayakawa to the U.S. Senate. His electoral victory, like Japan's current membership in the Western alliance and on the Trilateral Commission, was inseparable from Japan's strong international position.

Though impressive, Young's participation in the decision-making process did not alter American policy toward Africa from what had been established in the Kennedy Administration. His rhetoric on the importance of Africa to American economic and strategic interests merely had a transitory impact on State Department regionalists—that is, the advocates of pegging U.S. policy to specific regions and countries of the world—as opposed to the globalists, who approached American worldwide interests from the standpoint of anti-Sovietism. As an Africanist, Young never succeeded in gaining priority for African policy issues, and as a Black American, his ambitious effort to "ebonize" U.S. policy met similar defeat.

Several political factors beyond Young's control accounted for his failure. In the country at large, there was general opposition to strong pressures against South Africa. This was partly revealed by the Council on Foreign Relations in a 1979 survey of its 2,300 elite members and affiliated committees nationwide.[85] This survey confirmed that Young's pro-Africa advocacy ran counter to the preferences of the predominant White groups. Among Black Americans, Young did not organize a group constituency that potentially could have strengthened his influence in the Carter Administration. Within the Administration, Young and his occasional supporters, who included Carter and Vance, seriously underestimated the intractable antagonisms between the liberation movements and the White supremacy regimes. Whereas the Patriotic Front and SWAPO demanded unconditional political independence, Ian Smith clung to die-hard resistance, and Pretoria was committed to no basic change in apartheid. All of this meant that Young's ingenuous "civil rights" formula for race relations in the White-dominated areas was doomed from the outset. Overriding all these obstacles was the relentless and finally effective opposition of Brzezinski.

As Young's successor at the U.N., McHenry did not inspire any of the earlier momentous interest in Africa. The constraints which defeated Young also impinged on him. However, McHenry's lack of policy impact stemmed particularly from his own belief that *"the best interests of blacks, the United States, and Africa are best served by the failure of efforts to build policy for Africa largely on the basis of a constituency of black Americans."*[86] His predilection for "objectivity" in foreign policy was inherently devoid of meaning in a political system responsive to the force of interest-group politics. As a professional bureaucrat, he was out of touch with the interest-group basis of political influence, and he represented a viewpoint that sharply clashed with the raison d'être of such groups as TransAfrica.

With the end of the Carter Administration came a decline of the Black presence in American foreign policy. The Reagan Administration returned to what the decision-making nucleus had always been: White and male. Thus, despite the promising inroads of the Kennedy-Johnson era, and Young's emergence under Carter, the reality of Blacks' powerlessness was once more very evident.

Blacks, of course, are sufficiently cognizant of the great achievements certain members of their race have made, which provide indubitable evidence that high-level decision-makers of the United States have sometimes made exceptions toward the nation's biggest and oldest minority. Even in slavery there were Black poets, scientists, shipowners, and inventors. Blacks were also involved in U.S. foreign policy, as in the colonization of Liberia, and a Black man was the first person to die fighting in America's war of independence. However, like the contemporary wave of Blacks integrating giant corporations, "big" law firms, and city halls, these Blacks are also exceptions. They do not share the socioeconomic conditions afflicting the masses of Blacks, who remain imprisoned by poverty and indifference, and whose basic mobility, as Martin Luther King put it, is from a smaller ghetto into a larger one. Thus, the emergence of a few Blacks into the middle-class mainstream is not a signal for applause; on the contrary, it is another compelling impetus for reflection on past injustices.

The contemporary neoconservative reaction against Black mobility culminated in 1978 with the U.S. Supreme Court judgment in the *Bakke* case. This judgment recalls the various post-Reconstruction decisions, such as *Plessy* v. *Ferguson,* which canceled out the political and economic gains that Blacks had realized in the aftermath of the Civil War. The neoconservative reaction, however, not only includes such White critics as Carl Gershman,[87] whose specious logic and questionable purpose imbue anti-Black doctrines with a semblance of scholarly rigor, it also includes such Black bedfellows as William Julius Wilson, whose study *The Declining Significance of Race* purports to show that race has become a decreasing influence in the economic sector for certain categories of Blacks who acquired middle-class status during and after the civil rights movement.[88] However, such critics completely miss the point of Blacks' attachment to foreign policy. Policy-minded Blacks have never thought for a moment that their quest for equality in America could be culminated merely by the achievement of middle-class status, for their ultimate objective has always been power at the upper echelons where wealth holds the hand of political policy.

Black Americans will increasingly align with Africans, as they did during the Pan-African congresses, and with new Third World forces, as they have begun to do with the PLO,[89] to strengthen their anti-apartheid pressures for change in Namibia and South Africa. The overthrow of White supremacy in South Africa represents much more than a moral or racial interest to Black Americans. For them the rise of Black majority rule in the wealthiest country on the African continent would be the cutting edge for Black power and prestige everywhere.

# U.S. ECONOMIC RELIANCE ON AFRICA: Petroleum and the "Persian Gulf of Minerals"

The United States has become "dangerously reliant" on southern Africa for minerals essential to the American economy, warned Representative James Santini, Chairman of the House Mines and Mining Subcommittee, after his fact-finding trip to Zaire, Zimbabwe, and South Africa in 1980.[1] As stunning as this discovery may have been to most Americans, it overlooked a still larger and more critical reality: the United States depends on a host of other African countries for various vital minerals. It depends particularly on Nigeria, which is the second largest supplier of oil to the United States, and Libya, the third largest supplier. Indeed America has developed a commodities dependence on Africa, north as well as south, for such diverse resources as petroleum and cobalt. The seriousness of the U.S. dependence is discernible in Santini's judgment that a cutoff of the African minerals could bring much of American industry to a standstill.

The Arab oil boycott of 1973–1974 first demonstrated the usefulness of a vital natural resource as a weapon of political policy among Third World producers. African minerals have become similarly essential to the American economy and therefore have established their role in the future of America as a world power.

Certain minerals are concentrated in only a few regions of the world. Southern Africa, for example, contains 86 percent of the world's reserves of platinum group metals, 53 percent of manganese, 52 percent of cobalt, 64 percent of vanadium, and 95 percent of the world's reserves of chromium.[2] The indispensability of these minerals to U.S. productivity arises from a variety of reasons: domestic deposits of the platinum group metals, used as catalysts in automobile exhaust converters, are poorly defined and undeveloped; manganese, unavailable in domestic reserves, is essential to steel production; cobalt, also unavailable in domestic reserves, is an unsubstitutable ingredient of cutting tools as well as high-temperature parts of jet engines and turbines; vanadium, used in the production of iron, steel, and synthetic rubber, exists in domestic reserves, but these are small and insufficient for more than fifteen years at annual consumption levels.[3] Chromium's strategic value is like that of petroleum not only because the United States lacks domestic reserves, but especially because American industries depend on chromium to make a wide variety of vital commodities, including automobiles, computer components, heat-resisting alloys, stainless steel, and even hospital equipment. Because of southern Africa's abundant wealth in these resources, the region is now being characterized as the "Persian Gulf of minerals."

Altogether the African continent is the repository of 30 percent of the world's known mineral resources.[4] These facts assume additional strategic significance when one recalls that the Soviet Union is another major source of minerals indispensable to the American economy—chromium, manganese, and vanadium in particular. This raises the possibility that a political impasse between Washington and Moscow could precipitate a cutoff of Soviet supplies, leaving the United States at the mercy of African suppliers, some of whom are hostile to the United States.

All the imported minerals can be divided into either fuel or nonfuel resources. In the fuel category, Americans began in 1976 to recognize their dependence on foreign sources for nearly half their annual oil consumption. Four African states—Nigeria, Libya, Algeria, and Gabon—supplied about 40 to 45 percent of the imported petroleum. Unknown to most Americans, these African suppliers have surpassed Saudi Arabia, the leading single supplier of U.S. oil imports, and all other Middle Eastern producers in the total volume of American petroleum imports.

## OIL: THE ULTIMATE POLITICAL WEAPON

Nigeria, on the threshold of industrialization in 1980, is one of the world's richest countries in natural resources, and oil represents the key to its new wealth. Concomitant with this wealth has come an emergent position of political leverage vis-à-vis the United States and other industrial countries. Nigerian petroleum producers in 1980 averaged a daily yield of 2.2 million barrels of the country's crude petroleum.[5] It is prized by Americans because it is a high-quality, low-sulfur oil that can yield more gasoline per barrel than the heavier Middle Eastern crude.[6] American importers bought a million barrels, or almost half the production, every day. U.S. imports of Nigerian oil grew so rapidly in the decade between 1970, when the United States imported none, and 1980, when Nigeria provided as much as 16 percent of American oil imports, that this African country emerged as a creditor to the United States. The fashionable theories by which social scientists point woefully to dependency as an outcome of decolonization in developing societies no longer apply in the case of Nigeria, which comfortably approached the industrial giants from its position of strength.

By the standards of Saudi Arabia, Nigeria's proven reserves of about 20 billion barrels are comparatively small.[7] But Nigeria's "sweet" is in great demand both in the United States and Western Europe. Americans spent $6 billion for 350 million barrels of this oil in 1978, when Nigeria ranked sixth among the world's leading oil producers. American imports from Nigeria accelerated so much in the next two years that the United States ended with a trade deficit with Nigeria of nearly $13 billion in 1980—the biggest U.S. debt with any country.[8]

Nigeria had earned about $10 billion annually in overseas oil trade before the Khomeini revolution in Iran sent oil prices skyrocketing. Whereas Nigeria suffered a drop in oil revenues in

1978 mainly as a consequence of a worldwide decline in the demand for oil, with production falling to 1.5 million barrels a day, the country increased daily production to 2.3 million barrels a day in the first half of January 1979 as the Ayatollah Khomeini smashed the Shah's regime. Nigeria's oil revenues then leaped to $17 billion in 1979.[9] The boom in trade continued, and foreign exchange revenues, which had plummeted to a low of $2.4 billion in 1978, jumped to nearly $22 billion in 1980. As oil flowed into the barrels, the Nigerians, who were OPEC's obdurate advocate of high oil prices, watched in satisfaction as the American debt mushroomed.

Thanks to petroleum, Nigeria benefited from an average annual growth in its gross national product (GNP) of more than 13 percent between 1973 and 1978. This rapid accumulation of capital outdistanced South Africa and even oil-rich Algeria. With a GNP of $560 million in 1977, Nigeria had a per capita income of about $600, among the highest in Africa and the Third World generally. Although South Africa retained its status as the economic giant of the continent, Nigeria was now conducting twice as much trade with the United States.

Petroleum, which regularly accounts for about 85 percent of Nigeria's annual income, also attracts the bulk of American investment. The total value of the investment increased from $1 billion in 1974 to about $1.5 billion by late 1977.[10] Much of the oil, located in Nigeria's offshore wells and southern swamps, is pumped by five American multinationals: Gulf, Mobil, Texaco, Ashland, and Standard Oil of California.[11] The Nigerian government retains 60 percent interest in the operation, allowing the foreign firms a 40 percent stake. (European oil companies were represented by Elf, Agip-Phillips, and Shell-BP; the last was the country's largest producer until the government nationalized BP's 20 percent share in 1979, although not the 20 percent interest of the Royal Dutch/Shell Group.) Nigeria exported as much as 35 percent of its annual output to the United States until the Khomeini revolution stopped Iranian supplies in late 1978; afterward, Americans imported 55 percent of Nigeria's oil, enlarging their oil dependency and increasing their trade deficit with the African nation.

Natural gas represents another element of Nigeria's booming petroleum industry. Natural gas reserves are generally believed to be far greater than oil reserves. The latter may be depleted by the year 2000. The gas operation, still in an embryonic stage of development, used only about 5 percent of production and the rest was flared. In May 1978 Nigeria concluded an agreement with European firms to build a multibillion-dollar liquified natural gas plant with a daily production capacity of 2 billion cubic feet of gas. The plant, in which Nigeria retains a 60 percent interest, is scheduled to begin full operation in 1983.[12] Natural gas thus provides an economic potential of stupendous proportions. Whether the number of gas pumps continues to swell, or declines to a dribble, Nigerians, unlike Africans in resource-poor countries, can still look for their golden age in the future.

An American beneficiary of the natural gas industry was the Pullman-Kellogg Company, which the Nigerians granted a $340 contract in September 1979 to build a fertilizer plant.[13] This deal, the consummation of which resulted from the intervention of Ambassador Andrew Young at a critical point in the negotiations, had a dual impact: it lifted U.S. corporate investment outside the petroleum industry by 80 percent, and it induced a tremendous increase in the Nigerian activity of the U.S. Export-Import Bank, which provided $230 million in financing. Before this deal, Ex-Im's venture in Nigeria had amounted to $25 million, a small sum compared to British investment of $2 billion and West German investment of $4 billion.

Nigeria, with a population of nearly 100 million, is the largest Black nation in the world.[14] It has more people than any country in Europe except the Soviet Union. One of every four Africans is Nigerian, and with an annual growth rate of 2.5 percent, the population is sure to climb still higher during this decade.[15] The large population has made Nigeria the biggest consumer market in Africa. Its immense territory of 356,669 square miles more than doubles the size of California. Nigeria also claims the largest and best-equipped armed forces in Black Africa. After the changeover from a military to a civilian government in October 1979, wealthy Nigeria also became the world's fourth largest democracy.[16] These unique and powerful assets enable the Nigerians to boldly articulate the Pan-African aspirations of the Black world, whenever they choose to do so, and to suffer no fear in challenging U.S. power in Africa.

The challenge Washington preferred to avoid came during 1980 when Nigerian President Alhaji Shehu Shagari announced before the Foreign Policy Association in New York that his government "shall use any means at our disposal, including oil" to induce the United States to employ its international economic power to discourage and ultimately to destroy apartheid.[17] U.S. corporate interests in South Africa reacted with alarm, and not without reason, because Shagari's senior advisor Chuba Okadigbo further warned of Nigeria's disposition to build a nuclear bomb "if it is necessary to bring South Africa to the negotiating table."[18] Here, then, was an explicit demand that active opposition to apartheid be made an integral part of U.S. policy toward Africa. Although Nigeria lacked a nuclear reactor and fissionable materials, the United States could not dismiss the challenge because of the oil exports, as well as private American business investments in Nigeria.

In July 1979 the Lagos government indicated the kind of punitive action it might take by nationalizing Great Britain's Barclay's Bank, the biggest in the country, after disclosure of Barclay's subscription to a South African defense bond issue. The Nigerians soon nationalized the holdings of the British Petroleum Company, terminating its daily shipments of 360,000 barrels of Nigerian oil in retaliation for British oil exports to South Africa.[19] A year later the Shagari regime blocked British Airways from introducing the Concorde supersonic airliner on its London-Johannesburg route by denying use of Lagos airport. The airport, according to British Airways official Gerry Draper, was the only realistic stopover for a supersonic airliner bound for South Africa.[20] Thus, without protest or threat, the British company shelved its plans for this Concorde route indefinitely. Such British acquiescence would have been unimaginable thirty years earlier when Nigeria was a British territory and Winston Churchill rose to power declaring that he had not become Prime Minister to preside over the dissolution of His Majesty's empire.

Whether the Nigerians mean to use oil as a political weapon against the United States, as they did against Great Britain, will probably depend on their assessment of the economic risks. In one sense, America's economic dependence on Nigeria's oil stimulated a countervailing dependency: that is, as the dominant buyer of Nigerian oil, the United States held some claim on Nigeria, which needed to maintain a good market for its prime product. A given crisis could always provoke the Nigerians to seek new trade partners, as in 1974 when they replaced Britain with the United States as their largest export market. Alternatively, the United States could find new suppliers, or it could perhaps fulfill President Reagan's promise to break U.S. dependency by increasing domestic production and developing alternatives to fossil fuel, including coal, available in ample domestic deposits. However, the ultimate test for Lagos and Washington will undoubtedly hinge on America's willingness to alter its established relations with the apartheid government of South Africa.

Libya, under the radical leadership of Muammar Qaddafi, is more willing than Nigeria to use oil as a political weapon. Since he seized power in an army camp in 1969, at age twenty-eight, Colonel Qaddafi has left no doubt of his capacity to successfully challenge the United States, Libya's main oil customer. Libya has nationalized the subsidiaries of Texaco and Standard Oil of California, contributed to Ethiopia's purchase of Soviet arms, served as Africa's foremost supporter of the Ayatollah Khomeini, and—perhaps as a final symbol of defiance—burned the American embassy in Tripoli. The North African Arab state has also led OPEC in defeating the erstwhile invincible alliance between the Western multinational oil industry and the industrial nations. Under Qaddafi, Libya, while formalizing its own genre of socialism, has become a battering ram of the new international economic order.

The Carter Administration, like the Nixon-Ford leadership, generally acquiesced in the face of Qaddafi's defiance for very persuasive reasons. As America's third largest supplier of oil, Libya sent 600,000 barrels of its high-quality, low-sulfur oil to the United States daily, providing 10 percent of the fuel Americans consumed each year. Libyan oil reserves, estimated at more than 25.3 billion barrels, remain the biggest in Africa.[21] No less important is the fact that four of the five largest oil multinationals in Libya consisted of American companies, including Mobil, Exxon, and Occidental.[22] Washington has not been oblivious to the possibility of Libyan reprisal against the companies in the event of hostile U.S. action against Qaddafi.

Libya's reserves of natural gas reinforce its national power. Estimated at 28,500 billion cubic feet in 1977, these reserves were the third largest in Africa, exceeded only by those of Algeria and Nigeria.[23] Additionally, Libya undertook the construction of a 440-megawatt nuclear power plant under contract with the Soviet Union. This plant, Libya's second nuclear reactor, promised to become its first commercial producer of nuclear power.

Consistent price increases have become the benchmark of Libya's oil policy toward the West in general, and Qaddafi has articulated his indifference to the possibility of reprisal from Western customers:

> It's these same Western countries that are responsible for the rapid rise. The oil companies too. . . . We'd probably be better off just stopping oil production. That will take care of all consumer and producer problems, as there won't be any more oil to worry about. . . . We could use our oil for whatever we need for our own consumption. We're under no obligation to export it.[24]

This was clearly a dangerous wager, though not an idle threat, based on the Libyans' belief (shared by other African producers) that they can survive longer without revenues from oil trade than the West can survive without imported oil. Qaddafi knew that Americans were obliged to import oil, and at the end of 1979 he took the lead with a new price hike that would earn Libya more than $60 million per day, or $22 billion annually. These revenues provided Libya's small population of 2.5 million with a per capita income of $9,000, the highest in Africa, and one of the highest anywhere in the world.

Qaddafi's challenge to the United States may be deemed more symbolic than real because U.S. relations with Libya have operated at two different levels at the same time. The first level consists of the rhetorical threats and challenges as discussed above. The second has been a very viable, growing, and mutually lucrative exchange between Libya and American companies, including Exxon, Mobil, Occidental, Conoco, and Marathon. The interplay between these levels has frequently enabled Qaddafi and the United States to denounce the other's political policy while trade flourished. Consequently, when the Reagan Administration expelled Libyan diplomats from the United States in May 1981 on vague and impetuous charges, oil production by American companies in Libya remained stable. Libya, still the third largest foreign supplier of America's crude oil imports, accounted for 640,000 barrels a day, 10 percent of total U.S. oil imports and over 3.5 percent of total U.S. energy needs.[25]

Another notable instance of United States retaliation against Qaddafi has been the State Department's refusal since 1974 to allow the delivery to Libya of eight C-130 transport planes, for which his government had already paid the Lockheed Corporation a sum of $60 million.[26] Evidently Washington intended to punish Libya for nationalizing the two American oil subsidiaries (Texaco and Standard) during 1973 and 1974. President Carter maintained the embargo.

However, neither U.S. action impeded Libya's acquisition of the most advanced machinery because Qaddafi obtained a plethora of weaponry and matériel from the Soviet Union; these included one squadron each of Mig-25s and Tu-22 strategic bombers, the first ever sold by Moscow to a "friendly nation" outside the Warsaw Pact.[27] America's allies also helped to diminish the effect of the embargo; France delivered an additional 130 Mirage jet fighters, Italy several hundred Bell helicopters, and British and French companies sold 200 tanks to Libya.[28]

Instead of punishing Qaddafi, however, the embargo revealed

that America's declining ability to influence events in Third World countries stemmed not only from its own decreasing national power, but also from divisiveness produced by competing national self-interests within the Western alliance. The Europeans had their own substantial stakes in Libya. France, for instance, was anxious to retain the deposits of the Paris-based Banque Internationale Arabe, owned jointly by Libya and Algeria. West Germany and Italy received much of their petroleum from Libya. Above all, perhaps, in 1977 the Libyans purchased a 9 percent share in Fiat, Italy's biggest investor-owned concern.[29] Under the terms of the $415 million deal, Libya's holdings expanded to 13 to 15 percent as bonds converted to common stock. This de facto purchase of a large share of Fiat gave Libya, Italy's former colony, significant power in a business that produced 1.3 million vehicles annually, and sold billions of dollars worth of automobiles, ships, airplanes, capital goods, and armaments.

Qaddafi, who regarded himself as a Mao Tse-tung of the Sahara, used petrodollars to intrude his influence into other areas where it conflicted with U.S. foreign policy. Early in 1980 there were perhaps seven thousand foreign recruits in Libya, and many of these included SWAPO and ANC guerrillas training for confrontation against South Africa. Arms and trained guerrillas from Libya helped the Polisario, the Western Sahara liberation movement, in its war of independence for the phosphate-rich Western Sahara, where in March 1980 two thousand casualties were inflicted on the armed forces of Morocco, one of the United States' main allies in North Africa. Also troubling were Qaddafi's maneuvers to undermine the Camp David peace treaty at the very moment that President Carter was enjoying his ostensible success; the CIA claimed to have uncovered a Libyan plot to shoot down Sadat's plane on his way to Washington to sign the treaty.[30] Because the United States imported 35 percent of Libya's annual oil production, the White House had to face the nettling evidence that many of Qaddafi's worldwide ventures were paid in U.S. dollars.

To put the Libyan challenge to U.S. policy into full perspective, it is important to stress that Qaddafi's approach has been neither monolithic nor free of contradiction. This was illustrated by his exemption from public control of petroleum, banking, and insurance—industries of major concern to capitalist investors—despite his demand in 1978 for workers' control of other enterprises, in accordance with the socialist doctrine of *The Green Book,* Qaddafi's exegesis on ideology. Contradiction was also evident in the substantial increase in Libyan imports of American goods, despite fundamental political differences. Such inconsistencies explain why the American Embassy in Tripoli advised American businesses that they should "not be deterred by the political factor from seeking export markets in Libya."[31]

American-Libyan trade ties will probably be augmented, not reduced, under the conservative Republican Administration of President Reagan, because the Republicans' probusiness orientation would favor such an outcome a priori.

Economic cooperation in a context of political and ideological conflict has also defined America's relations with two more revolutionary African states, Algeria and Angola. After Saudi Arabia, Nigeria, and Libya, socialist Algeria is the fourth major supplier of U.S. oil,[32] reaching a record of 638,000 barrels per day in 1978, which amounted to 8 percent of total American imports. The American stake in Algeria crystallized soon after its independence as the United States replaced France, the former colonial power, as Algeria's main trading partner. The French continued to provide most of Algeria's imports, but as much as 56 percent of its oil production went to Americans. One result was an American trade deficit of $3.1 billion with Algeria in 1978.

Natural gas represented another American interest in Algeria, both because of U.S. imports and also because of the U.S. corporate role in developing the industry. American imports of liquified natural gas amounted to only about 5 percent of Algerian production in 1978 (the bulk was taken by Western Europe), but U.S. companies obtained contracts to play a major role in the construction of gas liquification plants and lines. These companies included Bechtel International, Pullman-Kellogg, and the Foster Wheeler Corporation. Like Nigeria, Algeria's premium-quality oil reserves may be depleted by 2000. However, its national power will likely be sustained by natural gas exports scheduled to soar from 13 billion cubic feet to a projected high of 80 billion in coming years.[33] The greater the U.S. need for natural gas, the more America's stake in Algeria's future increases.

In its relations with the United States, Algeria has shared with Nigeria and Libya a fierce determination to avoid neocolonial influences, as indicated by its firm control over its oil and gas resources. In February 1971, for example, President Houari Boumedienne nationalized oil production by taking the controlling share (or 51 percent) of the French oil companies. After organizing an international boycott in retaliation, France was soon shocked as El Paso Natural Gas Company moved into a market that heretofore had been a reserve of France. Although President Nixon blocked a deal between El Paso and the Algerians until they agreed to compensation settlement with France, the latter had in fact lost, for now El Paso was leading the way for the huge U.S. trade that followed.

America's need for African oil made clear the overriding U.S. dependence on African resources, and the dependency laid the groundwork for future political action that could be used in the event of African-American conflict. If the "big three" producers— Nigeria, Libya, and Algeria—decided to stop oil shipments to the United States, they would ipso facto eliminate more than a third of annual U.S. fuel consumption, precipitating a possible suspension, if not breakdown, in vital national activity in periods of fuel scarcity.

In the case of Angola, the United States has enjoyed the graceless distinction of being the only Western power that did not recognize the socialist regime after it wrested independence from Portugal in 1975. U.S. nonrecognition prevailed in the presence of certain irrepressible economic realities: Gulf Oil had had substantial operations in Angola's oil-rich Cabinda province even before independence and was still producing 150,000 barrels a day in 1979. Texaco then had a $360 million contract with the Angolan government,[34] although the company started an offshore rig only a year after independence. U.S. imports from Angola, oil mainly, reached $463 million in 1975 and remained at a high level of $347 million by 1980.

By comparison with the big three, Angola is a small trade partner of the United States, even if its natural gas production is included. However, the private investment in Angola of such American companies as Gulf, in which Angola retained 55 percent ownership, represented a significant corporate stake. Given the U.S. oil imports from Angola, and Angola's strategic contiguity with Zaire and Namibia, two highly sensitive areas of U.S. policy interest, neither reason nor enlightened self-interest supported the policy of nonrecognition.

Gabon, meanwhile, has become an important U.S. petroleum supplier while it has continued intimate economic ties with France, its principal trade partner and former colonial overlord. As the most important sector of Gabon's economy, petroleum has also attracted about $200 million in American investment; this foreign private interest is exceeded only by that of France. Like Angola, Gabon's exports to the United States have been small (see Table 2). However, the economic significance of this staunchly pro-Western nation should be seen in a larger context, because its multimillion-dollar annual production has elevated it not only to OPEC membership, but also to rank as Africa's fifth largest producer.

A high level of production in Gabon, as in the other countries, is not foreseeable without substantial new petroleum discoveries. In fact, its proven reserves began to decline in 1978, although price increases in the international market returned increasing income. Exploration thus became nearly as important as production; the American firms of Ocean Drilling and Exploration Company and Ocean Oil and Gas Company, which helped to bring an offshore field into production in 1976, collaborated with Gabon in these tasks. Projections for future discoveries remain positive, and new production could catalyze a rapid expansion of U.S. trade and investment with this nation.

Similar prospects exist for the small but promising African producers: Liberia, the Congo, Ivory Coast, Cameroon, Morocco,

Tunisia, and Egypt. Even several African states without known reserves, such as Niger, are digging underground in hope of finding oil. Some of these countries could become important in the world market depending on the magnitude of their resources. Such a thought is not farfetched. After all, who in America had heard of Libya a few years ago?

Whether the big three, singly or collectively, would use oil as a political weapon against the United States, their main customer, is the key factor U.S. policymakers must begin to consider in their formulation of policy toward Africa. Thus far, there has been no hint of an African cartel, the advent of which is universally feared among Western importers. Still, it is worth noting that Algeria, Libya, and Nigeria have coordinated price rises to prevent mutually harmful competition.

Coordination among the big three leads to a second critical political consideration for U.S. policy, namely, the degree to which American policy impinges on the dominant foreign policy interests of these countries. These interests refer primarily to apartheid South Africa in the case of Nigeria, and to the Israeli-Palestinian issue in the case of Libya and Algeria. Because American involvement in such areas could provoke one or more of the African states into reactions detrimental to American oil needs, Washington must now include this second factor in future formulations on U.S. policy toward Africa.

## "HIGH AFRICA": THE NONFUEL MINERALS

American vulnerability in minerals has become as acute as its oil dependency in many respects. The point was underscored by the Santini congressional report, which concluded that "no issue facing America in the decades ahead poses the risks and dangers to the national economy and defense presented by [U.S.] dependence on foreign sources for strategic and critical minerals."[35] Still another alarm was sounded by Allen G. Gray, technical director of the American Society of Metals: "A cutoff of our chromium supply could be even more serious than a cutoff of our oil supply. We do have some oil but we have almost no chromium."[36] However, chromium is not the only mineral missing from U.S. domestic supply, nor is U.S. dependency limited to "High Africa," as the region of central and southern Africa is sometimes called.

South Africa and Zimbabwe together have about 95 percent of the world's reserves of chromium, and each is a major supplier to the United States and Western Europe.[37] A single mine in Zaire provides the bulk of America's (and Western Europe's) cobalt. As with chromium, the United States imports almost 100 percent of its cobalt needs. African countries provide a host of other critical minerals, including tin, tantalum, lithium, and beryl, which support American space-age technology and missile requirements.

The indispensability of African minerals for the United States can be compared with the mineral needs of America's chief ally, Great Britain, which has a total import dependence on nickel, manganese, antimony, chromium, cobalt, titanium as well as uranium.[38] The West German economy is as dependent on foreign sources for cobalt and vanadium as for petroleum. These strategic minerals ushered African states into the new international economic order, as Western nations, including the United States, slipped inexorably into a dependence on African resources.

A high standard of living in any industrial society is sustainable only by a regular consumption of key nonfuel minerals as well as petroleum. Although the United States has domestic deposits and stockpiles of many minerals, often these minerals are not produced in sufficient quantities for domestic needs or they are not produced at all because of prohibitive conservation laws. The consequence is that Americans are obliged to import more than half of all the critical industrial minerals, from amounts as low as .5 percent of consumption for coal, to as high as 75 percent or more for cobalt and manganese.[39] Because the American economy is intermeshed with that of the European Economic Community (EEC) and Japan, it is quite germane to point out that these Western partners import equally high amounts of African resources. The Soviet Union, by contrast, has major deposits of many of the critical minerals.

Today the United States depends on foreign sources for twenty-four of the thirty-two minerals that have been designated as essential to American national survival.[40] Africa possesses at least twenty of them in plentiful supply. Table 1 identifies the African minerals which are critical to the American economy, and which constitute 25 percent or more of world production or reserves.

## TABLE 1

AFRICAN MINERALS
(25 percent or more of world production or reserves)

| Mineral | Percent of Estimated 1978 World Production | Percent of World Reserves |
|---------|------------------------------------------|---------------------------|
| Arsenic | 8.0 | 25.0 |
| Asbestos (crocidolite) | 100.0 | 100.0 |
| Bauxite | 15.0 | 30.0 |
| Cesium | | 30.0 |
| Chromium | 40.0 | 97.0 |
| Cobalt | 66.0 | 40.0 |
| Corundum | 85.0 | 75.0 |
| Diamond | 65.0 | 90.0 |
| Fluorspar | 13.5 | 32.5 |
| Gemstones | 75.0 | 65.0 |
| Germanium | 30.0 | 22.0 |
| Gold | 57.0 | 48.0 |
| Kyanite | 35.0 | 5.0 |
| Manganese | 31.0 | 50.0 |
| Phosphate | 25.0 | 75.0 |
| Platinum group | 45.0 | 72.5 |
| Tantalum | 22.0 | 70.0 |
| Uranium | 29.0 | 32.0 |
| Vanadium | 41.0 | 49.0 |
| Vermiculite | 40.0 | 40.0 |

Source: U.S. Bureau of Mines

The U.S. dependency on African minerals was well established by 1976. Africa then provided the following percentage of U.S. nonfuel imports: industrial diamonds (100 percent), uranium (38 percent), manganese (44 percent), antimony (40 percent), platinum (39 percent), cobalt (36 percent), beryl (30 percent), chromium (48 percent), and columbium-tantalum (21 percent).[41] Petroleum from Africa then accounted for 33 percent of U.S. imports. By 1979 Africa also supplied 20 percent of U.S. copper imports.

Africa's natural wealth, not confined to any single region, extended over the whole continent. Morocco, the dominant world supplier of phosphate, accounted for one third of the world trade in this mineral, which is used in the production of fertilizer, glass, steel, incendiary shells, and safety matches. Already rich in oil, Gabon is also wealthy in manganese ore, providing 41 percent of U.S. supplies (1975–1978).[42] Guinea, with the world's biggest reserves of bauxite, supplied 24 percent of U.S. imports.[43] Zambia remained the world's fifth largest producer of copper, while Zambia and Zaire together contained two thirds of the world's reserves of cobalt. Zimbabwe, rich in forty different minerals, counts chromium, nickel, copper, coal, gold, and asbestos among them. Botswana, whose mineral industry the U.S. Bureau of Mines characterized as "not significant in the mineral economy of the world"[44] in 1976, later discovered enough diamonds to become the world's third largest producer.

Comparing the resources of mammoth Nigeria with those of tiny Rwanda sharply illustrates the range of wealth among African states. In addition to oil, tin and coal comprise an important portion of Nigeria's exports, and its sizable deposits of zinc, limestone, and iron ore await development. Moreover, Nigeria produces nearly 95 percent of the world's industrial requirements of columbium,[45] used mainly in the steel and aerospace industries. This mineral-rich behemoth was also a net exporter of food until the government concentrated economic activity on the development of the petroleum industry following the discovery of oil in 1956. Although it subsequently suffered a drastic decline in agricultural output, Nigeria continued to compete with Ghana as a major world producer of cocoa, increasing export revenues from $302.7 million in 1975 to $664.3 million in 1979.[46]

Rwanda, by contrast, is a poor, landlocked nation that saw scant relief from survival on subsistence agriculture until it recently discovered that its naturally abundant pyrethrum flowers could be converted into powerful, biodegradable pesticides. The world demand for pyrethrum—the source of highly toxic but environmentally safe pesticides whose use is increasing in agriculture, forestry, and public health projects—has consistently outstripped supply.[47] Beginning with a $3.5 million investment in a pyrethrum refinery in 1980, Rwanda expects to become the world's third largest producer of this mineral, behind neighboring Kenya and Tanzania.

African wealth set the stage for an expansion of U.S. investment and trade during the 1970s. Traditionally, Africa has attracted a minor share of total U.S. direct investment abroad, only about 3 percent of the whole, and South Africa has consistently been the main recipient. However, American investment in Africa, $2.6 billion in 1970 (excluding South Africa), increased to $3.4 billion in 1978, almost doubling the level of 1968. In the same decade, investments in South Africa grew from $868 million to $1.7 billion. Nearly 60 percent of all direct investment outside South Africa was located in four countries—Nigeria, Libya, Egypt (after 1975), and Liberia (a traditional ally).

Trade relations accelerated between the African nations and the United States as the United States grew dependent on foreign minerals. Whereas the African nations accounted for $1.1 billion of U.S. imports and $1.6 billion of exports in 1970, they supplied almost $17 billion in U.S. imports and purchased nearly $6 billion in U.S. exports in 1978. The bulk of this trade concerned energy. Although South Africa tripled its exports to the United States between 1970 and 1976, the five energy producers (Nigeria, Libya, Algeria, Gabon, and Angola) multiplied their exports to Americans in the same period by an astronomical 5,000 percent![48] The swift pace of U.S. trade with Africa, as represented by imports and exports with leading trade partners, is shown in Table 2.

American private investment in the newly independent states of

Africa increased in particular during the Nixon-Ford Administration. Official encouragement to direct investment in Black Africa was promoted in large part by the Overseas Private Investment Corporation (OPIC), a U.S. government agency which insures American foreign investments against expropriation by host nations. However, most big companies self-insure to avoid OPIC's high premiums. OPIC actively sought new opportunities for American business in Africa, where its role had been negligible in the past. These OPIC initiatives probably ignored Nigeria's partial nationalization of the oil assets of British Petroleum, an action that so frightened U.S. investors that it precipitated a drop of 6.5 percent in American private capital investment in Black Africa during 1974.[49] Notwithstanding this temporary panic, the White House proceeded with its proinvestment drive, keenly aware of the growing U.S. need for Africa's natural resources.

Secretary of State Kissinger introduced the shrewd idea of a new international resources "bank," a mechanism that would have safeguarded private companies against nationalization, but whose principal objective was to enhance American access to vital African commodities through continually expanding investments. Nothing came of the bank plan, presented during his visit to Nairobi in 1976, but it confirmed that Washington had reversed itself on the traditional policy of neglect, and was now rushing headlong for an American foothold in African products.

It was no coincidence that American imports of Rhodesian chromium continued despite a United Nations embargo. The Byrd amendment, passed by Congress in 1971, nullified economic sanctions voted a decade earlier expressly to prohibit U.S. trade with the illegal regime of Ian Smith. Scuttling the embargo quickly enabled Rhodesia to supply the United States with 11.1 percent of its chromium needs in 1975 (and to earn $40.7 million in the exchange).[50] South Africa provided another 37 percent. Because the Soviet Union supplied the remainder, or about 50 percent of U.S. chromium needs,[51] a political impasse between Washington and Moscow at that time could have made the United States totally dependent on Rhodesia and South Africa.

**TABLE 2**

U.S. IMPORTS FROM AFRICA
(in millions of U.S. dollars)

| Trade Partner | 1970 | 1971 | 1972 | 1973 | 1974 | 1975 | 1976 | 1977 | 1978 | 1979 | 1980 |
|---|---|---|---|---|---|---|---|---|---|---|---|
| WORLD | 42,452 | 48,355 | 58,879 | 73,592 | 108,012 | 103,417 | 129,566 | 157,546 | 183,091 | 218,926 | 252,804 |
| AFRICA | 844 | 987 | 1,321 | 2,300 | 6,358 | 7,999 | 12,393 | 16,527 | 15,381 | 22,877 | 33,605 |
| NIGERIA | 75 | 138 | 287 | 690 | 3,519 | 3,525 | 5,251 | 6,499 | 4,977 | 8,650 | 11,316 |
| LIBYA | 42 | 54 | 123 | 229 | 1 | 1,120 | 2,406 | 4,043 | 3,993 | 5,544 | 7,395 |
| ALGERIA | 11 | 21 | 111 | 227 | 1,167 | 1,448 | 2,344 | 3,270 | 3,698 | 5,462 | 6,881 |
| SOUTH AFRICA | 288 | 287 | 325 | 377 | 609 | 841 | 925 | 1,261 | 2,259 | 2,617 | 3,428 |
| EGYPT | 23 | 19 | 17 | 26 | 70 | 28 | 93 | 170 | 105 | 381 | 487 |
| IVORY COAST | 98 | 88 | 97 | 115 | 101 | 172 | 263 | 313 | 439 | 379 | 303 |
| ANGOLA | 73 | 96 | 96 | 177 | 404 | 463 | 287 | 349 | 240 | 347 | 559 |
| GABON | 10 | 14 | 12 | 13 | 174 | 215 | 206 | 245 | 194 | 342 | 278 |
| ZAIRE | 43 | 47 | 45 | 75 | 74 | 72 | 200 | 179 | 234 | 291 | 370 |
| GHANA | 97 | 112 | 85 | 95 | 136 | 160 | 162 | 223 | 223 | 232 | 214 |
| CAMEROON | 27 | 21 | 25 | 32 | 30 | 20 | 26 | 40 | 81 | 221 | 638 |
| LIBERIA | 54 | 52 | 56 | 76 | 104 | 117 | 116 | 124 | 154 | 159 | 148 |
| ZAMBIA | 2 | 8 | 3 | 7 | 6 | 0 | 168 | 105 | 121 | 125 | 205 |
| ETHIOPIA | 71 | 65 | 62 | 84 | 69 | 53 | 99 | 97 | 100 | 114 | 91 |
| TUNISIA | 3 | 6 | 9 | 35 | 24 | 28 | 59 | 12 | 23 | 101 | 63 |
| UGANDA | 50 | 46 | 52 | 61 | 73 | 57 | 113 | 254 | 85 | 85 | 131 |
| CONGO | 0 | 3 | 3 | 8 | 2 | 21 | 60 | 34 | 86 | 81 | 95 |
| MADAGASCAR | 34 | 42 | 39 | 42 | 65 | 51 | 64 | 80 | 112 | 73 | 97 |
| KENYA | 24 | 27 | 29 | 28 | 44 | 40 | 66 | 98 | 56 | 56 | 59 |
| MOZAMBIQUE | 19 | 23 | 27 | 36 | 50 | 40 | 45 | 73 | 42 | 55 | 113 |
| MOROCCO | 11 | 8 | 13 | 14 | 22 | 11 | 18 | 24 | 49 | 49 | 41 |
| TANZANIA | 25 | 21 | 22 | 29 | 29 | 32 | 52 | 83 | 86 | 49 | 34 |
| SUDAN | 13 | 13 | 13 | 10 | 30 | 9 | 26 | 20 | 15 | 17 | 19 |
| SENEGAL | 1 | 1 | 3 | 2 | 3 | 2 | 4 | 2 | 2 | 5 | 10 |
| MAURITANIA | 1 | 0 | 1 | 1 | 0 | 0 | 0 | 0 | 2 | 0 | .4 |

U.S. EXPORTS TO AFRICA
(in millions of U. S. dollars)

| Trade Partner | 1970 | 1971 | 1972 | 1973 | 1974 | 1975 | 1976 | 1977 | 1978 | 1979 | 1980 |
|---|---|---|---|---|---|---|---|---|---|---|---|
| WORLD | 43,231 | 44,137 | 49,787 | 71,347 | 98,521 | 107,586 | 115,006 | 121,228 | 143,660 | 181,798 | 220,705 |
| AFRICA | 914 | 987 | 866 | 1,297 | 1,989 | 2,895 | 2,984 | 3,420 | 3,580 | 3,339 | 9,060 |
| NIGERIA | 129 | 168 | 115 | 161 | 286 | 536 | 770 | 958 | 985 | 632 | 1,150 |
| LIBYA | 104 | 78 | 85 | 104 | 139 | 232 | 277 | 314 | 425 | 468 | 509 |
| ALGERIA | 62 | 82 | 98 | 161 | 315 | 632 | 487 | 527 | 374 | 404 | 542 |
| SOUTH AFRICA | 563 | 622 | 602 | 746 | 1,160 | 1,302 | 1,348 | 1,054 | 1,080 | 1,413 | 2,464 |
| EGYPT | 77 | 63 | 76 | 225 | 455 | 683 | 810 | 982 | 1,134 | 1,433 | 1,874 |
| MOROCCO | 89 | 102 | 58 | 113 | 184 | 200 | 297 | 371 | 406 | 271 | 344 |
| TUNISIA | 49 | 42 | 55 | 60 | 87 | 90 | 82 | 111 | 83 | 175 | 174 |
| IVORY COAST | 36 | 22 | 22 | 69 | 49 | 78 | 64 | 89 | 94 | 128 | 185 |
| ZAIRE | 62 | 84 | 37 | 110 | 145 | 188 | 99 | 114 | 83 | 113 | 155 |
| LIBERIA | 46 | 43 | 41 | 46 | 70 | 90 | 85 | 91 | 108 | 107 | 113 |
| ETHIOPIA | 26 | 26 | 24 | 25 | 33 | 70 | 78 | 58 | 25 | 104 | 72 |
| SUDAN | 7 | 6 | 18 | 39 | 64 | 103 | 106 | 87 | 157 | 103 | 143 |
| ANGOLA | 40 | 37 | 27 | 40 | 62 | 53 | 35 | 39 | 32 | 93 | 111 |
| GHANA | 59 | 55 | 44 | 63 | 77 | 100 | 133 | 146 | 125 | 91 | 127 |
| ZAMBIA | 31 | 38 | 34 | 39 | 68 | 86 | 48 | 49 | 44 | 68 | 96 |
| KENYA | 34 | 41 | 24 | 39 | 49 | 49 | 43 | 77 | 138 | 61 | 141 |
| MADAGASCAR | 7 | 8 | 12 | 15 | 7 | 7 | 6 | 7 | 9 | 61 | 7 |
| CAMEROON | 19 | 14 | 37 | 15 | 20 | 30 | 40 | 54 | 52 | 61 | 93 |
| TANZANIA | 12 | 13 | 12 | 11 | 51 | 66 | 36 | 39 | 48 | 36 | 62 |
| GABON | 7 | 6 | 13 | 19 | 33 | 59 | 46 | 30 | 97 | 32 | 48 |
| SENEGAL | 8 | 9 | 14 | 24 | 34 | 33 | 41 | 36 | 48 | 31 | 41 |
| MOZAMBIQUE | 22 | 21 | 16 | 32 | 35 | 18 | 13 | 13 | 20 | 30 | 69 |
| CONGO | 0 | 6 | 6 | 5 | 8 | 12 | 14 | 12 | 9 | 14 | 22 |
| MAURITANIA | 4 | 7 | 5 | 9 | 11 | 14 | 19 | 18 | 8 | 7 | 20 |
| UGANDA | 4 | 7 | 3 | 2 | 8 | 15 | 6 | 14 | 3 | 1 | 12 |

Sources: International Monetary Fund, *Direction of Trade Annual Survey 1980* (Washington, D.C.: IMF, 1980); U.S. Department of Commerce, *Statistical Abstracts* (Washington, D.C.: Government Printing Office, passim 1972–1980; and U.S. Department of Commerce, *Highlights of U.S. Export and Import Trade* (Washington, D.C.: Government Printing Office, March 1981).

American private investment in African minerals soon expanded from the Mediterranean Sea to the Cape Coast. Before the end of President Ford's tenure, Union Carbide had established subsidiaries in Ghana, the Ivory Coast, Kenya, Sudan, as well as in South Africa and Rhodesia. Kaiser Aluminum expanded its bauxite operations in Ghana. Standard Oil of Indiana acquired interests in a Zairian copper mine. Bethlehem Steel invested in developing titanium deposits in Sierra Leone, Gulf Oil negotiated its future relations with Angola, and Reynolds Metals and Kaiser Aluminum maintained their plants in socialist Guinea. Bethlehem Steel even obtained rights to a fluorite mine in Mozambique before its independence. Overnight, it seemed, the race for African minerals was on, and by the end of 1975 it revealed itself in an unprecedented U.S. trade deficit of $4 billion with African countries other than South Africa and Rhodesia.

Nigerian oil, of course, accounted for the bulk (or $3 billion) of the deficit,[52] but it resulted also from several other nonfuel imports, including coffee and palm products from the Ivory Coast, groundnuts from Mozambique, and iron ore from Liberia, where U.S. mining interests have been ensconced for many years. Algeria provided 23 percent of America's imports of mercury, used to make electrical apparatus. Whereas the total value of American trade with South Africa tripled from 1969 to 1975, it multiplied sevenfold with the rest of Africa.

A parallel U.S. policy interest in African minerals concerns their general availability for Western Europe. More than the United States, such key NATO allies as Great Britain and West Germany depended on resources from foreign sources. What troubled Washington about this vulnerability early in 1980 were reports that the Soviet Union had begun major overseas purchases of numerous strategic materials, including cobalt, copper, lead, and aluminum.[53] Because Soviet self-sufficiency already existed in such minerals, U.S. policymakers speculated that Moscow maneuvered, at least in part, to limit or deny Western access to minerals necessary for arms production. To illustrate the potential danger of Soviet action to the NATO alliance, Table 3 lists the net imports of selected minerals by the United States, the EEC, and the Council for Mutual Economic Assistance (COMECON), the economic community of Soviet bloc nations.

### Table 3

NET IMPORTS OF NONFUEL MINERALS
(percent of consumption, 1977)

|  | U.S. | EEC | JAPAN | COMECON |
|---|---|---|---|---|
| Manganese | 98 | 100 | 99 | 3 |
| Cobalt | 97 | 100 | 100 | 68 |
| Bauxite | 91 | 97 | 100 | 28 |
| Chromium | 91 | 100 | 98 | 2 |
| Asbestos | 85 | 90 | 98 | 1 |
| Nickel | 70 | 100 | 100 | 13 |
| Zinc | 57 | 91 | 74 | 9 |
| Iron ore | 48 | 82 | 100 | 5 |
| Silver | 36 | 93 | 71 | 10 |
| Copper | 13 | 100 | 97 | 4 |
| Lead | 13 | 76 | 78 | 3 |
| Phosphate | Major exporter | 99 | 100 | 23 |

Source: U.S. Bureau of Mines

Soviet bloc presence in central and southern Africa sharpened U.S. agitation over possible preemptive Soviet purchases. Disquiet also spread from Washington to Bonn because of the fifteen thousand Cuban troops in Angola, which borders on Zaire, Zambia, and Namibia, coupled with perhaps eighteen thousand more in Ethiopia, which reinforced the influence of Soviet military advisors in the whole region. Western fears were momentarily calmed when economists explained that the Soviet purchases were made simply as a hedge against the future, when world prices of various minerals were expected to rise rapidly.[54] However, the possibility also existed that Moscow had begun to stockpile minerals, precipitating a simultaneous reduction of supplies available to the Western nations and, consequently, a sense of urgency regarding minerals they imported from Africa. Thus, as the decade of the 1980s began, there were unmistakable signs of new East-West competition for African resources.

Related to the expansion in African-American trade was Africa's vast potential in undeveloped resources and agriculture. Cameroon and Zaire, for example, possess nearly one fifth of the world's hydroelectrical potential, or an abundant reservoir of inexpensive hydroelectric power for irrigation that conceivably could convert the African heartland into one of the world's breadbaskets. Zimbabwe already has enough cultivable land to play such a role. Though little noticed, Liberia arose as a minor oil-exporting country. Niger, where arid land and drought made food shortages a condition of permanent crisis, became a new zone of strategic interest to Western powers after a Japanese-French-Niger team enlarged known uranium reserves with huge discoveries in 1979. The Fluor Corporation of California wasted no time in obtaining a contract to build a $550 million uranium development complex. In contrast to Niger's production of 220 tons of uranium in 1978, an output of 9,000 tons annually was projected for the 1980s as a result of new investments. Poor though it was, Niger ranked as the world's fifth largest producer of the ore, supplying 10 percent of total world output. Among its agricultural products, Africa supplied more than one half of U.S. cocoa imports, one fifth of the tea imports, and one fourth of the coffee poured into Americans' coffee cups.[55]

The entrenchment of a wide array of U.S. interests in Africa's wealth emerged as the dominant feature of African-American relations in the 1970s. Trade became the hallmark of this new phenomenon in international relations, reflected in U.S. imports of $12.5 billion in African fuels and lubricants in 1978, or nearly 30 percent of total U.S. energy imports.[56] Other major imports from Africa included unfinished metals ($1.8 billion) and agricultural commodities ($1.5 billion). Thus, the continent that had been primarily an object of U.S. neglect at the start of the decade ended it as one of America's critical trade partners.

Petroleum accounted for about 60 percent of total U.S. trade with Africa in 1978. An additional 15 percent involved mining and smelting, while 8 percent of U.S. investments went to manufacturing.[57] Although investments remained a small proportion of U.S. economic relations worldwide, the most salient aspect of the new economic relations with Africa did not concern the volume of interests, but the strategic character of the goods involved. In the end, therefore, Africa assumed a significance that matched the vital resource needs of the United States, not to mention those of its Western allies. Without fanfare or much notice, African states gained a comparative advantage as the United States slid into a dependence on their resources.

## CRITERIA FOR U.S. POLICY

Mutual interdependence between the United States and African countries resulted naturally from America's need for African resources and from Africa's corresponding need for American industrial products and technological assistance. American reliance on Africa went hand in hand with African nations' entry into the new international order, despite the considerable economic problems of certain African states—drought, food scarcity, refugees[58]— for which they often appealed to the United States as a benefactor of preferred but not last resort. African states, underdeveloped here, politically unstable there, have become connected to Americans' material well-being, and it seems inconceivable that they will continue to supply the American house of plenty while their own tables go bare.

African suppliers have not embarked on a "resource war" policy against the United States precisely because of the economic interdependence. Nevertheless, numerous nonfuel producers of minerals have entered into price and policy cartels, as exemplified by the Cocoa Producers Alliance, formed by such states as Nigeria and Ghana to coordinate cocoa production. Guinea, Sierra Leone, and Ghana participate in the International Bauxite Association. Several other African nations were members of either producer groups or commodity agreements between producing and consuming countries in a variety of products, including coffee, tea, sisal, and sugar. The Arab oil boycott of 1973–1974, which forced Americans to attend to the incipient new international economic order, stimulated a widespread movement among producers in various commodity fields to form cartels. With regard to petroleum, the big three producers have refrained from forming an African cartel mainly because of their membership in OPEC. On the other hand, they have collaborated on oil prices, often taking the lead in stimulating general OPEC increases. When Libya increased its price by $4 per barrel in December 1980, for example, Nigeria followed the next day with a $3 increase, and Algeria soon followed suit. The three countries have thereby exercised indirect but pivotal influence on OPEC policies. As a consequence they also have usually set the price pace for North Sea producers, which do not belong to OPEC. In this way the big three have exercised decisive influence on the world price of fuel.

Foreign cartels, of course, have traditionally been spurned in this country as anathema to American national interest (despite American corporate control of certain industries, such as computers, that is tantamount to cartel control). The National Strategy Information Center, a private group that acts as a watchdog in matters of national security, has posited the possibility that the Soviets and their allies in Africa could create cartels in certain critical minerals by integrating such socialist states as Angola or Ethiopia into the economic union of Warsaw Pact countries.[59] However, this viewpoint not only fails to appreciate the countervailing pressures of economic interdependence, it also ignores the fact that the paramount goal of African states is economic independence from all superpowers.

It has been proposed that the United States stockpile vital minerals as an antidote to foreign cartels. This alternative was well articulated in 1980 by a sixteen-member forum of the World Affairs Council of Pittsburgh, consisting of such experts as Murray L. Weidenbaum, Chairman of the Council of Economic Advisors in the Reagan Administration, who stated that the United States "should generate promptly public policies to enable the nation to maintain an adequate strategic stockpile of non-fuel minerals and other commodities on a consistent and long-range basis to underpin national security needs."[60] However, such stockpiles are almost universally regarded as impracticable because of the formidable effort necessary to acquire and maintain them. And if this were possible, it would not obviate the very sensitive task of selecting the precise minerals needed for every eventuality; even the experts may disagree on what constitutes "adequate" supplies. Stockpiles may provide temporary remedies for certain mineral needs, but they cannot safeguard the long-range durability of the American economy.

An extreme American defense in a war of resources has been proposed by John R. Block, the Illinois farmer who became Secretary of Agriculture in the Reagan Administration: "I believe food is now the greatest weapon we have for keeping peace in the world."[61] The Republican official argued that Washington should "tie other countries" to the United States through their dependence on imports of American grain and meat, because—until the year 2000 he supposed—such countries would "become more dependent on American farm exports and become reluctant to upset us." With respect to African countries, he was evidently unaware that as recently as 1978 Africa bought only one eighth of U.S. wheat exports and one fourth of U.S. rice exports.[62] These levels are so low that they could hardly bring defiant recipients to their knees, especially when alternative sources existed. Block also ignored Carter's 1980 embargo on grain to the Soviet Union, which failed because of transshipments of U.S. grain from East European nations, as well as because of expanded and redirected exports of grain to the Soviet Union from places other than the United States.[63] This failure led one analyst to conclude that "the longer any U.S. embargo continues, the more likely it becomes that new sources of supply will emerge."[64]

What is needed is an urgent and large-scale revitalization of U.S. economic and technical assistance to Africa. An enlarged foreign aid program would assist African states in their fundamental task of acquiring economic autonomy over their own resources, while providing them with an inescapable rationale for maintaining constant trade with the United States. Expressed differently, this approach would guarantee the United States continuing access, via trade, to the African resources. It has the additional advantage that it avoids diplomatic and commercial complications from the political instability or shifts in ideological orientation in these trade partners, except violence-prone South Africa. Such a policy would largely preclude the use of mineral resources as political weapons by African states.

Since 1960 U.S. assistance to African countries has been quite modest. American developmental assistance to Africa in the past decade has accounted for only about 10 percent of total donor assistance through bilateral and multilateral channels.[65] In 1978, for instance, U.S. bilateral aid amounted to $1.1 billion for the whole of Africa—that is, for nearly 500 million people—and Egypt obtained most of it ($751 million). Multilateral aid totaled only $305 million. The biggest recipient of U.S. assistance has regularly been Israel, a small country with a small population, which in 1978 received $792 million in economic aid.[66] Israel and Egypt together accounted for about 57 percent of total American foreign assistance to all countries in the world.

Table 4 shows the different categories of economic assistance scheduled for African states during 1980–1982. The figures represent actual obligations for fiscal year 1980, and planning levels for fiscal years 1981 and 1982. The U.S. aid program under Public Law 480, which was established by the Agricultural Trade Department and Assistance Act of 1954, provides agricultural goods as foreign assistance. Title I authorizes the sale of farm goods to developing countries for their "soft" or nonconvertible currencies. Title II authorizes outright donations of surplus commodities to countries for famine relief and other related purposes. Title III authorizes the use of surplus commodities for other types of donations and for barter transactions.

Increased U.S. assistance to developing but mineral-rich African states is consistent with American national interest because the increasing independence of these nations, and the resultant control

**Table 4**

U.S. ECONOMIC ASSISTANCE TO AFRICA, 1980–1982
(in millions of dollars)

| Country | Development Assistance | | | Economic Support Funds | | | PL-480 Title I/III | | | PL-480 Title II | | | Total Assitance | | |
|---|---|---|---|---|---|---|---|---|---|---|---|---|---|---|---|
| | 1980 | 1981 | 1982 | 1980 | 1981 | 1982 | 1980 | 1981 | 1982 | 1980 | 1981 | 1982 | 1980 | 1981 | 1982 |
| Angola | — | — | — | — | — | — | — | — | — | 4.9 | 1.1 | 1.1 | 4.9 | 1.1 | 1.1 |
| Benin | 2.6 | 4.7 | — | — | — | — | — | — | — | .9 | 1.3 | 1 | 3.5 | 6 | 1 |
| Botswana | — | — | — | 13 | 10 | 10 | — | — | — | 5.3 | 4.4 | 1.8 | 18.3 | 14.4 | 11.8 |
| Burundi | 4.4 | 4 | 5.1 | — | — | — | — | — | — | 2.5 | 2.9 | 2.5 | 6.9 | 6.9 | 7.6 |
| Cameroon | 6.3 | 17.9 | 21 | — | — | — | — | — | — | 1.8 | 1.6 | 1.9 | 8.1 | 19.5 | 22.9 |
| Cape Verde | 3.1 | 3 | 3.5 | — | — | — | — | — | — | 2 | .4 | .2 | 5.1 | 3.4 | 3.7 |
| Central African Republic | — | — | 1 | — | — | — | — | — | — | .5 | .4 | .1 | .5 | .4 | 1.1 |
| Chad | .2 | — | — | — | — | — | — | — | — | 1.2 | — | — | 1.4 | — | — |
| Comoro Is. | — | — | — | — | — | — | — | — | — | .3 | .2 | .1 | .3 | .2 | .1 |
| Congo | .2 | 2 | 2 | — | — | — | — | — | — | .7 | .6 | .1 | .9 | 2.6 | 2.1 |

**Table 4 (cont.)**

U.S. ECONOMIC ASSISTANCE TO AFRICA, 1980–1982
(in millions of dollars)

| Country | Development Assistance | | | Economic Support Funds | | | PL-480 Title I/III | | | PL-480 Title II | | | Total Assitance | | |
|---|---|---|---|---|---|---|---|---|---|---|---|---|---|---|---|
| | 1980 | 1981 | 1982 | 1980 | 1981 | 1982 | 1980 | 1981 | 1982 | 1980 | 1981 | 1982 | 1980 | 1981 | 1982 |
| Djibouti | 1.1 | 2.1 | — | — | 2 | 2 | — | — | — | 1.9 | 1.2 | 2.2 | 3 | 5.3 | 4.2 |
| Egypt | — | — | — | 865 | 850 | 750 | 299.5 | 300 | 313 | — | 25.6 | 24 | 1,164.5 | 1,175.6 | 1,087 |
| Ethiopia | — | — | — | — | — | — | — | — | — | 13.5 | 5.6 | 3.4 | 13.5 | 5.6 | 3.4 |
| Eq. Guinea | — | 1 | 1 | — | — | — | — | — | — | .5 | — | — | .5 | 1 | 1 |
| Gambia | 4.7 | 6.2 | 5 | — | — | — | — | — | — | 1.6 | 1.2 | 1 | 6.3 | 7.4 | 6 |
| Ghana | 10 | 4.9 | 8 | — | — | — | 12.7 | 12.7 | 14 | 4.9 | 7.8 | 6.6 | 27.6 | 25.4 | 28.6 |
| Guinea | 5.2 | 2.4 | 2.5 | — | — | — | 6 | 7 | 7 | 1.5 | 3.2 | .2 | 12.7 | 12.6 | 9.7 |
| Guinea-Bissau | 1.7 | 1.6 | 1.9 | — | — | — | — | — | — | .4 | 2.7 | .6 | 2.1 | 4.3 | 2.5 |
| Ivory Coast | — | — | — | — | — | — | — | — | — | .007 | .011 | — | .007 | .011 | — |
| Kenya | 17.3 | 21.1 | 34.5 | 14.5 | 5.5 | 10 | 16.9 | 11 | 15 | 5.1 | 7.7 | 4.4 | 53.8 | 45.3 | 63.9 |
| Lesotho | 9.8 | 9.3 | 9.9 | — | — | — | — | — | — | 7.9 | 8.7 | 8.8 | 17.7 | 18 | 18.7 |
| Liberia | 10.8 | 11.6 | 8.0 | 5 | 7 | 10 | 5 | 5 | 5 | .3 | .5 | .2 | 21.1 | 24.1 | 23.2 |

| | | | | | | | | | | | | | | | |
|---|---|---|---|---|---|---|---|---|---|---|---|---|---|---|---|
| Madagascar | — | — | — | — | — | — | — | — | — | .03 | 2 | 1.8 | .03 | 2 | 1.8 |
| Malawi | 4.4 | 5 | 7.3 | — | — | — | 5 | 5 | — | .7 | 1.4 | .9 | 5.1 | 11.4 | 12.3 |
| Mali | 15.5 | 13 | 9.9 | — | — | — | — | — | — | .5 | — | — | 16 | 13 | 9.9 |
| Mauritania | 2.7 | 8 | 9.2 | — | — | — | — | — | — | 7 | 3.3 | 3.1 | 9.7 | 11.3 | 12.3 |
| Mauritius | .3 | — | — | — | — | 2 | 2.8 | 3.5 | — | .5 | 1.4 | .6 | 3.6 | 4.9 | 2.6 |
| Morocco | 9 | 10 | 10.2 | — | — | — | — | — | — | — | 15.4 | 13 | 9 | 25.4 | 23.2 |
| Mozambique | — | — | — | — | — | — | 10 | 5 | 10 | 7.5 | 3.1 | 1.5 | 17.5 | 8.1 | 11.5 |
| Niger | 9.5 | 13 | 14.2 | — | — | — | — | — | — | 1.1 | 1.7 | .5 | 10.6 | 14.7 | 14.7 |
| Rwanda | 1.9 | 2.9 | 6.7 | — | — | — | — | — | — | 2 | 3.9 | 3.2 | 3.9 | 6.8 | 9.9 |
| São Tomé | — | 1.6 | — | — | — | — | — | — | — | .06 | .3 | — | .06 | 1.9 | — |
| Senegal | 10 | 13.8 | 18 | — | — | — | 7 | 7 | 7 | 8.8 | 7.3 | 7.8 | 25.8 | 28.1 | 32.8 |
| Seychelles | .6 | .5 | — | — | — | 2 | — | — | — | .2 | .5 | .4 | .8 | 1 | 2.4 |
| Sierra Leone | 2 | 2.6 | 2.3 | — | — | — | 16.4 | 1.3 | 1.2 | 1.5 | 2 | 2.1 | 4.7 | 5.9 | 4.4 |
| Somalia | 12.3 | 12.6 | 16.2 | 5 | — | 20 | 25 | 15 | 17.7 | 27.9 | 19.6 | 5.5 | 62.9 | 47.2 | 58.1 |
| Sudan | 30.1 | 22.9 | 27 | 40 | 50 | 50 | 25 | 25 | 25 | 1.5 | 7 | 3.3 | 96.6 | 104.9 | 105.3 |
| Swaziland | 7.5 | 7.5 | 6.8 | — | — | — | — | — | — | .1 | .4 | .7 | 7.6 | 7.9 | 7.5 |

## Table 4 (cont.)

U.S. ECONOMIC ASSISTANCE TO AFRICA, 1980–1982
(in millions of dollars)

| Country | Development Assistance | | | Economic Support Funds | | | PL-480 Title I/III | | | PL-480 Title II | | | Total Assitance | | |
|---|---|---|---|---|---|---|---|---|---|---|---|---|---|---|---|
| | 1980 | 1981 | 1982 | 1980 | 1981 | 1982 | 1980 | 1981 | 1982 | 1980 | 1981 | 1982 | 1980 | 1981 | 1982 |
| Tanzania | 14.9 | 13.5 | 15.9 | — | — | — | 7.5 | 7.5 | 7.5 | 5.8 | 5.7 | 1.7 | 28.2 | 26.7 | 25.1 |
| Togo | 1.9 | 2.2 | 2.6 | — | — | — | — | — | — | 2 | 3.4 | 2.7 | 3.9 | 5.6 | 5.3 |
| Tunisia | 10.2 | 25.1 | — | — | — | — | — | 10 | 10 | — | 3 | 3 | 10.2 | 38.1 | 13 |
| Uganda | — | — | 5 | — | — | — | — | — | — | 7.9 | 2 | — | 7.9 | 2 | 5 |
| Upper Volta | 9.2 | 14.1 | 18.2 | — | — | — | — | — | — | 11.5 | 17 | 11 | 20.7 | 31.1 | 29.2 |
| Zaire | 6.9 | 9.4 | 10 | — | — | — | 15.7 | 10 | 10 | — | — | — | 22.6 | 19.4 | 20 |
| Zambia | — | — | — | 24 | 20 | 20 | 12.5 | 10 | 10 | 6.5 | .1 | — | 43 | 30.1 | 30 |
| Zimbabwe | — | — | — | 22.9 | 25 | 75 | — | — | — | 1.8 | — | — | 24.7 | 25 | 75 |

Source: U.S. Department of State

over their economies, enables them to ward off external domination inimical to U.S. interests. Viewed in global terms, the more that African states move toward economic self-sufficiency, the more they gain the capacity to prevent the continent from serving as another theater of Great Power confrontation. From the American standpoint, confrontation with the Soviets in Africa is no more desirable than a collision in Europe, because a bipolar conflict anywhere could provoke the nuclear conflagration that has thus far been avoided. Ineluctably, independent African states have been thrust into a new international system. America's interest lies in assisting them to become partners in peace, rather than agents in conflict.

There is no region of the continent which is not a potential cornucopia of natural wealth. The Atlas Mountains are more than uninhabitable rocks and boulders, because trees for timber push forth from them; and the Sahara is more than barren sand, because petroleum lies below. It is no wonder therefore that Africa has become a region of superpower interest and will undoubtedly come to play a decisive role in world affairs in the coming century.

# 6

# U.S. MILITARY AND STRATEGIC STAKES: From the Mediterranean to the Cape

In 1976 Chester A. Crocker summarized the recent military and strategic role of the United States in Africa: "Apart from its brief venture into African grand strategy in conjunction with the British during World War II, the United States has never considered itself an African power in military or strategic terms."[1] But by early 1981, when Crocker was designated Assistant Secretary of State for African Affairs in the Reagan Administration, American military interests stretched over virtually every region of the African continent. The United States had obtained special rights for naval and air forces in some African states and had concluded military sales agreements totaling billions of dollars with many others. The new Rapid Deployment Force depended on African states for most of its foreign bases of operation. Moreover, the White House pursued a host of African allies, some old, others newly found, to strengthen America's cold war challenges across the continent. Within five years, the United States had not only acquired extraordinary military and strategic stakes in Africa, but had enveloped the continent in its global competition with the Soviet Union.

The United States was also involved indirectly in a wide spectrum of issues and events intrinsic to African nations. These ranged from American policy toward Morocco, a traditional ally that was waging war for control of the Western Sahara, to U.S. opposition to the foreign military alignments of Ethiopia and Libya, former American allies whose enormous support by Soviet bloc military forces threatened to provoke anti-Soviet challenges from Washington. The Republic of South Africa, a dominant ally ruled by a White supremacy dictatorship, generated a reign of such racial conflict that it rendered the United States susceptible to involvement there in a potential upheaval of unimaginable magnitude.

In almost every region of Africa, however, the United States continued to promote military policy that was primarily related to its extra-African objectives, and only indirectly related to indigenous African needs or imperatives. U.S. operations in North Africa, for example, mainly concerned NATO forces in the Mediterranean Sea (or Western Europe). One North African state, Egypt, joined states in the Horn of Africa to assist in the Persian Gulf objectives of the U.S. Rapid Deployment Force. Only in South Africa, where the United States retained both strategic and economic stakes, did American policy concentrate on issues directly related to African conditions.

## THE RAPID DEPLOYMENT FORCE

The Rapid Deployment Joint Task Force, organized in March 1980 as a strike force capable of moving swiftly into the Persian Gulf, represented America's latest use of the African continent for non-African military purposes. A direct outgrowth of U.S. cold war doctrine, it was conceived as a preemptive force against Soviet threats to this oil-rich region, which the United States identifies as vital to its interests. The Rapid Deployment Force recruits its manpower from all four branches of the armed services. Scheduled to become fully operational with 250,000 troops by 1985, it functions under a single command headquarters responsible for peacetime planning and responding to non-NATO emergencies. Although its strategy centers on the Middle East, four of its five original bases abroad were established in African countries.

The concept of the Rapid Deployment Force was not new.

France's *force d'intervention,* for instance, had operated for some time under the joint command of its parachute troops, marines, and other soldiers. As early as July 1977, the staff of Harold Brown, the U.S. Secretary of Defense, produced a classified study proposing a strategy for general-purpose forces in non-NATO situations. The study, known in the Carter Administration as Presidential Review Memorandum-10, anticipated the strike force, although the original conception encompassed South Korea as well as the Middle East and the Persian Gulf. President Carter announced the creation of the deployment force in October 1979. The Soviet invasion of Afghanistan in December 1979, which gave the Soviet Union closer access to the Persian Gulf as the anti-Western revolution was continuing in Iran, quickened Washington's anxiety over U.S. interests in this critical region. After the President issued the so-called Carter doctrine in his State of the Union message of 1980, declaring that the United States would employ military force if necessary to protect such vital interests as oil in the Persian Gulf, the mission of the strike force was finally established.

Egypt provided a military base for the fourteen hundred soldiers airlifted there in November 1980 for the strike force's first training exercise abroad. From Egypt's Cairo-West air base, the American soldiers rehearsed simulated contingencies akin to what might be expected in an actual intervention in the Persian Gulf. The initiative for use of the Egyptian base originated from President Sadat, who had offered the United States air and naval bases. Sadat's offer specified that there could be no permanent American military presence in Egypt, no extraterritorial enclaves, and no installations that excluded Egyptian officers, as had been the case when British and Soviet soldiers used Egyptian territory. In the terms of this gentleman's agreement, the United States thus acquired use of Egyptian bases as military bridges to the Persian Gulf in the event of a Soviet threat or other emergencies.

In contrast to Egypt, Somalia and Kenya accepted written agreements to provide the United States with bases for the Rapid Deployment Force. The strategic location of these countries is on the Indian Ocean, approximately a thousand miles from the Persian

Gulf. Somalia agreed to the strike force's use of its port at Mogadishu on the Indian Ocean, as well as its port and air bases at Berbera on the Gulf of Aden. The port at Mogadishu has long been well equipped for maritime trade, and Berbera's two Soviet-built air strips of 14,500 and 17,500 feet, respectively, accommodated any aircraft in the Soviet inventory during the period of Somalia's alliance with the Soviet Union from 1974 to 1977.[2] In exchange for use of the bases, the Carter Administration granted Somalia $40 million in military credits together with $5 million in economic assistance (although the Somalis had originally demanded a total of $2 billion in economic assistance alone).[3] Because of their size and versatility, the Somali bases constituted a quantum leap in America's access to the Persian Gulf.

Kenya, a longstanding recipient of American military and economic assistance, provided access to port and air facilities at Mombasa, a coastal city on the Indian Ocean. The United States rewarded Kenya with roughly $50 million for use of the base.[4] Mombasa is the main developed harbor accessible to American forces on Africa's east coast. It had already served as a naval port of call before the formation of the strike force. With 4,000 troops, the Navy's 40,000-ton amphibious warship U.S.S. *Tarawa* and two escort ships visited Mombasa in February 1981, when thirty-four other American warships circulated in the Indian Ocean to strengthen Washington's ability to accelerate an emergency deployment of forces.[5]

Neither the Somali nor the Kenyan bases equaled the huge U.S. base on Diego Garcia Island, the only American base in the Indian Ocean, located 2,300 miles from the Persian Gulf. Named after the Portuguese navigator credited with discovering it in 1532, Diego Garcia today belongs to Mauritius, an African island-nation in the Indian Ocean that was under British colonial control until its independence in 1968. In preindependence negotiations, Great Britain purchased Mauritius' Chagos Archipelago, in which Diego Garcia is the largest atoll, on the understanding that the island group would not be used for military purposes. The United States, in turn, leased the island from Britain in 1966 for a period of fifty years, secretly arranging to defray half the cost of the island purchase with $14 million in military credits to Britain.[6] In 1971 U.S. Navy Seabee teams arrived and began to construct what has since become a complete air field, with a 12,000-foot runway, a base with permanent barracks for hundreds of troops, and a harbor capable of accommodating the Navy's biggest aircraft carriers. Diego Garcia also contains an Anglo-American communication facility with electronic surveillance equipment for eavesdropping on Soviet warships in the Indian Ocean.

Most American ships have since operated from Diego Garcia. In his farewell budget, Carter recommended about $700 million for new construction there to support the new deployment forces.[7] The Reagan Administration planned to widen the runway in order to put America's mainstay bomber, the B-52, within close striking range of the Persian Gulf.

Several African states thus became clients involved in America's global cold war policy, not as partners but as launching pads for potential crises exogenous to Africa. Among the five countries that originally provided operational bases for the Rapid Deployment Force, Oman, a small independent nation at the eastern tip of the Arabian Peninsula, is the only one directly connected to the Persian Gulf region. The four other countries—Egypt, Somalia, Kenya, Mauritius—belong to Africa. Thus, the tradition of U.S. military policy by which African territories function mainly as transit points for American forces, as in World War II, survives in the nuclear age.

Political complications, however, have impinged on future U.S. use of Diego Garcia. These have included the OAU summit in 1980, which denounced the American base as "a threat to Africa and the concept of a zone of peace in the Indian Ocean."[8] The assembled African leaders, representing Africa's fifty independent states, demanded the island's unconditional return to Mauritius. Above all, a bipartisan majority of the Mauritian parliament undertook talks with London for Diego Garcia's return to Mauritian patrimony. To Washington's dismay, these developments ensued even as the island became firmly integrated as a central staging point in the emergent strategy of the new strike force.

All four African states prohibit permanent stationing of American forces on African bases, although the U.S. lease of Diego Garcia has permitted a decidedly long-term installation there. Mohammed Siad Barre, the President of Somalia, has notably defended his country's agreement with the United States by avowing that it provides only for the supply of fuel to U.S. naval vessels and aircraft in case of emergency; he said that the Somali government "did not give them bases, nor do they have any presence there."[9] However, the permanent, or impermanent, use of African bases by the United States is a moot point with respect to the Rapid Deployment Force precisely because the strike force requires only temporary installations for its missions. Prepositioning—or the advance emplacement of military equipment for future use by strike forces summoned to action—is a primary element of rapid deployment strategy, and it has obviated the presence of standing armies according to old conventional standards of ground warfare. Consequently, even the transitory U.S. use of African bases has not exempted the host countries from involvement in America's strategic competition with the Soviet Union.

It is important to emphasize that the use of African bases for non-African purposes does not correspond to American economic interests in Africa. The principal strategic value of the Persian Gulf applies to broader interests of the Western alliance, specifically to the NATO powers of Europe, and only secondarily to the United States itself. The Strait of Hormuz, through which half of the world's petroleum exports pass from the Persian Gulf to the Arabian Sea, is the focus of the West's strategic interest. It is an essential artery in the lifeline of Western Europe. The United States, on the other hand, has been receiving a substantial percentage of its imported petroleum from states on Africa's Atlantic and Mediterranean coasts. As of July 1980, the United States obtained 37 percent of its 1980 oil imports from Nigeria, Gabon, Algeria, and Libya in contrast to 25 percent from Saudi Arabia,[10] America's major oil supplier in the Middle East.

The evolving defense strategy of the Reagan Administration has indicated an expansion of strike force arrangements on African soil. The first budget of Defense Secretary Caspar W. Weinberger requested new expenditures for sundry developments of the Rapid Deployment Force, including improvement of the Indian Ocean bases at Diego Garcia, Berbera, and Mombasa. Most critically, Weinberger proposed in March 1981 the establishment of permanent American bases: "I think what we need is enough of American . . . military presence in that area, to lead the Soviets to conclude correctly that there would be an unacceptable risk to them to try the sort of thing they're trying in Afghanistan. . . . It's essential that we have facilities of that kind [that is, permanent military bases] to carry out that policy which is very much in our national interest and, indeed, in the interest of all of our NATO allies."[11] The Defense Secretary included Saudi Arabia among the possible host countries, but it seemed evident that the weight of the enlarged strategy would fall upon those African states where bases already provided the main springboards of rapid deployment policy.

The Soviet Union, of course, is also an Indian Ocean power, and the development of the Rapid Deployment Force has localized considerably American-Soviet tension in the region, exposing African and Middle Eastern states to the risk of potential or actual conflict arising from superpower rivalry. During September 1980 the Soviet Navy maintained thirty-two ships in the Indian Ocean from bases in Ethiopia, Mozambique, and South Yemen,[12] three countries allied to Moscow. A Soviet base also existed on tiny Socotra Island, located south of the Arabian Peninsula. Simultaneously the United States had forty-two ships deployed in the ocean, including the U.S.S. *Eisenhower* and *Constellation,* the Navy's largest aircraft carriers. Great Britain retained a task force of six ships there, perhaps temporarily, while France had reestablished its Indian Ocean presence with fifteen ships on Mauritius and on the adjacent French island territory of Réunion. This concentration of potentially hostile traffic has transformed the Indian Ocean into one of the world's most volatile military zones.

The militarization of the Indian Ocean by nuclear powers explains the OAU's insistence on maintaining this waterway as a "zone of peace." It also explains why South African ports, to which the White House suspended U.S. Navy visits in 1967 as a protest against apartheid, have resurfaced as an interest of some American strategists after the creation of the Rapid Deployment Force. The South African naval bases at Durban and Simonstown have occasionally been useful to the U.S. Navy in cases of emergency since the voluntary cessation of naval visits.[13] These ports became more attractive after the Angolan and Mozambican ports, available to the United States during Portuguese hegemony, began to service Soviet ships. Renewed American use of the South African bases would not only exacerbate tension in the Indian Ocean, but could also wreak intolerable domestic and international repercussions on American society.

Even before the new dangers brought on by the Rapid Deployment Force, the United States was running the risk of entanglement in local African conflicts. A prime example is the Somali-Ethiopian war over the Ogaden, claimed by Somalia as one of its "lost territories" but located within the national boundaries of Ethiopia. The Soviets, who had built the Berbera airport and harbor, switched support from their old ally Somalia to new ally Ethiopia after the war erupted in 1977. The subsequent arrival of about $1 billion in Soviet arms and perhaps seventeen thousand Cuban troops in Addis Ababa soon shifted the war decisively to Ethiopia, one of America's staunchest allies until its alliance with the Soviet Union. Somalia, which did not renounce its demand to the Ogaden, has in the past also laid irredentist claims to northern Kenya. Although Washington insisted on the removal of regular Somali forces from the Ogaden as a condition of the 1980 agreement providing U.S. arms assistance, the specter of recurrent warfare persisted, possibly exposing the United States to the risk of conflict with Soviet bloc forces loyal to Ethiopia.

Despite the political or military pitfalls, the United States seems increasingly determined to expand the operations of the Rapid Deployment Force beyond its African perimeters. Such determination results in large part from a deliberate drive by the Reagan Administration to restore America to preeminent world power at a time when countervailing tendencies of the new international economic order are constantly eroding American capability. Some of the principal beneficiaries of America's economic decline are the OPEC oil producers in the Persian Gulf. Transfers of Western capital to the Middle East from oil trade not only enabled Saudi Arabia to purchase advanced U.S. equipment such as the F-15 jet fighters, the capital shifts have also produced cracks in the edifice of an international system formerly under the undisputed sway of the United States. In this sense, the strike force symbolizes the military expression of an American drive that is fundamentally economic.

At the military level, the U.S. determination has been generated by a post-Vietnam quest for superiority over the Soviet Union in various regions of the globe, but particularly in the Third World. The Soviets' long-range naval aviation and worldwide client-state bases have given the Soviet Union a capability to cut sea lanes and to project power. Their projection capabilities had become clearly superior to those of the United States by the time the Rapid Deployment Force came into being.[14] For example, whereas the Mediterranean Sea was once regarded as "an American lake," by 1980 the Soviets enjoyed predominance in the eastern Mediterranean. The African countries providing bases for the strike force have thus become enmeshed, willy-nilly, in America's forward strategy for potential warfare on the terrain of Third World countries.

Anti-Sovietism, of course, is the motor force behind the new U.S. military ambitions. Washington seems relatively uncognizant that the decline in American power has come from sagging domestic productivity as well as Soviet and Third World challenges, and it has remained fixated on the Kremlin for virtually every threat to America's international position. A virulent expression of this phenomenon was exclaimed by Secretary Haig at the beginning of the Reagan Administration: "A great deal of what we're saying and doing today is focused on the Soviet problem. . . . It does no good to pretend in our policies or our proclamations that [Soviet activity] is not the most serious threat to world peace that we're facing today."[15] Thus there reappeared an assertion of extreme and reactive American cold war doctrine unheard since the time of John Foster Dulles.

Prudence may eventually impel American policymakers to

reconsider the utility of the Rapid Deployment Force in view of the numerous impediments to its development. Not the least of these is the establishment of military bases on African soil for extra-African objectives. Amelioration of the procedural and technical problems that beset its early organization—such as faulty command coordination among the four branches of the armed services, inadequate long-range transport aircraft for both troops and equipment, poor planning—is within the competence of the American government, while resolution of the external political complexities is not. From the standpoint of U.S. policy toward Africa, the greatest concern must be the possibility of endangering African nations with the threat of nuclear war under peacetime conditions that scarcely promote their interests.

## REGIONAL INTERESTS

The spectacular expansion of U.S. military and strategic interests in Africa is traceable to World War II, when the United States disbursed $5.5 million to Liberia for the construction of Roberts Field,[16] an air base where American aircraft maintained special landing and overflight rights in pursuit of Allied war objectives. Franklin D. Roosevelt became the first American President to set foot in Africa where he passed through Roberts Field in 1943 en route to Morocco to meet Churchill and Stalin at the Casablanca Conference. The establishment of Kagnew Station, a communications installation in Ethiopia, also occurred during World War II. These initial inroads were followed in the Korean War epoch by the construction of U.S. air bases and a naval port in Morocco. Libya, under its first postindependent ruler, King Idriss I, permitted the United States to build Wheelus Air Force Base in 1954 just three years after Libya's independence from Italy. In exchange for the military bases, the United States set an early precedent of providing modest but increasing monetary and military assistance.

With the subsequent termination of these initial operations after 1960, military assistance evolved as a consistent feature of American military policy toward African states. U.S. arms sales, grants, and training of African troops remained very low, averaging less than 5 percent of the worldwide U.S. total until 1976.[17] The chief beneficiaries of this assistance, in descending order, then consisted of Ethiopia, Libya, Morocco, Zaire, Tunisia, South Africa, Liberia, Kenya, and Nigeria. However, after the emergence of Marxist regimes in Angola and Mozambique during 1975, the United States multiplied its assistance to African states in an effort to shore up moderate or pro-Western governments.

Table 5 shows official tabulations of U.S. military sales agreements to the eighteen major recipients in Africa from 1950 to 1980. Egypt, which obtained by far the greatest amount of military assistance, over $2.4 billion in fiscal 1980 alone, led the way in the expansion of U.S. commitments. It was followed by substantial aid to Morocco, Sudan, Kenya, Tunisia, Ethiopia, and Zaire. The United States banned assistance to South Africa in 1963; nevertheless, as discussed later, the embargo failed to arrest all American arms exports, public as well as private, to the apartheid state.

The military sales catapulted the United States into the role of arms exporter to the African continent, though not the leading supplier. Until 1975 France had this position, with clients concentrated in *Afrique noire*. The Soviet Union then rose to first place after providing huge supplies to Angola and Mozambique. The other major Soviet customers included Ethiopia, Libya, and Algeria. The Soviet Union remained the dominant arms supplier to African states by 1981, although the United States trailed close behind as a result of its new outlays to Egypt, Somalia, and Kenya.

American arms supplies to African states have now established U.S. interests throughout the continent. To the military sales must be added such ancillary support as training of African troops from several states, including Egyptian soldiers, who have participated in joint exercises with the Rapid Deployment Force. Perhaps most critical to American policy are the African nations that have placed their military bases and ports at the disposition of U.S. forces. Finally, for separate reasons, South Africa has remained an element of American strategic preoccupation. America's fundamental military and strategic interests, as defined by the aggregate of the above

## TABLE 5

## U.S. FOREIGN MILITARY SALES AGREEMENTS IN AFRICA

(in thousands of dollars by fiscal year)

| | 1950–1970 | 1971 | 1972 | 1973 | 1974 | 1975 | 1976 | 1977 | 1978 | 1979 | 1980 | Total 1950–1980 |
|---|---|---|---|---|---|---|---|---|---|---|---|---|
| Cameroon | — | — | — | — | — | — | — | — | 1,922 | 3,606 | 4 | 5,532 |
| Egypt | 373 | — | — | — | — | — | 62,192 | 1,671 | 162,883 | 449,693 | 2,408,920 | 3,085,733 |
| Ethiopia | 723 | — | 10 | — | 6,272 | 17,301 | 82,108 | 6 | — | — | — | 106,418 |
| Gabon | — | — | — | — | — | 145 | — | 2,094 | — | — | — | 2,239 |
| Ghana | 54 | * | — | — | 193 | 7 | — | 93 | — | — | 125 | 473 |
| Kenya | * | — | — | — | — | — | 67,769 | 2,802 | 2,208 | 45,899 | 12,583 | 131,261 |
| Liberia | 1,226 | — | — | 1,283 | 334 | 422 | 149 | 37 | 28 | 952 | 80 | 4,510 |
| Libya | 26,147 | 632 | 2,672 | 130 | 12 | — | — | — | — | — | — | 29,594 |
| Mali | 89 | — | 48 | — | — | 17 | — | — | — | — | — | 154 |
| Morocco | 26,866 | 2,259 | 7,490 | 2,499 | 8,192 | 281,324 | 105,374 | 37,228 | 7,377 | 3,580 | 321,410 | 803,558 |
| Niger | — | — | — | — | 8 | — | — | — | — | — | — | 8 |
| Nigeria | 352 | — | 2,345 | 639 | 4,200 | 2,818 | 1,763 | 6,735 | 9,593 | 8,026 | 21,685 | 58,157 |
| Senegal | — | — | 4 | — | — | — | 6 | — | — | — | — | 10 |
| Somalia | — | — | — | — | — | — | — | — | — | — | 40,000 | 40,000 |
| South Africa | 3,145 | 1 | 2 | 1 | — | — | — | — | — | — | — | 3,149 |
| Sudan | — | — | — | — | — | — | — | 91,605 | 135,658 | 69,898 | 397 | 297,558 |
| Tunisia | 2,885 | — | — | 2,137 | 722 | 383 | 2,247 | 42,670 | 2,156 | 33,802 | 21,833 | 108,835 |
| Zaire | 1,588 | 16,326 | 286 | 684 | 1,320 | 1,596 | 11,758 | 12,426 | 178,13 | 6,196 | 10,374 | 79,738 |

* Less than $500.
Source: U.S. Department of Defense, *Foreign Military Sales Agreements and Military Assistance Facts, December 1980* (Washington, D.C.: Government Printing Office, 1980).

factors, are now encompassed within three particular regions—North Africa, the Horn of Africa, and southern Africa—and each therefore deserves special scrutiny.

**North Africa.**   The United States established its very first relations in Africa with this region nearly two hundred years ago, when the infant American Republic acquiesced to the payment of tributes, or fees, as the price of trading with the coastal powers then known as the Barbary States of Morocco, Algiers, Tunis, and Tripoli. Seizures of ships and crews, even enslavement, characterized the policies of these masters of the Mediterranean. Until the end of the eighteenth century, such European powers as Great Britain promptly paid the price to guarantee safe maritime passage. Anxious to increase American trade with Mediterranean markets at a time of fledgling U.S. naval strength,[18] the Confederation Congress commissioned a delegation including Thomas Jefferson and Benjamin Franklin to arrange treaties of peace and commerce with the dreaded Barbary powers. Seizure of the frigate *George Washington* by the dey (ruler) of Algiers in October 1800 humiliated the new Republic.

Today the strategic interests of the United States in the Mediterranean are interrelated with Soviet-American competition in the Maghrib, or in the four independent nations—Morocco, Algeria, Tunisia, and Libya—which are the historic heirs to the Barbary States. Libya's close alliance with the Soviet Union and Soviet bloc military presence in Libya constitute the primary concern of American policymakers. A related aspect of this fundamental interest involves the war of independence in the Western Sahara, where Libya and Algeria have supported the Polisario liberation movement against Morocco for the political independence of the phosphate-rich territory. For its part, Tunisia, a longstanding American ally in the Maghrib, has regularly placed its ports at the availability of the United States Sixth Fleet, the major force of the Western alliance in the Mediterranean.

Historically the Mediterranean Sea has served Western maritime and strategic interests. In recent years, France and West Germany have obtained 40 to 45 percent of their oil supplies via this busy body of water. Its economic and strategic serviceability to NATO countries depends on the Suez Canal to its east and the opening to the Azores Islands (and support bases) in the Atlantic Ocean to its west. The Mediterranean, in brief, has been vital to the functions of the Western world.

Though not a part of the Maghrib, Egypt is intimately connected to the region by geography, history, and culture as well as its strategic front on the Mediterranean. The recent reopening of the Suez Canal, now widened and deepened to allow the passage of huge supertankers (with 68-foot draft), has enhanced Egypt's maritime and strategic significance to the entire Western bloc. The United States has fixed on Egypt particularly as a staging zone for the Rapid Deployment Force.

Each of the five Muslim-Arab nations of North Africa has thus become a factor, in one form or another, in U.S. strategic interests. Soviet invasion of Afghanistan in late 1979, and the attendant deployment of Soviet forces within closer range to the Persian Gulf, heightened Washington's anxiety about its interests along the Mediterranean.

The Soviet Union, having emerged as a Mediterranean power, has established its own vital interests in this strategic body of water, called the American lake two decades ago when the United States enjoyed absolute dominance through the NATO Southern Command. From the mid-1960s the Soviets progressively increased their naval presence in the Mediterranean, notably in the eastern basin, and arrived in 1981 with as many as forty to fifty ships in regular operations. The Soviet Mediterranean fleet, often coming from bases in the Black Sea, contained vessels with sophisticated weaponry, including the gigantic *Kiev*-class aircraft carriers, from which planes and helicopters could take off. Soviet ships maintained access to anchorage in such locations as Malta and near Latakia, Syria. These advantages have since resulted in a perceptible superiority of Soviet projection capabilities in the eastern Mediterranean.

In the eyes of American strategists, Libyan leader Muammar

Qaddafi has contributed to an expansion of the Soviet power in the Mediterranean. The Soviet Union now stations in Libya about two thousand Soviet military advisors, while a comparable number of East German security personnel exercise with the Soviets a degree of custodianship over Libya's stocks of Soviet tanks, aircraft, artillery, military electronics, and other sophisticated weaponry, estimated at $12 billion by 1981.[19] Such gargantuan stocks of military hardware are regarded as far beyond the capacity of Libya's forty-thousand-man armed forces to absorb or use.

The possibility of Soviet use of Libyan air bases represents the other salient aspect of the Soviet threat. Although Libya lacks runways long enough to accommodate the new Soviet supersonic bomber "Backfire" (as code-named by NATO), the CIA identified eighty-one usable air fields in Libya, including nineteen with hard-surface runways;[20] some of these could be widened to receive aircraft such as Backfire. Such additions would probably alter the military balance of the entire Mediterranean in favor of the Soviet Union. To forestall speculation about Libya as a site of Soviet bases, Qaddafi emphasized in March 1981 that "from the revolution [1969] until now, we have not permitted naval warships either of the United States or Russia to enter Libyan territorial waters."[21] But his reassurance did not seem to dispel the concern of the men in the Pentagon, nor of such strategists in the field as Admiral William J. Crowe, Jr., the American Commander of Allied Forces South, the Mediterranean area of NATO.[22]

For the first time since World War II, the United States thus faces the prospect of falling to a secondary strategic capability in the Mediterranean. No longer master of the sea, the United States has watched its regional power dwindle relative to the Soviets' enlarged naval presence and Libya's bulging store of arms and petrodollars. Qaddafi specified that Libyan armaments be intended for worthy African or Arab liberation movements, but they can also be quickly activated by Soviet or surrogate troops airlifted from outside Africa.[23] This explains why Allied intelligence analysts wonder whether the arms might also represent prepositioned equipment for Soviet use in the Middle East, Europe, or even in another world war.

Despite Qaddafi's foreign policy, U.S. decision-making concerning Libya is constrained by a high volume of crude oil imports, which resulted in an American balance of payment deficit of nearly $8.5 billion with Libya in 1980.[24] The U.S. oil purchases, amounting to more than $9 billion in that year, accounted for almost 4.5 percent of total American oil consumption. Two NATO partners, West Germany and Italy, shared a much greater dependency on Libya's high-quality crude. The economic factor consequently weighed upon U.S. strategic thinking toward Libya, deterring Washington from punitive actions pondered by certain policymakers, especially a few high-level cold war zealots of the Reagan Administration.

Elsewhere Libya has waged the Arab world's most militant opposition to Egypt, America's North African ally par excellence under Sadat. Without Egypt, which the Arab League suspended because of its separate peace with Israel in the Camp David Accords, the United States would lose a key pivot of the Rapid Deployment Force; without Sadat, who had been constantly opposed by his neighbor, the United States could lose Egypt altogether. For the construction or expansion of bases for the strike force, the Carter Administration had proposed expenditures of $367.4 million, a figure the Reagan Administration raised to $472.6 million in March 1981.[25] This included $106.4 million that was scheduled in 1982 to improve Egypt's port and military base at Ras Banas, a coastal town on the Red Sea across from an important oil terminal in Saudi Arabia. The designated improvements involved runway expansions and aprons for jet fighters and military air transports, shelter for prepositioned supplies of U.S. naval forces, and a staging area for dispatching ground troops into the Middle East. These preparations enlarged America's investment not only in the Rapid Deployment Force but also in Sadat's precarious regime.

Sadat, on the other hand, grew noticeably ambivalent toward Egypt's inexorable incorporation into U.S. strategy, especially as it related to the port and air field at Ras Banas. Not only did Washington solicit Egyptian approval for nuclear-powered warships to pass through the Suez Canal under a formula of safety standards that would exclude Soviet vessels; the United States also pressed Sadat to sign a contract for American use of Ras Banas, which the Pentagon proposed to spend $400 million improving.[26] Sadat denied both requests, intensely aware, as the Reagan Administration was not, of his internal and external risks that such thorough immersion in American military policy would engender. In 1981 the Egyptian leader still found himself between a Scylla of Islamic fundamentalists at home, and a Charybdis of Libyan and other anti-Sadat Arabs abroad.

In view of Libya's anti-Western posture and Egypt's political ambivalence, Morocco, a historic ally of the United States, assumed special significance to American policymakers. Morocco first resurfaced as an object of American strategic policy during the 1950s, those early cold war years when the United States committed itself to the defense of Western Europe as a goal of American national interest. Like France, which ruled Morocco under a quasi-colonial protectorate until its independence in 1956, the United States found a receptive ally in the traditional Moroccan monarchy whose orientation was patently pro-Western. In keeping with the network of mutual security alliances Washington was then establishing, the United States and France selected five sites in Morocco for the construction of strategic air bases. Three of these became bases for the Strategic Air Command and were not phased out until 1963. An American naval communications facility at Port Lyautey functioned until its termination by U.S. initiative in 1978. Yet the conclusion of these operations did not terminate Moroccan-American military association, for Morocco continued to permit port visits by U.S. naval vessels and transit rights to U.S. military aircraft.

The United States also became indirectly involved in Morocco's struggle for the annexation of the Western Sahara, a territory of no vital interest to the United States that was claimed by Moroccan King Hassan II as part of Morocco's historic domain. The war began in 1975 when Spain, the colonial ruler, arbitrarily relinquished control of the territory's northern two thirds to Morocco and the southern one third to Mauritania. The Polisario—an acronym for the Popular Front for the Liberation of Saguia el-Hamra and Rio de Oro, the two major sectors forming a single entity under Spain's domination—resorted to guerrilla warfare against both Morocco and Mauritania. At the request of the United Nations, the International Court of Justice at The Hague ruled in 1975 that neither country should have territorial sovereignty over the Western Sahara and, further, their administrative function should cease as soon as the problem of Saharan self-determination could be resolved. Algeria, the second largest U.S. oil supplier in Africa, joined Libya in prompt military and political support to the Polisario.[27] In August 1979 Mauritania dropped its irredentist claims after devastating attacks by Polisario guerrillas.

The United States meanwhile pursued a dualistic, if not contradictory, policy; it recognized Moroccan administrative control but not its claim to sovereignty over the territory. As can be seen in Table 5, U.S. military sales to Morocco, amounting to about $105 million in 1976, later declined as the Carter Administration restricted arms sales to equipment deemed suitable for use only within Morocco's internationally recognized boundaries, or what Harold Saunders, the Assistant Secretary of State for Near Eastern and South Asian Affairs, identified as "the Morocco proper."[28] (Incongruously, the State Department and other U.S. governmental agencies situate North African countries in the State Department jurisdiction responsible for the Near East and South Asia.)

Given Washington's inability to control the use of American-supplied weaponry after its arrival in Morocco, the Moroccans obviously had a free hand to utilize it in the Western Sahara as well as in "Morocco proper." A congressional study mission headed by Stephen J. Solarz, Chairman of the House Subcommittee on Africa, visited Morocco during April 1979 and found that it had used such American equipment as F-5 jet fighters and recoilless guns (106-millimeter) in the Western Sahara.[29] This discovery similarly confirmed the unrealistic nature of American arms policy toward Morocco.

The Carter Administration nonetheless maintained its guideline of "forthcomingness," or action by Morocco toward a negotiated settlement of Saharan self-determination, as a condition for U.S. military assistance. Congress largely supported the President. Then came the so-called Carter doctrine in January 1980, and the flames of a cold war resurgence were lit, reversing American strategic considerations on several issues, including congressional opposition to military support for Hassan II. The Administration subsequently approved the sale of additional reconnaissance planes and jet fighters,[30] though without relinquishing the old guideline or delivering the equipment.

In one of his first decisions as Secretary of State, Alexander Haig approved the sale of 108 M-60 tanks to Morocco.[31] This equipment, previously requested by Morocco, had been denied by the Carter Administration. Haig also approved the scheduled delivery of the reconnaissance planes and jet fighters approved conditionally by the Carter Administration. The policy of the Reagan Administration, which imposed no requirements on Morocco, was a clear departure from past policies. An extreme reliance on the supply of weapons as a substitute for diplomacy quickly became a trademark in Reagan's approach to foreign policy generally.

The immediate effect of the new policy was to recharge Morocco's resolve to continue its struggle for annexation. It also indirectly placed the United States in opposition to Saharan decolonization. In prolonging a war that cost Morocco perhaps $1 million daily, and which it probably could not win, King Hassan II also enlisted Washington's firmer commitment to Moroccan defense. These developments raised the likelihood of increasing Libyan and Algerian military assistance to the Polisario. Most critically, the expanding American military role sowed the seeds of Soviet bloc support to the Polisario, and thereby of a greater and more dangerous militarization of the region.

In the whole of North Africa, the United States thus encountered unresolved and potentially explosive problems at the beginning of the 1980s. None of the strategic problems, moreover, could be resolved by unilateral American action. Curtailment of Soviet expansion in the Mediterranean seemed unlikely in view of Soviet preeminence in the eastern basin, not to mention its growing military ties to Libya. The expansion of U.S. military stakes in Egypt neither enhanced Sadat's viability nor guaranteed the future positions of the Rapid Deployment Force. Prolongation of the war in the Western Sahara invited cold war regional alignments reflective of the American-Soviet competition. Above all, the anti-Soviet retrenchment of the Reagan Administration was certain to lead to a new test of will in North Africa. That test came in August 1981 when jet fighters from the Sixth Fleet shot down two Libyan planes near Libyan territory in the Gulf of Sidra.

*The Horn of Africa.*   This region emerged as a realm of U.S. strategic interest after Soviet bloc military forces arrived there during the 1970s. Strategy for the Rapid Deployment Force later augmented America's interest in the region. In addition to Ethiopia, which aligned with the Soviet Union and Cuba in 1977, the Horn is comprised of Sudan, Djibouti, Somalia, and Kenya. The Horn's strategic value derives from its location on the Red Sea and the Indian Ocean, or, stated in terms related to U.S. strategic interests, from its proximity to the Persian Gulf. With neighbors Djibouti and Somalia, Ethiopia shares geographic command of the Straits of Bab al Mandab, which form the narrow passageway from the Indian Ocean and the Gulf of Aden to the Red Sea and the Suez Canal. The countries of the Horn touch upon some of the world's most critical waterways and have therefore appealed strongly to strategic planners in the White House and the Kremlin alike.

Kenya and Somalia became associated with America's global strategy through their military bases put at the disposition of the Rapid Deployment Force. Kenya, whose capitalist system has contributed to its alliance with the United States since independence, has been a major African recipient of American aid, securing more than $131 million in military sales agreements from 1950 to 1980 (see Table 5). Somalia, having signed a treaty of friendship and cooperation with Moscow in 1974, remained an ally of the Soviets until it expelled them three years later in retaliation for their growing support to Ethiopia, Somalia's adversary in the

Ogaden war. As a result of an American-Somalian agreement in 1980, the United States became the beneficiary of the excellent Soviet-built airport and harbor of Berbera on the Gulf of Aden.

For the benefit of the Rapid Deployment Force, the Reagan Administration committed $24 million to Somalia during 1982 to repair oil storage and other facilities at the port of Berbera.[32] In Kenya, another $26 million was earmarked to dredge the port at Mombasa as well as to provide it with additional fleet support. These changes were endorsed by Defense Secretary Weinberger immediately after taking office, and thus indicated the Administration's plan for long-term access to the African bases.

In view of the U.S. foothold in Kenya and Somalia, American policymakers continued to perceive Ethiopia as their central strategic problem because of nearly twelve hundred Soviet military advisors and thirteen thousand Cuban soldiers still there in late 1981 supporting the Marxist leadership of Colonel Mengistu Haile Mariam. His military regime had come to power in the aftermath of a revolution won without external support. During the long reign of Emperor Haile Selassie, the United States had been Ethiopia's main ally; the singular importance Washington conferred on this alliance was revealed by the fact that Ethiopia remained the major African recipient of U.S. military and economic assistance in the two decades between 1950 and 1970. At Kagnew, near the city of Asmara, the United States operated a large communications base that was not dismantled until 1974 by agreement. The electronic surveillance equipment at Kagnew base had enabled the United States to monitor Soviet activities in Africa and around the Indian Ocean.

However, after the revolution of February 1974 toppled the emperor and elevated Mengistu to power, Ethiopia's new socialist leadership embarked on a radical foreign policy that culminated in November 1978 with a twenty-year treaty of friendship and cooperation between Ethiopia and the Soviet Union. The Dergue, as the ruling Provisional Military Administrative Council was called, had adopted Marxism-Leninism by this time. It had also expelled the U.S. military advisory mission from the country and settled Soviet and Cuban advisors in the plush houses previously inhabited by the Americans.

The Soviet Union was motivated as well by those strategic assets of Ethiopia that earlier had solidified its alliance with the United States. Ethiopia's location directly on the Red Sea and close to the Straits of Bab al Mandab, its proximity to the Arabian Peninsula, its potential control of the Blue Nile flowing through the Sudan and Egypt, and its suitability as a staging point for other activities in both Arab and African nations must have entered Soviet strategic thinking.[33] The Soviets were also excited by the prospect of using the two Eritrean ports of Assab and Massawa, which seemed fortunate substitutes for their loss of the Berbera port.

What followed was the Soviets' most massive assistance program in Africa, amounting to roughly $2 billion by 1981. Consisting of military aid primarily, the Soviet program was enlarged by additional assistance from several other Eastern European countries. This included a $46 million loan from Czechoslovakia in 1978 for plant construction; a $20 million loan in 1977 from East Germany for plant equipment, and a later $2 million loan for expansion of the Assab port.[34] Fidel Castro, who visited Ethiopia in March 1977, soon provided five hundred medical personnel, two to three thousand scholarships for Ethiopians to study in Cuban schools, and perhaps sixteen thousand soldiers to assist Ethiopia against internal opposition and Somalia. The East Germans took over the training of Ethiopian police and security forces. Thanks to the Soviet bloc assistance, Ethiopia developed one of Africa's biggest armies by 1980, equipped with modern weapons, including the first Mig-23s in any Black African state. These factors enabled the army to defeat Somalia in the Ogaden as well as the Eritrean guerrillas fighting for secession in the north of Ethiopia.

During the early phases of the Ethiopian revolution that led to the overthrow of Haile Selassie the Ford Administration resisted the temptation to rupture relations with Ethiopia, hoping that continued ties would give the United States some leverage with the new regime. As a matter of fact, Washington approved an agreement for $82 million in military sales to Ethiopia in fiscal

1976 (see Table 5). Congressional opposition to Secretary of State Kissinger's policy toward Angola largely precluded strong U.S. reaction in any case. But in February 1977, as Jimmy Carter settled in at the White House, American-Ethiopian relations reached a watershed when the Dergue declared its intention to henceforth seek arms from countries more attuned to its new ideological orientation. Apparently unknown to Washington, Ethiopia had already, in December 1976, initiated its relationship with Moscow through a secret arms deal.

The subsequent influx of Soviet assistance and Cuban soldiers has produced a cleavage unmatched in U.S. relations with any African country except Angola. Though continuing humanitarian assistance to Ethiopia, the Carter Administration suspended developmental assistance and preferential trade treatment because of Ethiopia's expropriation of certain U.S. properties without compensation. The Administration further publicized its willingness to consider African requests for assistance to maintain security in the region. Pressed for demonstrative anti-Soviet action by his National Security Advisor Zbigniew Brzezinski, the President thus served notice of a stiffening American response to Ethiopia's realignment with Moscow. The militant anti-Soviet posture of the Reagan Administration later widened the chasm in American-Ethiopian relations.

Although the new Ethiopian regime was socialist, this was not a decisive factor in the strained U.S.-Ethiopian relations. The United States had established diplomatic relations with the Marxist government of Mozambique. Strategically, however, Ethiopia's alliance with the Soviet Union facilitated Soviet maneuverability in the Indian Ocean, and this lodged an intractable wedge in the future of American-Ethiopian relations. Although the Carter Administration retained diplomatic ties, the strategic issue none-theless became a prime concern in Washington amid the resurgent cold war fervor.

Ethiopia's offensive in the Ogaden war, which provoked an influx of thousands of refugees into Somalia during 1979, also catalyzed African alliances that more or less reflected American-Soviet polarization in the Horn. Egypt and Sudan, for instance, extended military or moral support to Somalia. Libya, on the other hand, supported Ethiopia. (Kenya also backed Ethiopia, but for a nonideological reason—namely, Somalia's irredentist claim to northern Kenya.) The impact of bipolar competition between the superpowers on inter-African relations was to increase divisiveness among the countries.

Djibouti, France's last colony in Africa, also became involved in these developments because of the internecine rivalry between the country's minority Afar population and its dominant, Somali-speaking Issas. Until Djibouti's independence in 1977, Djibouti port served as Ethiopia's main export route. The French retained a large naval base there during the colonial era, and the port remained an object of Western, especially French, interest. Djibouti held considerable strategic importance because of its location at the point where the African coast approaches the Arabian Peninsula forming the Straits of Bab al Mandab, the vital passageway between the Red Sea and the Indian Ocean. The American-Soviet polarization tended to spread into Djibouti as a result of the Issas' affinity with Somalia and the Afars' with Ethiopia.

The cold war dimension of U.S. policy assumed acute significance after the formation of the Rapid Deployment Force. Through its massive support to Ethiopia, the Soviet Union revealed both a policy of resolute support to a new African ally as well as a perception of Ethiopia as a Soviet beachhead of long duration. A profound ideological stake further attached the Kremlin to Ethiopia. As David and Marina Ottaway observed in *Afrocommunism,* the Soviets "saw in Ethiopia with its class conflicts a much greater revolutionary potential than in any other African country, even shades of their own revolution."[35] The huge contingent of Cuban soldiers reinforced the Soviet commitment.

The United States, with a base at nearby Berbera, clearly risked potential Soviet bloc challenges in the very region where the strike force had established military installations. Furthermore, the Soviet bases at Aden in South Yemen (on the Arabian Peninsula) and at

Dahlak Island in the Red Sea multiplied the potential for Soviet-American collisions in the area. Late in 1981, Washington prepared for a long-range regional presence by establishing military ties to Sudan, Africa's largest country.

The Horn of Africa thus became integrated into America's strategy toward the Persian Gulf, while being turned into a hotbed of tension through the strategic competition of the superpowers. Barring contrary vicissitudes of regional politics, the Soviet Union will resist being dislodged from its position in Ethiopia just as the United States will cling to its stakes in Kenya and Somalia. The Horn's sudden transformation into a new theater of the cold war has resulted from the expanding cold war developments. Though largely unnoticed by the general American public, even by Congress, these unprecedented events portend unpredictable but dangerous problems for the United States in an age of nuclear vulnerabilities.

**Southern Africa.** This region stretches from Mozambique around the Cape of Good Hope up to Angola. The strategic interest of the United States in the region centers on the Republic of South Africa. These interests have been determined by three critical stakes. The first stake is the concentration of U.S. corporate interests in the apartheid state. The second stake, economic and strategic in nature, is the maritime route around the Cape of Good Hope, which is a passageway for petroleum and nonfuel minerals shipped to Western Europe and, to a far lesser extent, to the United States too. The third stake, a security interest, concerns the perpetual state of racial conflict caused by South Africa's apartheid system, which threatens to engulf the United States in African racial warfare of gigantic proportions. Although Americans have established growing interests in Zimbabwe, and retain interests in Mozambique and Angola, South Africa and its apartheid control of Namibia represent the core of U.S. interests in the rim of southern Africa.

The corporate stake consists of about 350 American companies with aggregate direct investments of $2 billion in 1980 (see

Chapter 7). These constitute the bulk of U.S. investments on the African continent. The Cape sea route, which connects the South Atlantic and Indian Oceans, serves nearly 25,000 ships annually, about half of which call at South African ports with their cargoes of Middle Eastern oil. The ships transport 90 percent of Western Europe's petroleum imports, 70 percent of its strategic minerals, 25 percent of its food supply as well as 20 percent of America's oil imports.[36] Until recently the Mediterranean Sea had not been a practical alternative to the Cape route because the supertankers carrying Persian Gulf oil were too large to navigate the Suez Canal. Although the canal has been enlarged to accommodate the supertankers, it can still easily be closed in the event of Arab-Israeli hostilities (as in the Arab-Israeli wars of 1956 and 1967). The Cape route is therefore vitally involved in the economic and security interests of the United States and its NATO allies.

Today, however, the most sensitive U.S. interest in southern Africa—and the salient threat to peace in the entire region—is the racial conflict in South Africa. A dictatorial White minority has armed itself in preparation for a prospective confrontation with a Black majority increasingly in revolt against the inveterate system of White supremacy. This conflict extends also to Namibia, where the protracted war of liberation led by SWAPO could induce American or Soviet intervention, if not both. The United States will not be able to escape taking a final, definitive position on apartheid in the present decade. As explained by Colin Legum, the Africanist scholar born in South Africa, "it is difficult to see how the communal and other types of conflict in this important region—especially in the Republic of South Africa—can be resolved without violence or without international involvement."[37]

Beginning with the Kennedy Administration, a new American military policy toward South Africa was established. In 1962 the United States unilaterally declared an embargo on the sale of arms and military equipment that South Africa could use in the enforcement of apartheid. This basic policy was strengthened on August 2, 1963, when U.N. Ambassador Adlai E. Stevenson proclaimed the White House's intention "to bring to an end the sale of all military equipment to the government of South Africa by the end of this calendar year."[38] A U.N. embargo, approved by the United States, prohibited the sale and shipment to South Africa of arms, ammunition, and military vehicles as well as equipment and materials for the manufacture and maintenance of arms and ammunition there.

The new American policy, as implemented by the Johnson Administration during 1964, imposed two important guidelines: a prohibition on the sale of all military equipment of significant value to military, paramilitary, and police forces in training or combat; a prohibition on maintenance of arms and munitions. Omitted from these guidelines were foreign arms manufacturers using American components, but this was corrected in 1968 by a third guideline that outlawed the use of these components in the foreign manufacture of arms, ammunition, and other weapons-related items for South Africa.

A related aspect of the new policy concerned limitations on U.S. naval visits to South African ports, and on contacts with American officials or visits to the United States by South African military officials. Washington suspended U.S. Navy visits to South Africa in 1967. The Navy, which sometimes traversed South Africa's Cape route, had previously made stopovers at its Simonstown naval base, where Black American sailors encountered racial harassment on shore leave. Thus, the naval restrictions represented a protest against both apartheid and South Africans' racism directed at Americans.

The Carter Administration amplified the basic policy in 1977 by endorsing the U.N. vote to make the 1963 arms embargo mandatory. The Department of Commerce in 1978 further expanded U.S. export restrictions by prohibiting all exports an American exporter either knows, or has reason to know, are destined for use by the South African military or police. The latter prohibition was clearly the most comprehensive because it was not limited to weapons and other military equipment but applied to every item exported from the United States to South Africa.

America's policy on arms restrictions to the White supremacy dictatorship, now in effect for nearly two decades, has curtailed drastically South Africa's acquisition of U.S. military equipment. However, the policy has not blocked South Africa's access to all American equipment. Numerous loopholes exist in the restrictions. For instance, the guidelines exempted preexisting contracts for military items completed by August 1963, with the result that the South African government obtained roughly $30 million in U.S. military supplies from 1963 until April 1973.[39] The 1963 U.N. embargo, moreover, did not specify so-called dual-purpose equipment—items such as noncombat aircraft, computers, and electronic equipment, which can be used for both civilian and military purposes. The result was that sales of these unspecified materials continued despite their obvious utility to South African security forces. The Johnson Administration sought to close this loophole in 1964 by limiting sales of dual-purpose equipment to civilian end users.

The Nixon Administration deliberately relaxed certain restrictions on arms to South Africa in accordance with its Angola ("tar baby") policy. For example, when Henry Kissinger was National Security Advisor, he recommended that the United States "enforce [the] arms embargo against South Africa but with liberal treatment of equipment which could serve either military or civilian purposes."[40] President Nixon approved this National Security Council recommendation in January 1970, paving the way for the most permissive interpretations that tended to violate the spirit, if not the letter, of the 1963 embargo. One such subterfuge had already occurred in the mid-1960s with the sale of at least twenty-two Cessna Model-185 light planes, which the State Department classified as civilian equipment. The South African military magazine *Paratus* disclosed, however, that these planes were to be used in border surveillance against SWAPO guerrillas.[41]

Whereas the 1964 guidelines of the Johnson Administration prohibited exports of dual-purpose equipment without strong assurances that it would not be used by South Africa's military, the Nixon policy permitted such exports to both civilians and the military in the absence of strong evidence indicating an explicit combat-related use. The change amounted to a convenient device for Washington to supply Pretoria with certain equipment that otherwise would have been denied by the guidelines. In fact, the Nixon Administration did not publicly admit the existence of any guidelines for enforcing the embargo.

Under Nixon's permissive policy, South Africa obtained substantial quantities of dual-purpose items that could be adapted for use by the military. These included sixteen Lockheed L-100 cargo planes and seven Swearingen Merlin-IV transports. (The L-100 cargoes are comparable to Lockheed's C-130 Hercules cargo planes flown by the U.S. Air Force, and the Merlin-IV transports are executive-type transport planes capable of carrying fifteen to twenty paratroopers or five thousand pounds of cargo over distances of several hundred miles.)[42] Other U.S. civilian equipment adaptable to military purposes included computers, communications systems, navigational devices, and military vehicles. Much of this equipment was subsequently utilized by the South African military or police.

President Carter sought to reverse this practice in pursuit of his human rights approach to foreign policy. First, he rescinded Nixon's policy on the export of dual-purpose equipment. Second, the Commerce Department promulgated new and more stringent export regulations in February 1978 "to further U.S. foreign policy regarding the preservation of human rights by denying access to U.S.-origin commodities and technical data by the military and police entities of the Republic of South Africa and Namibia."[43] These regulations banned the knowing export and reexport of all commodities and technical data of American origin to the South African military or police. For the first time, Washington also publicized the specific items of military-related equipment that the new embargo covered.

In an extraordinary shift from the Nixon policy, Carter's regulations embargoed not only military-related commodities, but all items under the Commerce Department's jurisdiction, including technical data and consumer goods that an exporter knows, or has reason to know, are to be purchased or used by South Africa's military or police. The regulations applied both to exports and reexports, and therefore prohibited the export of items that passed through third countries en route to South Africa. These amendments constituted the most definitive interdiction of U.S. supplies to South Africa since the embargo of 1963. They indicated Washington's clear intention to at least deny U.S. support to the coercive forces of apartheid.

Strict as the Carter regulations were, they did not cause an absolute termination of American military-related equipment shipped to South Africa because of residual loopholes in the restrictions as well as outright legal violations by a few American exporters. For example, the regulations administered by the Commerce Department did not ban sales of noncombat military equipment and dual-purpose equipment to civilians and governmental agencies excluding the military and police. These sales pertained to such items as computer technology, civilian aircraft, and airborne and ground-based communications equipment that South African importers could easily convert to military uses. Although nominally these sales constituted commercial transactions between American firms and private South African buyers, the U.S. government was directly involved through the Commerce Department, which authorized all civilian exports to South Africa, and through the Export-Import Bank, which assumed the risk for local banks' loans at American taxpayers' expense. The State Department was responsible for ensuring that the South African military did not obtain military equipment in accordance with the 1963 embargo. Five weeks after the United Nations adopted the embargo of 1977, the State Department approved the sale to South Africa of six Cessna planes for civilian use, surely aware that Pretoria had used these for counterinsurgent border patrol in the past.

Intelligence cooperation between the United States and South Africa constituted another significant aspect of U.S. military policy not covered by the embargo of 1977. This omission pertained to exchanges of information between the CIA and the Bureau of State Security (BOSS), the espionage apparatus organized by the apartheid state in 1968. The two agencies maintained extremely close contacts.[44] South Africa had facilitated the CIA's development of a mercenary army to suppress the Congo rebellion, and South Africa's intelligence network subsequently shared the CIA's violent antipathy toward communism.[45] The CIA's role also involved South African race relations, and this particular collaboration has been sharply criticized by C. Clyde Ferguson, a Deputy Assistant Secretary of State for African Affairs under Nixon: "It is incomprehensible that the United States should be cooperating with South Africa's intelligence operation organization, knowing that its main job is to keep the Africans in check."[46]

American companies have provided South Africa with arms in flagrant violation of State Department restrictions and the U.N. embargo. For example, Colt Industries and the Winchester Group of Olin Corporation manufactured small arms as well as ammunition and exported them to South Africa via third countries from 1971 to 1975.[47] Similarly, the Space Research Corporation shipped 55,000 long-range (155-millimeter) artillery shells to the South African government during 1977 and 1978.[48] The company further equipped the South African army with the GC-45 howitzer, a cannon reported to be the most advanced artillery in the world.[49] Although the U.S. government prosecuted the violators, their infractions exposed the relative ineffectiveness of existing prohibitions.

The Carter regulations did not apply to an American exporter who did not know, or had no reason to know, that a dual-purpose item in question would be utilized by South Africa's military or police. Such loopholes permitted, if not encouraged, legalistic legerdemain with which U.S. exporters could flout the law. American exporters escaped all penalty if South African purchasers simply provided no clue or information that the equipment would be transferred to the forces of coercion.

Once in South Africa, the U.S. equipment comes under the jurisdiction of South African laws, which can easily nullify the intent of Washington's regulations. Although the Commerce Department may vigorously limit dual-purpose exports to South African civilians and governmental agencies other than the military or police, South Africa's National Supplies Procurement Act (1970) authorizes the seizure of any goods or services deemed necessary or expedient for the security of the apartheid system. Section 100 of South Africa's Defense Act (1957) authorizes Pretoria to commandeer any articles for a variety of military purposes, including maintaining internal order. Furthermore, the U.S. regulations are automatically rendered null and void by South African importers who act in collusion with their police or military when obtaining U.S. equipment. Thus it is safe to conclude that any U.S. exports susceptible to conversion or modification for military purposes, especially equipment requested by the apartheid regime, may end up in the hands of the South African security forces.

This conclusion applies in particular to U.S. assistance to South Africa in nuclear energy. Especially pertinent is a $4.5 million research reactor completed at Pelindaba in 1965 by Allis Chalmers, an American corporation. From 1965 to 1975 the U.S. government also provided South Africa with highly enriched uranium in addition to training South African nuclear scientists and engineers at laboratories of the Atomic Energy Commission (now under the Department of Energy).[50] United States assistance conformed to a 1957 American-South African agreement (later amended) that authorized the export of U.S. nuclear equipment and enriched uranium for use in a research reactor. The agreement expressly forbade the use of these materials for the development of atomic weapons or other military purposes.[51] A 1965 agreement (later amended) provided for the operation of the reactor under safeguards of the International Atomic Energy Agency, and it remains in effect, like the bilateral agreement, until the year 2007. South Africa further agreed in 1974 not to use nuclear materials supplied by the United States for the construction of a nuclear device, even for peaceful applications. In 1975, however, the United States stopped exports of uranium, heretofore supplied in small quantities in the form of prefabricated fuel rods, because South Africa refused to sign the Nuclear Non-Proliferation Treaty. This international treaty obliges nations that do not already have nuclear weapons to renounce their right to them.

South Africa's refusal strengthened a widely held assumption that

Pretoria was preparing to build an atomic bomb. Its industrial and technological infrastructure facilitated the production of nuclear weapons, and its own proven reserves of uranium—the Western world's third largest after those of the United States and Sweden—provided the apartheid regime with the potential to satisfy future supplies from domestic sources. The termination of U.S. uranium exports apparently forced the Pelindaba reactor to operate far below capacity. Eventually South Africa could overcome this impediment by obtaining the necessary enriched fuel from its own enrichment facility, or from an alternative supplier, such as France. Namibia, which is rich in diamonds, also contains large deposits of uranium that are already available to South Africa.

South Africa was hardly deterred by the U.S. decision to end uranium exports in 1975 because it began the construction of full-scale nuclear plants the following year. A French company contracted to install two 922-megawatt lightwater reactors in the town of Koeberg (near Cape Town).[52] A French banking consortium financed the project, estimated to rise in cost to $1 billion by 1984.

The world assumed that South Africa was prepared to launch an atomic weapon in August 1977 following Soviet satellite reports of nuclear testing in South Africa's Kalahari Desert. Data from American satellites confirmed the existence there of ground-based structures closely resembling facilities used in the experimental testing of nuclear devices. In its turn, the South African government not only denied detonating a nuclear device, but even insisted that no such structures existed. The Kalahari installations mysteriously disappeared after protests against future tests by France, Great Britain, and the United States. The Carter Administration subsequently yielded to Pretoria's denial. Washington's retreat raised serious doubts about its enforcement of the agreements outlawing South Africa's use of American-supplied materials for military purposes. Far more disturbing, this retreat opened to question U.S. capacity to detect and verify nuclear operations by other distant countries, including the Soviet Union.

An explosion in the South Atlantic in September 1979, also apparently unleashed by South Africa, underscored the uncertainty regarding America's nuclear detection capability. The Carter Administration failed to determine the source of the explosion, or even if a nuclear blast had actually occurred.

Whether South Africa possesses nuclear weapons has never been confirmed. There is no doubt, however, that it has the wherewithal necessary to produce nuclear devices from South African resources, thanks in large part to past U.S. assistance. The evidence suggests that the White supremacy state can now build atomic weapons, and in a short time; it may, in fact, have already done so.

Through various schemes, South Africa has clearly flouted certain features of U.S. military policy. For instance, the Piaggio P-166 patrol plane was built by an Italian company using American (Avco-Lycoming) engines; it carries as many as twelve passengers or 2,500 pounds of cargo, and can also be armed with a variety of bombs.[53] Without the cooperation of its allies, the United States cannot prevent South Africa from obtaining American-supplied equipment and materials.

France was the main source of arms exported to South Africa in the second half of the 1970s. The French supplied as much as 53 percent of South Africa's imports of major weapons. These included Agosta submarines, A-69 frigates, and Mirage F-1C airplanes.[54] France has also provided aircraft containing U.S. components, such as the Cessna Model-337 Skymaster. French Mirage jet fighters, the most sophisticated aircraft in southern Africa, have been used in South Africa's attacks on Angola.[55] French arms exports to South Africa dropped sharply after France endorsed the U.N. mandatory arms embargo in 1977; for instance, the French canceled South Africa's orders for four warships. Nevertheless, it is clear that past military sales from France, together with those from Italy, the second largest arms supplier to South Africa throughout the 1970s, assisted the White supremacy state decisively in the consolidation of its military arsenal.

Israel, the world's largest recipient of U.S. economic and military assistance, obtaining as much as $2.2 billion annually, has been another major supplier of military assistance to South Africa.[56] Indeed, the principal buyer of Israeli arms is the apartheid state, which received 35 percent of Israel's total export of weapons in 1979. Israel's Uzi submachine gun, manufactured under license in South Africa, is standard equipment in the South African army. Reshef-class fast patrol boats, armed with Gabriel ship-to-ship missiles, have been purchased by South Africa.[57] During 1976 South African naval personnel were trained in Israel to operate the boats. Israeli and South African military attachés have frequently consulted on counterinsurgency tactics. An Israeli private firm, Tadiran Electronics, was reported ready in 1977 to establish a subsidiary in South Africa for the manufacture of electronic devices for counterinsurgency.[58]

The Reagan Administration, after only two months in office, moved in a sudden new direction of U.S. support to the apartheid regime. This suggested a serious retreat from official policy toward South Africa of the last two decades. In reference to South Africa's rigid system of racial segregation, President Reagan defended U.S. support on both moral and strategic grounds: "As long as there's a sincere and honest effort being made [by the apartheid regime], based on our own experience in our own land, it would seem to me that we should be trying to be helpful. . . . Can we abandon a country . . . that strategically is essential to the free world in its production of minerals we all must have and so forth?"[59]

The first evidence of a rupture of established policy followed when five senior South African military officers, including the chief of military intelligence, secretly arrived in the United States and consulted with NSC officials and the Pentagon's Defense Intelligence Agency. Reagan's Ambassador to the United Nations, Jeane J. Kirkpatrick, holding a policy-level position in the Administration, received the South African intelligence chief, General P. W. Van der Westhuizen, in New York. The South Africans' visits and consultation with U.S. officials violated longstanding U.S. policy outlawing official business visits to this country by members of South Africa's armed forces. A proviso of the embargo on U.S. arms sales to South Africa had carefully specified this prohibition. Here then, in the interest of South Africa, was a blatant breach of U.S. law by the American government itself.

Although the White House expelled the South Africans and attempted to excuse the infraction by stating that they had obtained visas from the U.S. Embassy in Pretoria by concealing their identity as military leaders, the disingenuous excuse glossed over the chilling fact that they had already completed their clandestine consultations before the expulsion. What increased the insidious character of the U.S.-South African exchanges was their occurrence in the same week that the Administration declared its eagerness to repeal the Clark amendment, which prohibited covert U.S. assistance against the regime in Angola. The severity of these developments provoked the African Group at the United Nations, consisting of representatives from the fifty African member-states, to alert the U.N. Secretary-General of the "dangerous consequences" that could result from a change in U.S. policy toward South Africa.[60]

Past American arms sales to South Africa, coupled with those of America's allies, have helped the White supremacy dictatorship to modernize its armed forces and to develop them into the most powerful of any on the African continent. The net effect of the Western military assistance has been to reinforce South Africa's capacity to maintain apartheid domination internally as well as in Namibia.

South Africa, of course, is now a major arms manufacturer itself. Its productive capacity ranges from conventional to nuclear weapons. Over the years South Africa acquired this capability through the development of its industrial and technological infrastructure, which is more advanced than that of many European nations. Indeed, in developmental terms, the White portion of South African society is a completely modern and industrial entity in every respect. None of this development was possible without the essential support and cooperation provided by the United States and its Western allies. They therefore have a direct responsibility today in seeking to eradicate the system of racial repression which their past assistance helped to consolidate.

South Africa has also become a major arms exporter. As a critical case in point, the White minority regime of Rhodesia obtained

98.7 percent of South Africa's arms exports from 1970 to 1979, strengthening its capacity to fight the anticolonial forces that nonetheless managed to bring their war of national liberation to a successful conclusion. Military trade has further linked South Africa to Taiwan and South Korea. South Africa's production and export of armaments has thus intensified the spread of dangerous weapons in the world.

South Africa's objection to the Nuclear Non-Proliferation Treaty has heightened international tension regarding its likely production of nuclear weapons. The apartheid regime, systematically gearing itself for confrontation for many years, has developed what it calls "total strategy" to resist opposition from internal insurrection as well as external challenges from independent African governments.[61] In 1968 the Afrikaner government created the Armaments Development Corporation (Armscor), a state-owned company that either manufactures equipment for the defense forces or buys it from local or foreign contractors, overtly and covertly. Armscor is one of South Africa's fastest growing industries. In the aftermath of the U.N. embargo of 1977, and its endorsement by those who formerly supplied arms, such as France, items now produced by South Africa under license include the French Mirage interceptor aircraft, a local version of the Italian Miacchi jet-training aircraft, French-designed Panhard armored cars, Israeli-designed missile boats, air-to-air missiles, artillery pieces, and a wide variety of ammunition.[62] This formidable output has converted the White community into a fortresslike society, all of whose members have been trained to supplement the defense strategy with their personal firearms.

By comparison with the independent states of Africa, South Africa has predominated in the buildup of military weapons. It has ranked as the continent's biggest importer of arms for the past two decades. Military expenditures by the apartheid regime consistently consumed a dominant part of the governmental budget. For the year ending March 1980, for example, South Africa committed $2.3 billion, or 17.5 percent of the central government's budget, to military expenditures; in contrast, Nigeria, Africa's most populous nation, committed $1.7 billion, or about 9.7 percent of state expenditures, to the military.[63] The singularly huge South African allocations should also be seen in the racial context they were meant to serve: the expenditures were intended almost exclusively for the military and police purposes of the 4 million Whites in the country. Therefore these expenditures cannot, as in the case of Nigeria, be correlated with South Africa's total population of 22 million. On this basis it can be said that the White South Africans maintain one of the biggest ratios of arms expenditures to population size in the world.

South Africa's well-armed dictatorship, in short, has become a threat to international peace and security. With die-hard determination, the Whites struggle to maintain their supremacy in South Africa and Namibia. But the Black majorities under apartheid rule cannot be expected to continue to tolerate their domination; and they constitute a permanent reservoir of manpower for nationalist forces such as the ANC, who are committed to the defeat of apartheid at any cost. The great danger for the United States lies in being engulfed in South Africa's racial conflagration, or perhaps more ominously in being dragged into confrontation with the Soviet Union, a strong supporter of SWAPO. There is nothing so powerful, said Victor Hugo, as an idea whose time has come. And for many years the idea of war against White supremacy has been sweeping across southern Africa.

## THE MILITARIZATION OF AFRICA

The United States and the Soviet Union in tandem are the major arms exporters in the world today. In Africa, they have pursued competitive policies militarizing the continent from one end to the other. To be sure, the old colonial rulers have also played a part in Africa's militarization: unique among them, France resumed an expansive policy after Valéry Giscard d'Estaing became President in 1974. With a force of approximately ten thousand French troops deployed in seven countries at different times, in addition to military intervention in such states as Tunisia and Chad, France has been second only to the Soviet bloc in the number of foreign troops stationed on African soil. Moreover, African states have sometimes appealed to the industrial suppliers for weapons in response to various internal and intra-African conflicts. Such appeals increased during the 1970s with the rising independence of more nations. It was the superpower rivalry, however, that preceded all other factors in accounting for Africa's rapid progression from a low military profile at the beginning of 1970 to the position of second largest arms-importing area in the Third World by 1978.

The new armament of Africa is depicted in Figure 1 showing world arms imports in 1978 by geographic region. A major jump in Africa's share of armaments occurred within a single year. Africa accounted for 17 percent of the world share in 1977, when the Middle East took 39 percent.[64] However, by 1978 the African percentage increased to 25 percent while the Middle East's actually declined to 37 percent. The necessity of access to African military bases by the Rapid Deployment Force accelerated the process of African militarization. What the chart cannot reveal is how the transfer of potent weapons to African and other countries vitiated the superpowers' ability to limit or moderate potential warfare generated by their own arms policies.

The rapid militarization of the African continent has passed largely unnoticed by American politicians still indifferent to African developments. Even the makers of foreign policy have frequently ignored it, except in those instances where they recognized the resource-rich African states as prospective new markets for the sale of American armaments. The academic community has similarly overlooked this new phenomenon, perhaps because of a renewed lack of interest in African studies at American universities. *Daedalus,* the journal of the American Academy of Arts and Sciences, exemplified this lack of interest conspicuously in a two-volume issue on U.S. defense policy in the 1980s by printing twenty different articles on a plethora of American military interests in every geographic region but Africa.[65]

For a brief period, the United States attempted to control the spread of conventional arms to Africa as well as to the rest of the

WORLD ARMS IMPORTS, 1978 *Shares by Regions*

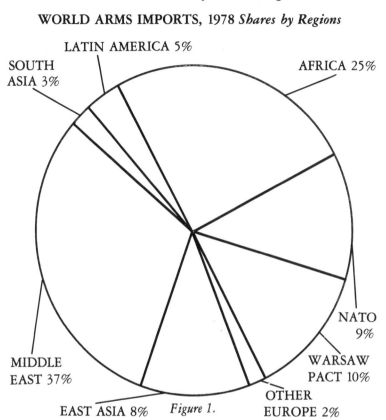

LATIN AMERICA 5%

SOUTH
ASIA 3%

AFRICA 25%

NATO
9%

MIDDLE
EAST 37%

WARSAW
PACT 10%

OTHER
EUROPE 2%

EAST ASIA 8%   *Figure 1.*

*Source:* U.S. Arms Control and Disarmament Agency, *World Military Expenditures and Arms Transfers 1969–1978* (Washington, D.C.: Government Printing Office, October 1979), p. 8.

Third World. President Carter in 1977 imposed an unprecedented limitation on the dollar value of arms transfers. The dollar ceiling, which became effective in 1978, affected foreign military sales and military assistance programs to all countries except the NATO allies, Japan, Australia, and New Zealand. The new policy promised to moderate arms buildups because the United States was the world's leading supplier of conventional arms. In Africa, meanwhile, the Soviets then stayed ahead in total export of weaponry, both conventional and strategic.

In addition to setting the good example, the Carter Administration also approached the Soviet Union, the second largest supplier, and other arms exporters to seek multilateral cooperation on arms restraint. It was not long, however, before the Carter doctrine counteracted Carter's own initiatives, nor before the Reagan Administration resumed American arms exports to numerous countries, including Morocco, as the first order of business.

Thus the problem persists. The militarization of Africa, which is actually a manifestation of a larger problem of arms buildups in the world generally, especially in the Middle East, cannot be regarded as beneficial to the long-range interests of the United States, nor to the regional stability American policy ought to promote in the interest of African-American relations. Similarly, the militarization does not advance the economic and developmental priorities of African nations. The United States should therefore take the lead in halting the process by which the African continent has been transformed into yet another battlefield of the cold war.

A secondary but also crucial policy change should be a retreat from the cold war doctrine which demands an alliance relationship as the sine qua non of U.S. assistance and cooperation. From the standpoint of U.S. decision-making, the impulse to anti-Sovietism has habitually predominated all other desiderata in the formulation of Africa policy. However, the needs of African states cover an enormous range, from trade to developmental assistance to national security, and these determine Africa's relations with the United States. These states have often ended up at loggerheads with Washington as a result of policymakers' proclivity to cold war policy.

This rigidity prompted Secretary of State Haig to announce as the Reagan Administration took office that policy toward Angola would begin with an extensive review of "what options are available to us to bring about an outcome which hopefully will result in an orientation of Angola . . . not to the East but, more importantly, to the Western family of nations."[66] Such intrusive designs, ignoring the political choices the Angolans had already made for themselves, were understandably perceived by the established government in Luanda as a threat to its existence, increasing its sense of urgency for military security and consequently for greater Soviet bloc assistance.

South Africa, of course, remains the principal threat to U.S. security interests in Africa. The Reagan Administration's sympathetic approach toward the apartheid regime incited widespread hostility in independent Africa, damaging the goodwill and workable relations that surfaced early in the Carter Administration. Africans became circumspect, even distrustful. This was evident in Assistant Secretary of State Crocker's tour of ten African nations in April 1981 when he attempted to clarify Administration policy and gain African commitment to the plan for negotiated settlement in Namibia involving constitutional guarantees for the White minority prior to independence. When Crocker arrived in Zambia, the Foreign Ministry sent a subordinate official to meet him in a pickup truck.

Washington should not only enforce an absolute cessation of American corporate exports of arms and arms technology to the White supremacy regime, it should also stop the legal export of dual-purpose equipment. The mandatory arms embargo of 1977 established the necessary basis for an effective policy; what has been missing is the political will to enforce it rigorously. An unconditional enforcement of the embargo together with appropriate pressures on America's allies for equal compliance should become Washington's constant practice until the violent system of apartheid, like fascism, changes. History has placed apartheid on the same track as European colonialism; hence, apartheid will not survive in the long run regardless of American policy. Still, it will be far more profitable to American future interests and prestige in Africa to take a final stand against apartheid, for opposition there represents a singular stake in which American national security and the interest of international peace converge.

# SOWETO:
# Decision Time for U.S.
# Policy in South Africa

South Africa, where a small and desperate minority of Whites depends on the West to preserve their supremacy in a Black nation they have converted into a racial powder keg, is destined to become the focus of a turning point in American policy during this century. Unfortunately for U.S. decision-makers, South Africa poses a challenge to political rationality as well as a test of national morality, because the racial situation there, more than anywhere else in the world, impinges directly on American security. In few other places do American economic and strategic stakes collide more sharply with Soviet interests. Nowhere else does an area of American foreign policy so directly call into question and threaten to inflame racial tensions at home. To state the problem differently, mass violence in South Africa, whether internally or externally caused, could hasten the nuclear confrontation that has thus far been averted, and it could also trigger a racial confrontation of disastrous and unbearable consequences within the United States.

America's cold war ideology has wielded its inexorable influence on policy toward the apartheid state as toward the rest of the African continent. However, it has been applied differently in South Africa because American policymakers have emphasized South Africa's strategic importance as a pro-Western bulwark against Soviet bloc penetration into the whole rim of southern Africa. The establishment of Marxist regimes in Angola, Mozambique, and Ethiopia during the 1970s magnified the role of anti-Sovietism in U.S. policy toward Pretoria. In fact, the strategic factor assumed a value far beyond the economic stakes represented by about 350 American corporations with total direct investments of $2 billion in South Africa during 1980. The cold war focus also frequently overshadowed Washington's concern for the racist suppression of the country's Black majority by the White minority.

The White minority dictatorship meanwhile remained the primary source of actual and potential conflict in southern Africa, not only because of apartheid domination of South Africa, but also because of its direct control of Namibia, which was declared illegal by the International Court of Justice in 1971.

Senator Dick Clark underscored the explosive nature of apartheid when he headed the Senate's Subcommittee on African Affairs: "The conflict between the races in South Africa promises only to become more intense and increasingly to pose a real threat to the stability of the entire region." [1] The realization that the Soviet Union could extend its military influence into southern Africa suddenly moved Africa center stage along with the Middle East and Western Europe as potential theaters of world war.

The ramifications of South Africa's racial crisis on American society were first apprehended on June 16, 1976, when South Africa's police fired on unarmed Black schoolchildren staging a peaceful demonstration in Soweto, the Black ghetto located twenty miles outside Johannesburg. The students were protesting the government's plan for compulsory education in Afrikaans (the Afrikaners' language) as a new feature of the bantu education system. When they marched to demonstrate their opposition, a frantic South African government sent well-trained, well-armed, and experienced policemen to stop them. Police violence ensued as policemen shot and killed a thirteen-year-old. [2] By the end of the year, the police had shot thousands of the youthful protesters, killing perhaps a thousand and maiming and wounding countless others.

In contrast to such decisive African events as the Congo crisis, Soweto seized the attention of Black Americans and shocked them. The sight of White police firing on Black youths was not unfamiliar to Blacks, especially among the residents of poor urban neighborhoods. But, more importantly, the uprising in Soweto presented Black Americans with an African problem that was clear-cut; namely, there was no uncertainty as to who the malefactors were. From television screens and portable radios, the news of a grave tragedy in the land of their ancestors swept into Black communities. Not coincidentally, TransAfrica, the Black American lobby on foreign affairs, was organized in the aftermath of Soweto.

The U.S. government began to scrutinize Soweto in relation to Black soldiers in the U.S. Army. By 1976 Black soldiers accounted for nearly 35 percent of the men under arms. This percentage was not only unprecedented, it was troublesome to American policy planners because it was uncertain how these troops would behave if ordered to intervene in a hypothetical crisis on African soil. Neither the strategists at the Pentagon nor those in the State Department wished to ponder the full implications of such an event. But the policymakers did draw a crucial lesson from Soweto: A widespread civil uprising in which Blacks were violently pitted against Whites in South Africa might rebound on American national interests, intensifying racial antagonisms at home while catalyzing Black dissent, if not outright mutiny, in the United States armed forces.

What caused the Soweto uprising to shake American leaders was the fact that it caught them, as it did most observers everywhere, completely by surprise. Until Soweto, South Africa's military capability was considered practically invincible, whether in response to an internal insurrection or an invasion of forces from independent African states. The judgment of the Nixon Administration, as rendered in Kissinger's secret National Security Council memorandum of 1969, was that "South Africa is the hard core of southern Africa," and that "its security forces are strong and effective."[3] American business's perception of South Africa was related by John Blashill in *Fortune* magazine: "The Republic of South Africa has always been regarded by foreign investors as a gold mine, one of those rare and refreshing places where profits are great and problems small."[4]

Suddenly the Soweto uprising, precipitated by defenseless schoolchildren rather than armed guerrillas, challenged the old assumption of South Africa's fortresslike invulnerability. It exposed the White dictatorship as vulnerable to upheaval in the urban areas, precisely those localities that had heretofore been regarded as impregnable White redoubts. A sudden drop in the price of gold on the international market reflected Western anxiety over South Africa, which remained the world's biggest producer of gold. The student demonstrations were not suppressed until six months later, forcing South Africa to declare a state of emergency, and revealing to the world that it was incapable of guaranteeing full protection of the Western interests. Ever since the uprising, Soweto has been a strong symbol of Blacks' determined resistance to apartheid.

The Soweto uprising thus marked a watershed in American strategic thinking about South Africa. No longer could United States policy be narrowly focused on corporate and strategic interests as far as South Africa was concerned. Now, for the first time, the American government walked a policy tightrope there because a wrong political or military decision could engulf the United States in cold war confrontation, and the flames of a racial conflagration there could leap across the Atlantic into American society. Kissinger's memorandum had hypothesized that, in the event of terrorist activity in South Africa, the Soviets and Chinese would become the main beneficiaries of the conflict because of their support to the Black majority. A consciousness arose in Washington that the time had come for a new approach in relations with southern Africa.

## SOUTH AFRICA: THE EXPLOSIVE SOCIETY

To understand the revisions that were required in United States policy after the Soweto uprising, it is important first to examine the peculiar political and economic structure of South African society. Apartheid, the official policy of racial segregation in South Africa, was formally adopted by the ruling Nationalist party in 1948. However, the policy merely applied the force of law to a de facto situation that was already well advanced by the Afrikaners, the Afrikaans-speaking White descendants of Dutch colonists who had begun to settle on the South African coast as far back as the seventeenth century. Goaded by the Afrikaners, the other Europeans (primarily British) joined in enforcing the system of segregation, which applied to Blacks and Coloureds (Afrikaners' term for persons of mixed-blood ancestry). By 1948 racial segregation had become such a tradition that the Christian churches also enforced it.

The theory of apartheid was formulated in 1947 by a number of professors at Stellenbosch University, then known as the heart of Afrikaner intellectual nationalism. A group including Dr. Theophilus Dönges, a future Minister of the Interior, Dr. Ernest Jansen, a future Minister of Native Affairs, Professor Werner Eiselen, a future Secretary of Native Affairs, and Professor Andries Cilliers developed a rationale for apartheid based on their unquestioning assumptions of European supremacy. They envisioned a system of racial divisions in which three major racial groups— Whites, Blacks, and Coloureds—would individually develop along their own lines, each group being governed by a federation of racial states under the control of Pretoria. This rationale formed the basis for the so-called Bantu Reserves, rural areas which would be partitioned for the country's Black majority, and which permitted the White minority of 2 million to preserve their residential redoubts in urban areas. Eiselen and Cilliers recognized the ingenuous character of the provision for Bantu Reserves, or "bantustans" as they were called in Afrikaans, but the race scholars still recommended a forcible removal of South Africa's 8 million Blacks to north of the Limpopo River, South Africa's northern boundary, without being able to decide whether Southern Rhodesia or the Belgian Congo should be the site of the people expelled.[5]

Today South Africa is the only country in the world where racial segregation and White supremacy are sanctioned by state policy. Apartheid, which refers to "separation" or "apartness" in Afrikaans, therefore provides both the ideological and legal basis for White dictatorship in South Africa.

Apartheid in practice was organized according to rigid political, economic, and social divisions that enabled Whites to maintain absolute and complete control in each sphere. The Whites' monopoly of power developed during the late nineteenth century as the European settlers finally defeated the anticolonial resistance of the indigenous African inhabitants. Great Britain, which established South Africa as a Crown colony in 1806, contributed significantly to the process of White domination by enacting the South Africa Act of 1909, which made the territory self-governing. This law extended a longstanding British policy of granting White settlers power to manage the country with no participation, or even consultation, of the native majority. Britain thus transferred its authority as a colonial master to the dominant White minority of European settlers, thereby producing the dual nature of the independent Afrikaner (South African) government as both a "mother country" and a colonial power. In other words, the Afrikaners, in their relation to the Black majority, assumed political control in Pretoria as a European elite in command of an internal colony with a subject population.

Mining and an abundance of fertile farmland lured successive waves of European settlers, especially Dutch and English, to South Africa. These, however, were not the only powerful incentives. Another was the cheap labor of African slaves, whom the Dutch East India Company introduced into the territory in 1658. The settlers thereby established their stake in African slavery, which was not abolished until nearly two centuries later. From the beginning, the quest for economic and material gain determined the Europeans' migration to South Africa.

European immigrants to South Africa were unlike White settlers in almost every other part of colonial Africa. They came to the territory not as traders or expeditionary forces seeking some limited or even temporary objective, as was often the case in the British Empire, but as settlers who had decided to build a permanent residence in the colony. Settler communities—or Europeans who made themselves organic additions to the indigenous society—cropped up here and there, first in the Cape Coast area, later deep in the interior territory now known as the Transvaal. The "Great

Trek," or the Afrikaners' mass flight into the interior to escape British control in the Cape Colony, followed a British law of 1828 giving free Coloureds legal equality with Whites; the movement accelerated after the abolition of slavery in 1834. Very early, the Europeans revealed a fervent antipathy to integrating with Africans, although European men never hesitated to seize and sleep with African women (which increased the Coloured population).

The Europeans in South Africa surpassed settler colonies in such countries as Angola and Algeria in their direct and total rule of an African society. These Whites also took the extraordinary step of changing their civil status from foreign settler to citizen of the territory. To facilitate this process, the settlers confiscated African ancestral lands and forcibly displaced the Africans into localities that Europeans did not desire. The transformation in land ownership was not completed until 1936, when the Land Act coerced Africans into moving onto new territories specifically designated for them. A strange metamorphosis unfolded as the Europeans defined themselves as the "citizens" or "natives" of South Africa, and the indigenous African inhabitants as "foreigners" in the territories that were newly occupied by the Europeans. Blacks were thus converted into strangers in their own land.

The basic structure of the political system was laid down in the South Africa Act of 1909. Not only did it restrict membership in Parliament to Whites, it applied the same restriction to the provincial councils and nearly all the municipal councils, except in the Cape province, where a few Coloureds were elected to office, and in Stanger, Natal, where once an Indian was elected to a town council.[6] Voting, of course, became the monopoly of Whites, as all Whites above eighteen years of age were eligible to vote. The civil service, like the court system, was similarly restricted to White control. Never was a Black or non-White person in a position of authority over a White person in South Africa. And the White dictatorship's authority was not circumscribed by the territorial boundaries of the four provinces that made up South Africa—the Cape, Natal, the Orange Free State, and the Transvaal—for it extended also to the neighboring territory of Namibia, or South-

West Africa, which South Africa acquired in 1920 as a mandate under the League of Nations. Apartheid was firmly established there as well. Until 1961 South Africa was known as the Union of South Africa and belonged to the British Commonwealth; but under the leadership of Afrikaner Prime Minister Hendrik Verwoerd, the Whites broke ties with the British to declare the Republic of South Africa, still a government of, by, and exclusively for White people.

The Europeans, or Whites, of South Africa, estimated at 4.3 million or 16 percent of the total population in 1980, can be divided into two main categories, Afrikaner and English. The Afrikaners, also known as Boers, descended from the Dutch Calvinists who first settled in the Cape of Good Hope in 1652. Many other European nationalities, including French, Germans, Italians, and Greeks later migrated to the territory, and were progressively assimilated into the culture of the Afrikaners, the ruling and numerically superior White element. The English settlers, on the other hand, did not reach South Africa in substantial numbers until it was annexed as a British colony in 1806. Jews, who have become well assimilated in the larger White society, primarily belonged to the English-speaking White group.

Nearly all the Europeans resided in the urban or "White" areas reserved for them, and the White population was roughly 87 percent urban by 1976.[7] Diamonds were discovered near Kimberley in 1870 and gold near the future city of Johannesburg in 1886, and these riches provided powerful magnets to further European immigration. The vast wealth of South Africa has continued to draw Europeans there; even today, perhaps a thousand new immigrants arrive every year.

The Blacks, or bantus as the indigenous Africans are named by Afrikaners, consist of about 20 million people and represent more than 70 percent of the South African population. The Afrikaner government has isolated them on native reserves known as "bantu homelands," or bantustans, in a system of territorial segregation first legislated in 1913 with the Natives Land Act. However, the idea of native reserves in which the Africans could be confined and which they would leave only to serve the Whites was almost as old as the European occupation of South Africa. Indeed, one of the first acts of the new Boer Republic of Natal, established in 1838, was the passing of legislation that restricted Blacks from the settled parts of the republic, except as servants of Whites. It also prohibited them from owning land, firearms, or horses; from participating in the political process; and from being at large without passes signed by White employers. According to the 1970 census of South Africa, there were about 7 million Blacks, or 35 percent of the Black population, living in the bantu homelands,[8] which mainly consisted of the country's most impoverished, rural terrain.

The official apartheid theory argues that the entire Black population belongs to one of the bantustans, and that all Blacks are citizens of the bantustans regardless of where they live. In terms of relative land distribution, the Black majority with more than 70 percent of the total population resides on 13 percent of the land, whereas the White minority with 16 percent monopolizes 87 percent of the land, including the most arable agricultural lands.

Under the guidance of Verwoerd, the Whites began to displace Blacks onto isolated terrains, far from the White cities, producing what he termed "a form of [social] fragmentation which we would not have liked if we were able to avoid it, thereby buying the white man his freedom and the right to retain domination in what is his country."[9] Verwoerd's relentless drive to relocate the Black masses led to the creation of the Transkei as the first of the so-called African states in 1962. In reality, Transkei and the seven additional bantustans that had been created by 1976 were no more than political appendages of the White dictatorship. This view was corroborated in June 1972 by the Chief Minister of KwaZulu bantustan, Chief Gatsha Buthelezi, who described the role of the bantustan chiefs over the population removals as "covering up naked and outright white domination inherent in presenting a draft prepared unilaterally by whites in the interests of whites."[10] The bantustan, defined by Pretoria as a central body controlling a conglomeration of areas inhabited primarily by members of one "tribe,"[11] was exposed as a political nonentity.

A plan for ten independent bantustans was ultimately approved by the South African government. If the plan is ever carried out fully, Africans, by South African law, will become "citizens" of the bantustans only. No Black person will then be accepted as a citizen of South Africa.

Because of the need for cheap labor in South Africa's industrial centers, about 8 million Blacks reside near the urban areas. Their proximity to the White industries has not given them similar access to the White political assemblies. In 1968 Prime Minister B. J. Vorster clarified Pretoria's plan for the political future of Blacks, urban and rural:

> The fact of the matter is this; we need the [Blacks], because they work for us, but after all, we pay them for their work. . . . But the fact that they work for us can never . . . entitle them to claim political rights. Not now, nor in the future . . . under no circumstances can we grant them those political rights in our own territory, neither now nor ever.[12]

Comparable conditions prevailed for the 2.5 million Coloureds and about 800,000 Asians. In November 1979 Vorster's successor, Pieter W. Botha, reconfirmed South Africa's opposition to equal political participation: "I say it again: one-man, one-vote is out in this country. That is, never."[13]

Prime Minister Botha promised to liberalize the apartheid caste system by authorizing trade union rights for Black workers and by dismantling such symbols of what he called "petty apartheid" as White-only restaurants, segregated sports events, and the official wage policy that excluded Blacks from the best-paid jobs. Evidently, however, these were symbolic gestures designed to reduce international criticisms of the apartheid system, because Botha refused to eliminate the hard-core aspects of apartheid, such as the pass laws, which require blacks to carry passes issued by their employers at all times, and prohibit free movement. He also stepped up racial segregation with plans to forcibly relocate another million Blacks onto the bantustans. The promised liberalization, meanwhile, applied only to Black workers in urban areas, that is, to those who were marginally integrated into the mainstream economy.

Economically, South Africa presents an extreme racial dichotomy between European wealth and Black poverty. On the one hand are the Europeans, who enjoy a living standard and a per capita income surpassed only in the United States, Canada, and Sweden. On the other hand are the Blacks, who provide the bulk of this wealth through their labor, but who have been reduced to the ranks of the world's most poverty-stricken people. With only 16 percent of the total population, the Whites take 75 percent of all income annually.[14] According to the South African Institute of Race Relations, Whites earned 4.4 times more than Blacks as recently as 1977.[15] In the same period, Whites earned three times more than Coloureds and more than twice as much as Asians.

Nowhere were the social inequalities more stark than in public education. South Africa approved the Bantu Education Act of 1953 to establish direct control of Black schools by the Ministry of Bantu Affairs, rather than by the provincial or even homeland governments. Whereas education for Whites between ages seven and sixteen is free and compulsory, Black pupils have to pay for most of their education. The gross injustice of apartheid is best illustrated by South Africa's per capita expenditures on Black and White education: during 1978–1979, for example, the government spent roughly $940 on each White child, $290 on each Coloured child, and $90 on each Black child.[16] Financial pressures and overcrowded schools usually result in huge drop-out rates among Black students, who often withdraw as functional illiterates.

A graphic illustration of the organization of inequality was the pass law legislation of 1952, which requires all Blacks to carry a "pass" or reference book containing their photograph; race identity; registration number; details of their tribal connections; the official authorization to be in an urban area; their current tax receipt; their permit to be employed or to seek employment; the name, address, and monthly signature of their employer; and various other specifications. Every Black male and female above sixteen is obligated to carry the pass at all times, and a failure to do so can lead to immediate arrest and prosecution. Suppression under pass laws account for a quarter of criminal prosecutions each year.[17] A major side effect of the pass laws is the disintegration of the African family caused by the prohibition against husband and wife living together when one spouse lacks the permit required to reside in the Black districts near the cities. In practice, husbands working in the White cities are forced to abandon their wives in distant rural settlements.

The term "Black" has traditionally referred to the indigenous inhabitants of South Africa, whether descended from South African ancestry or not. The ethnicities or "tribes" consist of such groups as the Zulus, the Xhosi, and Tswanas. Coloureds, people who are the product of Europeans' cohabitation with Blacks or Asians, are identified as a separate group. Lately, however, the Whites of South Africa have generalized "Black" to include native Africans together with Coloureds and Asians, except for the Japanese, who have been reclassified as "White" because of South Africa's substantial trade relations with Japan. These peculiar racial delineations have made it possible to dichotomize South African society into Blacks and Whites, the exploited and the exploiters. This explains why Waldemar A. Nielsen, a former President of the African-American Institute, concluded that totalitarianism was not the only problem of South Africa; it also represented "the most flagrant and clearcut case in the world today of oppression of colored people by white people as a matter of official policy." [18]

Capital punishment is another area of law that further illustrates South Africa's oppression of Blacks. Hangings in South Africa have represented about 90 percent of all legal executions in the Western world for many years. There were at least seven hundred such executions in the last decade (132 in 1978), and Black Africans have accounted for 80 percent of those hanged, or proportionately more than their percentage in the overall population. [19]

Apartheid can now be recognized as a racially unique and historically reactionary political system. It is a police state which has insulated itself from internal efforts seeking change through peaceful means. It is an ideology constructed on the notion of a superior White race, reminiscent of Nazi Germany. It is an inflexible racist dictatorship that is not amenable to a genuine application of democratic institutions and practices. Apartheid is also the culture of a society where fanatical European settlers have amassed enormous wealth and privileges by exploiting and alienating Africans in their own country. South Africa, in sum, is an unstable society ready for racial explosion.

## ECONOMIC INTERESTS AND
## THE SHARPEVILLE MASSACRE

South Africa had become the main object of U.S. relations in Africa long before the Black nations captured American attention by their achievement of political independence during the 1960s. The Afrikaner-ruled territory was already being courted by the few U.S. businesses on the African continent, importing American goods valued at $260,618,000 in 1955, or roughly half of all the American goods imported by all African States.[20] As a supplier of goods to the United States, South Africa, with $95,478,000 in exports, was exceeded only by the Belgian Congo, whose exports were worth $109,121,000. Liberia, Ethiopia, and Egypt, among the countries not ruled by Whites, maintained growing relationships with the United States. However, they were not treated on a par with South Africa, partly because Washington tended to view South Africa as a European territory, and especially because relations between the United States and South Africa had emerged as an exclusive link between U.S. policymakers and the Afrikaners. Not until January 1956, in fact, did the State Department transfer its South African desk from European Affairs to Near East, South Asian, and African Affairs.

Apartheid did not become an issue of concern to American policymakers until the Kennedy Administration. Washington's failure to challenge apartheid resulted not from official callousness, but from the fact that American leaders had not yet acted against the pervasive racist practices within the United States, particularly the de jure and hard-core segregation of the South. Through *Brown* v. *The Board of Education of Topeka,* the Supreme Court in 1954 terminated the "separate but equal" segregationist doctrine that had been in effect for nearly half a century. Nevertheless, the Court's ruling in favor of school desegregation could not bring about implementation, despite the Eisenhower Administration's first steps toward school integration in Little Rock, Arkansas. Taking office near the peak of the civil rights movement led by Dr. Martin Luther King, Jr., President Kennedy broached policy changes that would undo American segregation and revise the existing approach toward South Africa.

Economic stability in Great Britain, however, then dominated U.S. policy interest in South Africa's apartheid system. In 1961 South Africa sent about 33 percent of its total exports to Britain, in contrast to the 8.3 percent it sent to the United States.[21] In the same year South Africa imported about 29 percent of its foreign goods from Britain, as compared to the 18 percent from the United States. American exports to South Africa in the 1960s tended to rise faster than American imports from South Africa, with the result that the apartheid country soon represented only about 1 percent of U.S. foreign trade.

The strong economic ties between South Africa and Britain were well demonstrated by the fact that the British retained 58.9 percent of total South African foreign liabilities by 1965.[22] As South Africa's biggest trade partner, England had become dependent on South African commerce. What made this dependence so critical was that it occurred in a period of increasing instability in Britain's international trade balance. Because Britain was a pillar of NATO, as well as a principal U.S. trade partner, Washington was infinitely more concerned with the English trade connection than with South Africa's apartheid.

The horrors of apartheid were first noticed by Americans as a result of the police brutality that took place in the township of Sharpeville in 1960, the year which the United Nations anointed as the "Year of Africa." That was the year European colonies in Africa acquired new status and entered a new era as independent African states. In South Africa, on the other hand, White supremacy was entrenched deeper than ever, causing Nelson Mandela, a leader of the African National Congress (ANC), a nonviolent reformist party, to summon his followers for a nonviolent demonstration against the pass laws, the hated symbol of European domination.[23] Perhaps as many as twenty thousand marchers turned out on March 21, refusing to carry their passes, then surrendering themselves at a police station for their violations. Suddenly, without provocation, nervous White policemen fired on the unarmed marchers, leaving casualties of 69 killed and 180 wounded.[24] Police violence also hit Black demonstrators in a few other townships, such as in Langa (Cape Town), but none was as savage as in Sharpeville. Thus, as the new citizens of such nations as Ghana and Cameroon celebrated their political independence, the Africans of South Africa encountered new repression. (Mandela and other ANC leaders such as Walter Sisulu were sentenced to life imprisonment in 1964, and have since remained in the prison on Robben Island near Cape Town.)

The "Sharpeville massacre," as the police killings were known, soon drew Washington's attention toward apartheid. The violence erupted at a time when civil war loomed over the Congo, and the Ku Klux Klan waited in ambush for Freedom Riders on their way to Birmingham, Alabama. Although the U.N. Commission on the Racial Situation in South Africa had concluded in 1954 that steps toward political equality in the apartheid country were of prime importance, and moreover that these steps could not be deferred *"without serious danger,"*[25] the United States concurred in South Africa's view that apartheid belonged entirely to Pretoria's domestic jurisdiction. Great Britain took the same position. Still, the Sharpeville explosion exposed the instability of South African society, and thereby the potential danger to Western economic interests there.

G. Mennen Williams, a former Governor of Illinois, and then the Assistant Secretary of State for African Affairs, alerted the Kennedy team to the need for a review of the established U.S. policy toward South Africa. The new Administration recognized the threat to U.S. leadership in the United Nations and Africa because of Washington's longstanding solidarity with South Africa and the Portuguese territories under European domination. Williams urged the President that in order to protect U.S. interests in

Africa, he should consider a repudiation of apartheid as a step toward dissociation from the South African regime.

Subsequently, Secretary of State Dean Rusk held a private meeting in New York on October 6, 1962, with South African Foreign Minister Eric Louw, stressing the New Frontier's view that apartheid posed a danger to the security of Africa.[26] During the spring of 1963, the Administration queried nineteen foreign governments regarding their willingness to join the United States in putting pressure on South Africa to change its system of racial segregation. This was not difficult at all, because thirteen countries had already approved a U.N. resolution declaring that South Africa's racial policies and practices were "creating a dangerous and explosive situation, which constitutes both a threat to international peace and a flagrant violation of the basic principles of human rights and fundamental freedoms which are enshrined in the Charter of the United Nations."[27] The United States, which had consistently opposed this position during the 1950s, now edged toward a change in policy.

U.N. Ambassador Adlai Stevenson pronounced the change at the United Nations on August 2, 1963, declaring Washington's intention to terminate the sale of all military equipment to South Africa by the end of the year. That was the Kennedy Administration's gesture of disapproval of South Africa's racist system—and the first official rebuke of apartheid. This, however, was not a unanimous position, because in late August, Stevenson himself cabled the following to the Secretary of State:

> Black South Africans, unless they receive roughly equal rights, will undoubtedly pursue their efforts to point [of] civil war increasingly supported from outside. Under the circumstances, best hopes for a long-range situation compatible with our own interests may well come from urging South Africans forward along lines of partitioning countries between predominantly Black and predominantly White areas (in latter, Whites would constitute majority), united perhaps in some kind of federation.[28]

Stevenson, the liberal Democrat, a former Governor of Illinois, thus expressed a dominant viewpoint in the Administration that, although a system of rigid racial segregation had to be condemned, the United States did not demand a fundamental change in the apartheid society, especially not when the United States had not itself extinguished its own system of segregation.

## THE ROLE OF CHARLES ENGELHARD

Widespread Black unrest shook South African society in the aftermath of Sharpeville, producing a severe economic crisis, as foreign shareholders in the stock market and money market withdrew their capital, alarmed by Sharpeville's sudden revelation of the instability inherent in all racist societies. South Africa's foreign exchange fell by almost 50 percent owing to the flight of about $271 million in 1960 and $63 million in early 1961.[29] White investors in South Africa began to pressure their government for certain concessions to the Black majority, hoping thereby to forestall further divestments, which threatened to bankrupt the economy.

At this point the American industrialist Charles W. Engelhard, Jr., intervened on the side of the apartheid regime. Under his leadership, a group of U.S. financiers obtained a vital $150 million loan for the South African government from a number of sources, including the International Monetary Fund, the World Bank, Chase Manhattan Bank, and First National City Bank.[30] As the largest American investor in South Africa, Engelhard controlled twenty-three major enterprises there. Through his chairmanship of Rand Mines, he also controlled several gold and uranium operations. The foreign capital he marshaled was vital to South Africa, not only because it came at a time of crisis, but especially because it freed other South African money for new investments to rescue the economy and reinforce the apartheid system. Although there was a general pattern of net outflow of capital from 1960 to 1964, as British and other European investors hastily withdrew their capital, thanks to Engelhard there was a net inflow of U.S. capital into South Africa from 1961 to 1964.

Two years before Sharpeville, Engelhard had organized American–South African Investment Co., Ltd., a trust fund which held

$60 million in assets by 1965.[31] The portfolio of American–South African Investment consisted of gold mining stocks primarily; this was extremely significant, because gold speculation was rife when Engelhard founded the fund. At that time South Africa's gold reserves had dropped to 75 million pounds sterling, and Engelhard's enterprise brought in 12 million pounds that helped restore international confidence in the rand, South Africa's basic monetary unit. Later, in the wake of Sharpeville, American–South African Investment helped to attract American capital back to the apartheid economy and, like the loan, the new investments arrived just in time.

Engelhard based his worldwide business network on Engelhard Hanrovia, a family holding company with headquarters in Newark, New Jersey, which by 1965 had $95 million in assets.[32] The heart of the corporation's business, and its power, was its investment portfolio, the repository for Engelhard's investments in nearly twenty-eight companies on six continents. By far the major body of these holdings was Engelhard Industries, the world's biggest refiner and fabricator of such precious metals as gold, silver, and platinum. With subsidiaries in ten foreign countries, this company, which was 72 percent owned by Engelhard Hanrovia, became an international giant in its own right.

Engelhard established much of his giant empire in South Africa, where he had made a series of major investments. In 1965 his investments there amounted to $30 million, a small sum by the standards of an industrial society, but huge according to the capital standards of a developing country.[33] Furthermore, he owned large investments in several South African enterprises, such as S.A. Forest Investments (timberlands) and Penta Chemical (chemicals). But the most influential of Engelhard's investments were his interests in the Anglo-American Corporation, a giant conglomerate with assets of $462 million, profits of $38.4 million, 157 subsidiaries and affiliates, and control of $530 million in assets of the De Beers Consolidated Mines. De Beers owned about 80 percent of the noncommunist world's diamonds, 25 percent of its gold, and 9 percent of its copper. With assets valued at approximately $3 billion, Anglo-American dominated South Africa's economy as DuPont dominated Delaware's.

Through his investments and a close friendship with Harry F. Oppenheimer, chairman of the Anglo-American conglomerate, Engelhard became a real power in South Africa. Heir to a fortune estimated at $10 million to $20 million, Engelhard had originally been attracted to South Africa because "I wanted to do something different from what my father had done. Africa was different." [34]

Oppenheimer obtained a 10 percent interest in Hanrovia, and in return Engelhard acquired a similar interest in E. Oppenheimer and Sons, the Oppenheimer family holding company that controlled Anglo-American. [35] The relationship with Oppenheimer gave him influence on the development of the South African economy, and in this respect he proved to be a key supporter of the apartheid system. As a director of the South African Chamber of Mines, Engelhard was also in a position of direct influence on South Africa's domestic policies, including a determination of miners' wages, which in 1966 averaged $7.82 a day for Whites and 70 cents a day for Blacks. [36] *Forbes* magazine, published by Engelhard's friend Malcolm Forbes, has clarified the industrialist's impact: "In the development of Anglo [-American's] ambitions—not only in North America and elsewhere in the world but also in South Africa itself—few outsiders have played a more critical role than Harry Oppenheimer's close friend and American partner, Charles Engelhard, Jr." [37]

Engelhard's access to American policymakers enabled him to exercise influence on United States policy toward South Africa. A director of the Foreign Policy Association, Engelhard made sizable financial contributions to the Democratic party, switching from the Republican party in 1953, and maintained an intimate friendship with Lyndon Johnson. He belonged to the Committee for Economic Development, the NATO commission, and the President's Special East-West Trade Committee. When Gabon and Zambia reached independence, in 1960 and 1964 respectively, he represented President Kennedy at their independence ceremonies. Paradoxically, perhaps, Engelhard, the arch-American capitalist in Africa, was the President's representative in 1963 at the first independence anniversary of revolutionary, socialist Algeria.

The South Africa Foundation, Pretoria's publicity, or propaganda, machinery in the United States designed to influence American public opinion toward South Africa, was set up with Engelhard's assistance. Although he never publicly condoned apartheid, and disliked Prime Minister Vorster, Engelhard still believed that "there are not many countries where it is safe to invest, and South Africa is about the best of the lot."[38] By such statements he reinforced a prevalent viewpoint among critics of U.S. policy toward South Africa that economic interests predominated over other considerations vis-à-vis the apartheid society.

Engelhard clearly influenced the evolution of U.S. policy toward South Africa. He stimulated substantial trade and commercial ties with South Africa in a decisive period of its history, when economic decline menaced the viability of the country. He campaigned among American political and corporate leaders for more extensive relations, portraying the apartheid society as a desirable and profitable locus for American investments. He sought to create a favorable public attitude toward South Africa by way of the South Africa Foundation. On behalf of an Anglo-American affiliate he arranged, in the United States, a $30 million loan, which, according to Harry Oppenheimer, "was brought to South Africa, where it made a significant difference to the reserves of [South Africa's] foreign exchange"; as part of the emergency capital after Sharpeville, the loan provided "an interesting example of the great value of possessing financial institutions with international connections."[39] While Eisenhower warned about the dangers of unwarranted corporate influence on governmental policy in his valedictory on the military-industrial complex, Engelhard played a role in the development of American relations with a foreign country that few private individuals have equaled.

## APARTHEID AND AMERICAN INVESTMENTS

The growing economic relations between South Africa and the United States accelerated after Sharpeville, and continued until the Soweto riots of 1976, at which time there were about 350 American companies in business in South Africa. Between the Sharpeville and

Soweto crises, United States private capital flowed into South Africa, which continuously proved to be the highly profitable investment market that Engelhard had predicted. The American share of direct foreign investment in the apartheid economy, which amounted to 11 percent in 1960, had risen to at least 16 percent by 1976.[40] This amount represented about 40 percent of total United States investment in Africa, and provided 1 percent of all United States foreign earnings. American investments in manufacturing exceeded those in natural resources, and South Africa's abundant mineral wealth, coupled with the government's strict maintenance of a surplus of low wage labor, created a remarkable profit margin for American investors.

United States policy toward South Africa was improved by the comprehensive restrictions on arms exports imposed by U.S. approval of the mandatory U.N. embargo of 1977. Washington, however, did not discourage American investments in the apartheid society, and went so far as to endorse American corporations' compliance with the laws of the regime. Thus, no fundamental movement in American policy took place in the sixteen-year period from Sharpeville to Soweto.

American strategic interests in South Africa also took root during this same period. For instance, the United States acquired rights to the Simonstown naval base, located on South African soil, which served as a repair installation for American naval vessels. South Africa has an inherent strategic importance for the United States by virtue of its location along sea lanes to Middle Eastern oil; this factor assumes vital value in the event of a closing of the Suez Canal route, as was the case during the Anglo-French-Israeli attacks on Egypt in 1956, and again in the Arab-Israeli war of 1967. Under such conditions, the Cape Coast sea lanes offered the United States and Western Europe an alternative route to the closed customary route. At Simonstown the United States also maintained space tracking stations and intelligence operations that enabled the CIA to observe Eastern Europe and much of independent Africa.

American corporate investments constituted the heart of U.S. interests in South Africa by 1976. These investments were substantially more critical to South Africa than to the United States, because whereas South Africa held as little as 1.2 percent of all U.S. overseas investments, American firms provided as much as 20 percent of total foreign investments in South Africa.[41] American investments also took special significance from the fact that they were concentrated in the fastest-growing sectors of the South African economy, including oil, automobiles, banks, computers, heavy engineering, and high technology. Equally important, these six sectors comprised the main economic pillars of the apartheid system.

To examine the means by which the American multinationals bolstered South Africa's apartheid system, certain criteria have been identified. For instance, the size of a company's investment could be so large that, by the investment alone, the company could be said to contribute to the maintenance of apartheid. Also, a company's volume of sales in a given year could be so great as to represent a support to apartheid. Bank loans and tax payments to the South African government would likewise help to sustain the regime and the economy, while corporate assistance in new resources or technology would strengthen industrial development in the White regions. An American company maintaining operations in or near one of the bantustans would automatically be involved in promoting the policy of apartheid. However, the most salient criterion of support would be corporate assistance to South Africa's military and police forces, the backbone of the apartheid system. Consequently, any U.S. company engaged in business with these forces would ipso facto be a supporter of apartheid. So obvious was the nature of such business that in February 1978 the United States Department of Commerce imposed an embargo on all commodities, services, and other materials from the United States intended for use by the South African police and military forces, regardless of whether they operated in the Republic of South Africa or in Namibia.

South Africa has never possessed oil reserves of its own. It is almost totally dependent on foreign firms to import, refine and market its petroleum supplies. Although the country developed the world's only successful oil-from-coal plant in 1955, and was endowed with an abundance of coal reserves, oil imports still satisfied most of South Africa's energy needs because the conversion plant produced little oil. The foreign-supplied petroleum was so vital to South Africa's military security that the government decreed it a criminal offense for any oil company in the country to deny oil to the South African armed forces. Without the oil, the White minority would lose its capacity to employ the tanks, police vans, and airplanes that solidify the regime's police and military control.

Three American companies—Caltex, Exxon, and Mobil—once controlled about 44 percent of South Africa's petroleum market. In 1978, for instance, Mobil and Caltex together controlled 40 percent of the South African oil market, each with South African assets worth about $350 million. The combined assets of the two companies constituted more than a third of the total United States investments in the country. In 1976 the sales of these companies exceeded $500 million, nearly double the sales of any other American corporations in South Africa.[42]

The South African military, which by South African law maintains priority on all petroleum products in the country, relied on Mobil and Caltex. Mobil, for example, provided fuel for the army and air force in Northern Transvaal, the main location for these forces. The strategic significance of oil was suggested by the legal advice Mobil obtained from its South African solicitors: "As oil is absolutely vital to enable the army to move, the navy to sail and the air force to fly, it is likely that a South African court would hold that it falls within . . . the definitions of munitions of war."[43] Furthermore, as revealed in a 1978 United Nations report, the South African subsidiaries of the major oil companies—a group that included Mobil and Caltex—supplied oil for ten years to Ian Smith's Rhodesia in violation of U.N. sanctions.[44] This trade was conducted clandestinely via intermediary companies, and it exposed the American firms' lack of ethical and legal concern in supporting the illegal White minority regime in Rhodesia, as well as the apartheid system of South Africa.

The gravity of South Africa's dependence on foreign oil was

magnified by the Ayatollah Khomeini's decision in February 1979 to cut off oil exports to South Africa. Under the Shah's regime, Iran had provided about 90 percent of South Africa's crude oil imports. After the Iranian embargo, South Africa apparently bought its supplies on the spot market.

At this juncture, another American industrialist, J. Robert Fluor, came to South Africa's rescue by contracting to develop a major part of South Africa's coal-to-oil program. Fluor, who was Chairman, President, and Chief Executive of the Fluor Corporation, one of the world's biggest engineering and construction firms, signed a $4.2 billion contract with the apartheid regime to assist the South African Coal, Oil and Gas Corporation (SASOL), a state-owned company in charge of the coal conversion program.[45] Fluor committed itself to the management and coordination of the total project, including a major portion of the engineering, design, procurement, construction, and a multitude of other supportive functions. The American multinational also agreed to construct Secunda, a township located five miles from the plant, to lodge SASOL workers. South Africa's desperation for its own oil supplies was shown by the government's estimated $6.7 billion investment on the SASOL project, or a sum that was more than half of South Africa's national budget ($13 billion) for fiscal 1979–1980. The projected date for completion of the SASOL plants is 1982, by which time South Africa expects to be producing 35 percent of its petroleum needs from coal.

Like Engelhard two decades earlier, Fluor promoted South Africa's interests in the United States. For example, he applied for credit from the Export-Import Bank on SASOL's behalf in 1975, when the bank's policies prohibited direct loans to the South African government. He was a board member of the Heritage Foundation, an American organization which disseminates information projecting a favorable image of the apartheid society. The political fund of the Fluor Corporation contributed to the 1978 senatorial campaign of Roger Jepsen,[46] the Iowa Republican who defeated the incumbent Dick Clark, the Senate's leading critic of South Africa and head of the Senate Subcommittee on African

Affairs, which in 1976 had sponsored investigations exposing the racist, discriminatory, and oppressive nature of apartheid.

American corporations have played a critical role in South Africa's automobile industry, although their former dominance has ended as a result of recession and competition from other foreign firms. General Motors, Ford, and Chrysler accounted for about one third of all motor vehicle sales in South Africa during 1979, with a total investment of $300 million and assets valued at $500 million.[47] The importance of these firms was not limited to their employment power or market positions, however; they also contributed directly to South Africa's defense forces as suppliers of trucks and other vehicles to the military and police. In 1977 Ford was the leader in auto sales in South Africa, and General Motors captured 27 percent of all automobile sales as well as 23 percent of commercial sales.

Ford's involvement in the apartheid economy was perhaps best illustrated by the treatment of its Black workers in November 1979, when the company summarily fired all seven hundred Blacks at its Port Elizabeth assembly plant. Ford had provoked a crisis by dismissing Thozamile Botha, a Black foreman accused of anti-apartheid political activism in Ford's Struandale plant, the only one of several Ford factories with a predominantly Black labor force. To justify his dismissal, Ford alleged that he had been missing work to develop a new Black political group, the Port Elizabeth Civic Organization. Botha's fellow Black employees then walked off their jobs, demanding his reinstatement and condemning the racist policies which placed Whites in most of the plant's managerial and supervisory positions. Ford's reprisal was swift: it dismissed all its Black workers, establishing an action that was unprecedented in the history of American corporate investments in South Africa. (Simultaneously the General Tire and Rubber Company dismissed its 625 Black workers in Port Elizabeth, capital of South Africa's automobile industry.) Although Ford soon reinstated its Black workers, by then it had become firmly involved in a confrontation that was at least partly rooted in Blacks' frustrations over apartheid.[48]

In the event of a declaration of war by South Africa, South

Africa's National Supplies Procurement Act enables the apartheid regime to conscript the American automobile firms into the service of its Defense Ministry. Upon the government's declaration of a "national emergency," the factories of Ford and General Motors could be immediately converted into production of war material, as was the case during World War II. In 1977 South Africa issued a contingency planning report stating that General Motors South Africa, Ltd., together with other United States firms, had been designated as "National Key Points," meaning that the companies would be secured in a military emergency by a citizen force commando system, a kind of industrial militia.

American banks have provided support to the White minority regime in two important ways. First, through loans, they have buttressed the apartheid economy in periods of severe economic and political instability. As noted, Chase Manhattan and First National City (now Citibank) participated in the $150 million loan that counteracted the outflow of foreign capital after Sharpeville. From 1974 to 1976, and after the Soweto uprising, a number of American bank loans similarly reinforced the economy. Second, these loans have often been extended to South African parastatals, or state corporations directly under the control of the apartheid government. For instance, the Citicorp International Bank (a division of Citicorp, the holding company which owns Citibank) managed a $100 million loan to the government-owned Iron and Steel Corporation (ISCOR) in 1974, and two years later Citibank, Morgan Guaranty Trust, and the First National Bank of Chicago loaned $100 million directly to the government.[49]

Citibank affirmed in 1978 that it had made no new loans to South Africa in more than a year. Instead, the bank said it was limiting its credit selectively to certain private sectors. However, Citicorp acknowledged that loan money is fungible; that is, loans made to South Africa for one sector make possible the release of capital from that sector for use in another. For risk reasons, the bank placed a moratorium on lending to the South African government, but said it would resume lending if the risks decreased. Citicorp also refused to extend its temporary moratorium on loans to the South African government to include all forms of financing, including loans through subsidiaries, trade-related credits, and interbank lending.

Chase Manhattan, which had no subsidiary in South Africa, similarly disclaimed making any new loans to the South African government. However, Chase maintained 20 percent ownership of London's Orion Bank,[50] which did make loans to South Africa. Therefore, despite Chase's ban on loans to the South African government and its parastatals, some of Chase's capital undoubtedly reached Pretoria via interbank lending. That is why a United Nations report concluded that many banks involved in lending to South Africa still remain hidden.[51]

Several major American banks have joined Citicorp and Chase in declaring policies against new loans to the South African government. These policy reversals resulted from widespread public protests in the United States, especially among Blacks and college students, as well as from United Nations pressures.[52] Technically, the banks have maintained the prohibition on new loans; however, the larger banks, such as Citicorp, have refused to deny loans either to the private sector or to the financing of trade. Accordingly, the large banks have resorted to correspondent relationships or arrangements by which two banks (usually from different countries) agree mutually to provide services and credit facilities under conditions that do not involve direct ownership.

In the computer industry, South Africa has depended on U.S. data processing equipment because it does not have any major computer manufacturers. During the 1970s American companies controlled nearly 70 percent of the computer market in South Africa. A single American company, IBM, controlled 25 to 30 percent of the South African market, making IBM South Africa's biggest supplier and servicer of computers. Perhaps most indicative of IBM's orientation toward the apartheid regime was its decision in 1965 to bid in a contract to computerize the pass law system. IBM failed to obtain the contract, but the company's attempt to obtain it revealed an unmistakable policy. As explained by IBM Vice-President Gilbert Jones in 1976: "If you are going to go in South

Africa, it is our feeling that you have to sell to the South African government. . . . It is beyond me to believe that the South African government is going to buy your computers and allow you to stay in South Africa if you don't deal with the government."[53]

General Electric, the prototype of the heavy engineering and high technology firm, supplied and serviced equipment for ISCOR, the core of South Africa's iron and steel industry. Pretoria envisioned this industry as the foundation of its industrial and military self-sufficiency. General Electric and the Kennecott Copper Corporation also became involved in the implementation of apartheid; for instance, South Africa GE operated a small company located in Bophuthatswana, a bantustan created in conformity with South Africa's policy for Black segregation, while Kennecott retained majority ownership in a company established near Kwa-Zulu bantustan in an area that the Zulu people had inhabited until their expulsion to make way for the company.

By no means has the orientation of American companies toward apartheid been monolithic. On the contrary, in statements of their official positions, the corporations have covered a wide spectrum ranging from virtual approval to complete rejection of apartheid. At one extreme are the companies which have consistently refused to endorse the Sullivan Principles, the fair employment guidelines introduced in 1977 by Reverend Leon H. Sullivan, the Black board member of General Motors. These companies, which amounted to an estimated 164 (out of the total of 350 American companies in South Africa), manifested at least an acceptance of the apartheid system by their failure to sign the Principles.[54] At the other extreme are companies that have issued statements opposing apartheid, such as the Polaroid Corporation, which declared in 1977: "Polaroid has established a policy against selling to the South African government because it abhors that country's policy of apartheid."[55] Most American companies, however, have adopted positions between these two poles to justify a continuation of their operations in South Africa. Among the companies against apartheid, very few have imitated Polaroid in taking their opposition seriously enough to withdraw from sales to the government.

Given the favorable orientation toward South Africa of most U.S. corporations, not to mention their substantial investments there, the American firms have become uniquely placed to influence the racist and oppressive system of apartheid. U.S. investments in South Africa, as discussed earlier, have risen to 20 percent of all foreign investments in South Africa, making the United States South Africa's second largest investor. Yet, as revealed in 1977 by the U.S. Senate Subcommittee on African Affairs, the American corporations as a whole "have made no significant impact on either relaxing apartheid or in establishing company policies which would offer a limited but nevertheless important model of multinational responsibility."[56]

Originally, the Sullivan Principles were embraced by many American companies as a definitive step toward establishing ethical and morally responsible policies. The Principles consisted of six guidelines: (1) nonsegregation of the races in all eating, comfort, and work facilities; (2) equal and fair employment practices for all employees; (3) equal pay for all employees doing equal or comparable work for the same period of time; (4) initiation and development of training programs to prepare Blacks for supervisory, administrative, clerical, and technical jobs in substantial numbers; (5) increasing the number of Blacks in management and supervisory positions; and (6) improving the quality of employees' lives outside the work environment in such areas as housing, transportation, schooling, recreation, and health facilities. By the end of 1979, the Principles had been signed by 135 U.S. multinationals, including Ford, IBM, and Kennecott. However, a majority of companies had not signed them.

Endorsed by an initial twelve signatory companies in March 1977, the Sullivan Principles have since been perceived as a significant, though belated solution to the problem of discriminatory treatment and unequal occupational advancement affecting all Black employees in the apartheid economy. Indeed, the State Department went so far as to endorse the guidelines as a potential force for change in South Africa. To be sure, some progress has been made; one cause of the Blacks' walkout at the Ford plant was the anger of a White union over the integration of cafeterias and the union's loss of a variety of fringe benefits, which provoked an accusation from the White workers that Ford's management cosseted the Blacks and capitulated to them. The Arthur D. Little Company, which Sullivan retained to monitor his guidelines, has pointed to the reports of two commissions impaneled by Pretoria, the Wiehahn and Riekert Commissions, which, as hopeful signs of change, recommended modifications of laws and regulations to improve the working and living conditions of Blacks, Coloureds, and Asians. Another sign, also perhaps stimulated by the Sullivan program, was a decision of the Botha government to give Black unions the right to negotiate under South Africa's industrial conciliation law.

However, it is now widely agreed that the Sullivan Principles have not lived up to their expectations, and for numerous reasons. First, the Principles never addressed either bank loans, corporate expansion, sales to the police and the military, or investments in or near the bantustans. Second, the Principles completely overlooked trade union rights for Black unions until public protest in the United States compelled Reverend Sullivan to add them as a rider to his original guidelines. Third, the Principles did not demand political rights for Blacks, or challenge Pretoria's policy of forced migratory labor, or seek to abolish the pass law system. Furthermore, even if all 350 American companies had signed and enforced the Principles, they would have affected as few as 55,671 Black workers,[57] or a mere 1 percent of South Africa's Black labor force of an estimated 4 million. Above all, the Principles failed to challenge the so-called separate development policy by which Whites confined the Black majority to the 13 percent of the land that was devoid of mineral wealth and industrial development. The Sullivan Principles thus emerged as a limited and moderate statement of reforms that produced no fundamental changes in the apartheid system.

At the 1979 stockholders' meeting of General Motors, Reverend Sullivan attempted to defend his program: "The main goal for all our efforts is and must be the ending of the apartheid system . . .

for it is one of the most humiliating, degrading [sic], psychologically destructive instruments of political control . . . in the world today. . . . Whether we like it or not, American companies and other companies may have to leave in time anyway from that country."[58] Sullivan, who now endured increasing criticism by Black American groups and other individuals concerned about American policy toward South Africa, continued as the chief Afro-American apologist of American investments in the apartheid economy. His guidelines were resisted by a majority of U.S. multinationals on one hand, and condemned by Black and other American spokesmen on the other.

In roughly the same period, the South African Council of Churches, claiming to represent nearly half of South Africa's population, adopted a resolution that was decidedly at odds with Reverend Sullivan's program. In July 1978 the Council took the extraordinary and unprecedented initiative of "urging foreign countries and corporations to 'radically revise' their investment policies in South Africa in light of the bolstering effect that foreign investments were said to have had on the dominant position of the ruling White minority."[59] The South African church leaders suggested that if the foreign multinationals could not make the recommended revisions, then they should leave South Africa.

## RESURGENT COLD WAR: THE END OF INDIFFERENCE

"There is nothing to be gained in a debate about whether in the past America has neglected Africa or been insufficiently committed to African goals," Kissinger declared upon his arrival in Lusaka, Zambia, in April 1976, promising an urgent and basic revision in American policy toward Africa.[60] This was the first time he had set foot on the African continent after eight years in office, and the master of American foreign policy represented his new policy as a humanitarian concern for peaceful change in the struggle for Black majority rule and political independence in Rhodesia. Through his "shuttle diplomacy" the Secretary of State attempted to dramatize the concern with junkets between Pretoria and the capitals of independent African nations. However, the purported humanitarianism was discounted by such Black leaders as Nyerere, because racially oppressive conditions had long existed in all of southern Africa—Rhodesia, South Africa, and Namibia—without convincing evidence of American interest in alleviating them.

South Africa, of course, had become the pillar of American relations in the whole of southern Africa. Quite apart from the economic investments there, the United States also retained critical trade relations with Rhodesia, which annually supplied 10 to 20 percent of the chromium needs of American manufacturers. The United States grew very dependent on this trade because it was totally lacking in domestic chromium sources. The only alternatives to Rhodesia were South Africa, which provided about 31 percent of America's chromium, and the Soviet Union, which supplied the remaining 60 percent.[61]

Vital in the production of stainless steel, jet planes, and surgical equipment, chromium was essential to American industry. Until his death in 1970, Charles Engelhard insisted on strengthening American trade relations with Rhodesia, but without drawing attention to his controlling interest in the Eastern Stainless Steel Corporation, which shared a partnership with Oppenheimer's Rand Mines in the production of Rhodesian chrome. Senator Harry F. Byrd, Jr., a Virginia Democrat, successfully sponsored legislation empowering the Nixon Administration to buy chromium from Rhodesia in violation of the United Nations embargo on trade with Rhodesia. Under the threat of possible economic blackmail by the Soviet Union, American leaders preferred to reinforce their commerce with the bastions of White supremacy.

Namibia, which contains some of the world's most profitable base minerals and diamond mines, represents a further dimension of the economic stake the United States has in southern Africa. Regarded in the 1960s as the most important company in the base metal field, the American-owned Tsumeb Corporation took almost a third of Namibia's record mineral output of $63 million in 1961.[62] By 1965 nearly 93 percent of the territory's diamond production was controlled by Consolidated Diamonds of South West Africa, a South African subsidiary of De Beers Consolidated Mines, which was itself a subsidiary of the Anglo-American Corporation of South Africa. Between them, these two companies monopolized corporate investments in Namibia.

South Africa, the dominant investor in Namibia, also ruled it as an apartheid fiefdom. Namibia had originally fallen under South Africa's control in 1920 when the League of Nations entrusted it to Pretoria as a mandate. However, in 1966 the United Nations revoked this status, preparing the way for self-determination of the territory's Black majority of 700,000 who were then dominated by about 90,000 Whites. When, in 1971, the International Court of Justice upheld the U.N.'s legal right to take such action, South Africa rejected the world tribunal's opinion. By the court's judgment and subsequent U.N. decisions, all nations were enjoined to refrain from any act that might imply a recognition of South Africa's incorporation of Namibia, and to discourage their nationals from investing in the territory. American corporations, however, ignored these rulings and entered into commercial complicity with Pretoria. As American investments poured into the territory of Namibia, and Kissinger introduced his humanitarian policy, SWAPO guerrillas saw no reason to relent in their armed struggle for political independence.

Never did Kissinger's humanitarian approach divert attention from the realpolitik interests, or the concrete strategic and ideological stakes, of the United States—namely, the rise of Africa as a critical factor in the cold war. With Soviet bloc penetration into Angola and Mozambique, South Africa's economic and military importance to the United States became an issue of top priority. Although Nigeria was beginning to provide the United States with twice as much trade as South Africa, Washington still perceived the White supremacy state as a pro-Western outpost against Soviet, Cuban, and Chinese incursions in the region because of Pretoria's powerful military capability, including nuclear equipment. South Africa's mineral resources and the Cape Coast route to Middle Eastern oil were regarded as related stakes. Thus, even if the

United States could satisfy American oil needs from domestic sources, which became less and less likely after the 1973–1974 Arab oil boycott, Washington had to act promptly to preserve the economic and defense interests of the Western world alliance. The Soweto upheaval added additional urgency to the revolutionary changes converging in Angola and Mozambique. Already in 1969 Kissinger's National Security Council memorandum (Option 2) had anticipated the cold war prospect in southern Africa by warning that "there is a serious question whether pro-Western leaders of the [B]lack states could continue to justify their stance to their populations if the US officially declared its opposition to current liberation efforts. Radical and communist states would be the beneficiaries."[63] Through its desperate assistance to UNITA and the FNLA, the United States went far beyond a mere declaration of opposition to direct involvement with the forces which ultimately failed to stop the MPLA. Nor could American support to Portugal stave off its defeat in Mozambique. In no time at all, it seemed, the Soviet bloc forces had put capitalism and Western strategic interests on the defensive.

This background explains why the Carter Administration viewed Africa, and especially southern Africa, as areas of unavoidable policy priority. In 1977 what at first appeared as a breakthrough in the long-established policy toward apartheid occurred when Vice-President Walter Mondale, in a Vienna meeting with South African Prime Minister John Vorster, warned that unless Vorster initiated a "progressive transformation" of South Africa's White supremacist policies to allow full political and social equality for the Black majority, the Carter government would be compelled to begin diplomatic steps against Pretoria.[64] Without specifying what the steps would be, Mondale indicated that a new American policy toward South Africa was definitely in progress:

> I do not know what conclusions the South African Government will draw. It is my hope that [the talks] will lead to a reassessment, to a change of course. But I cannot rule out the possibility that the South African Government will not change, that our paths will diverge and our policies come into conflict.[65]

*   *   *

He stunned world opinion on leaving the talks by declaring that the United States favored a "one-man, one-vote" policy in South Africa,[66] advocating, in other words, a fundamental and revolutionary alteration in the political system of the White dictatorship.

Ambassador Young traveled to South Africa recommending social change during the same week that Mondale talked to Vorster. Young, who insisted on the supremacy of the free market system, advised a group of mostly White South African business leaders that they held the key to the change he deemed necessary to forestall the country's economic deterioration: "One of the good things about South Africa is that nobody has anywhere to go and you have no choice but to work it out or fight it out and I hope you work it out."[67] In Johannesburg he urged Black South Africans to seize their rights through American-style civil rights boycotts. Simultaneously, President Carter alluded to South Africa and other oppressive regimes in a defense of his human rights program at Notre Dame University: "We are now free of that inordinate fear of Communism which once led us to embrace any dictator who joined us in our fear."[68] In what consummated the Carter Administration's evidently well-synchronized broadside against apartheid, Mondale expressed his relief over the declared policy change: "I think most Americans feel very good about having come clean on this issue."[69]

Five months later, leaders in the Carter Administration completely reversed themselves, returning to the pro-apartheid position Henry Kissinger had issued in 1969. Not only had the historic opportunity of a basic revision in American policy toward South Africa been lost, the Administration, through its embarrassing volte-face after its momentous promise, was beginning to relegate all Black Africa to virtual insignificance in policy priorities. In an October 1977 interview with the *Rand Daily Mail,* a major South African newspaper, Mondale now stated that "we want a good relationship with South Africa," explaining that the United States had never proposed a plan for change in the apartheid country because Washington did not have one.[70] Ingenuously, the Vice-President contradicted himself: "If there was one central suggestion that I made [at the Vienna meeting], it was that the leaders of the South African Governmen. meet with the legitimate nonwhite leaders of South Africa and develop with them the reforms which made sense to all South Africans."[71] In the context of South Africa's apartheid system, Mondale was keenly aware, as had been Kissinger before him, that any official change would be dictated by the Afrikaner elites in the pursuit of their exclusive self-interests.

In addition to the resurgence of anti-Sovietism in the White House after Brzezinski's viewpoint waxed in influence, the eclipse of Carter's firm anti-apartheid approach resulted from a massive public relations campaign that South Africa had masterminded in the United States. The South Africa Foundation had always spent heavily on pro-apartheid propaganda; for instance, it allocated $112,779 in 1975 to distribute material depicting South Africa as a stable society, profitable for foreign investments and grossly misrepresented by its enemies in the United States.[72] Pretoria annually spent about $1.3 million on propaganda, or what it called official "information," to influence the opinions of American citizens. Through its own agencies, such as the Information Service of South Africa, and through the support of its defenders in Congress, South Africa staged a successful lobby in the United States. No Black African nation attained such influence, and South Africa's lobby is surpassed only by the representatives of nations with powerful followings in the United States, such as Great Britain and Israel.

## PATH TO INFAMY: THE REAGAN POLICIES

The Reagan Administration formulated its evolving policy toward South Africa almost exclusively within the context of American economic and strategic stakes. The fundamental economic stake, of course, consists of the U.S. companies in South Africa which in 1980 made the United States the top trading partner of South Africa for the third year in a row. For the first time, however, the United States led in both exports and imports; this two-way trade was worth about $4.2 billion compared to $3.4 billion in 1979, or an increase of 24 percent. (American exports to South Africa amounted to $2.28 billion, and imports totaled $1.92 billion.) West Germany and Britain followed the United States in volume of trade with South Africa.

The sea route around the Cape of Good Hope was perceived as both an economic and strategic interest because of its access to Middle Eastern petroleum. For Reagan policymakers, the apartheid state seemed to be especially valued as a pro-Western bulwark against Soviet bloc expansion in southern Africa, and welcomed as a potential ally in the Administration's boisterous cold war policy.

When Assistant Secretary of State Crocker visited several African states during April 1981, he attempted to win support for a negotiated Namibian settlement which proposed constitutional guarantees for Namibia's White minority as a precondition of independence. This was America's substitute proposal for the five-nation Western plan that Pretoria had endorsed in 1978 under pressure from the Carter Administration, but rejected as premature on the eve of Reagan's Presidency. The militant cold war orientation of the Republicans portended closer American relations with South Africa.

The Administration's willingness to align with the apartheid dictatorship was confirmed finally in May 1981 by the disclosure of State Department briefing papers affirming Washington's readiness to open a new chapter in bilateral relations in exchange for South Africa's cooperation in combating Soviet influence in southern Africa, notably in Angola, and Pretoria's support for an internationally acceptable solution in Namibia.[73] Not since Kissinger's ill-conceived "tar baby" policy had Washington so heartily embraced the White minority dictatorship.

The new approach ignored the negative impact of such a policy on America's relations with other independent African states. Yet American economic stakes with these countries, amounting to $4.5 billion in direct investments, and annual trade of $13.7 billion by 1980, had grown larger than those with South Africa. By aligning with South Africa, the Reagan Administration indicated the priority of its Africa policy at the risk of alienating the independent

African states. At their OAU summit in 1981, the fifty member-states condemned what they regarded as the Administration's "collusion with the South African racists."[74] Shortly thereafter Washington was again reprimanded when it unilaterally vetoed a U.N. Security Council resolution condemning South Africa's August 1981 invasion of Angola. The United States thereby parted company with its Western allies (France and Britain) to become the only Western power to stand openly with the White supremacists of South Africa.

At home the Administration has seemed unconcerned with the potential domestic reaction to its new approach toward South Africa. Coupled with considerable anti-apartheid sentiment in the universities and in various organizations is Black American alienation because of insensitivity or indifference to the interests and welfare of Black South Africans.

## A POLICY PROPOSAL: THE CASE FOR VOLUNTARY WITHDRAWALS

African resistance to apartheid quickened even as the Reagan team readjusted U.S. policy. Forces of the African National Congress operated underground guerrilla organizations seeking change through armed insurrection. Police stations, banks, and oil refinery and other apartheid facilities were hit by the African insurgents in urban localities once regarded as invulnerable to Black revolt. In the fiercest assault, African saboteurs bombed a Durban power plant in April 1981, compelling hundreds of businesses to close temporarily.

Nearly four thousand young Africans who fled South Africa in the aftermath of the Soweto uprising of 1976 made up the main columns of the paramilitary organization from their exile in neighboring countries like Mozambique. The anti-apartheid resistance has been strengthened by forces of the Pan-Africanist Congress, another underground nationalist movement, which was organized in 1959. The march toward mass upheaval in South Africa has thus begun in earnest, and the prospect of widespread racial confrontation there threatens to involve the United States and the Soviet Union on opposite sides.

What then should be the proper response of U.S. policy under these conditions of approaching revolution in South Africa? The United States is in the strongest position of all the Western powers except Great Britain to influence the White minority along the path of peaceful accommodation with the Black majority. This is so because American governmental and business relations with South Africa are in reality no more than a series of relations with the ruling Whites. The United States might successfully promote what can be termed a policy of voluntary reversals—or actions by the U.S. government and U.S. corporations to unilaterally reverse the existing pattern of political and corporate cooperation with the apartheid state. Washington, for example, could begin by prohibiting the sale of dual-purpose equipment, and eliminating military and intelligence collaboration of all kinds. The corporations, which would be as likely to deal with South Africa under Black-majority rule as under White domination, could phase down operations in such strategic sectors as heavy engineering and the automobile industry.

A policy of voluntary reversals would permit Americans to take the initiative in reducing ties with South Africa before these ties are severed indefinitely by African revolutionaries. Such a policy would also reduce the risk of Soviet-American confrontation in an upheaval where South African Whites are likely to fight to the end to preserve their power and privileges. Unlike the Reagan approach, this policy would place the United States on the side of a country that seems destined to become the most powerful Black nation in the World.

# CONCLUSION

The practice of defining American policy toward Africa in reaction to Soviet strategy has prevailed against all efforts to change it during the two decades from Kennedy to Reagan. Taking root during the Congo civil war, this attitude has become a tradition in U.S. relations with independent African nations, restricting American options almost invariably to issues of competition, if not confrontation, with the Soviet Union. The corollary to anti-Sovietism as the predominant factor in policy formulation has been the predisposition of American policymakers to establish alliances with regimes of personal leadership in response to their pro-Western ideological orientation. The unrepresentative and even undemocratic character of such regimes has not been an insurmountable obstacle to good relations with Washington. Policymakers have thereby discarded the most positive and exemplary features of American national ideals in the pursuit of cold war objectives.

In Africa this approach to foreign policy has minimized America's opportunities for influence. Often it alarms African leaders that the United States is attempting to confine their political choices to the anti-Soviet restrictions Washington has imposed on itself. Africans, however, have their own particular objectives; most states are still in full evolution, combatting adverse legacies of colonialism while seeking to integrate their diverse cultures and people into a modern body politic. They do not accept America's cold war dogma as a determinant of their own policy options, nor do they acknowledge a priori that Soviet foreign policy is both aggressively ambitious and inherently antagonistic. As explained by Stanley Macebuh, a member of the editorial board of Nigeria's *Daily Times,* "it is possible, of course, that Americans are willing to reconcile themselves to playing . . . a secondary role in history [by merely reacting to Soviet initiatives]. But they cannot expect other peoples to accept the same fate voluntarily."[1]

The United States, in other words, is isolating itself in its own ideological vacuum in approaching African states primarily from the standpoint of cold war ideology. American insistence on cold war objectives—in opposition to Africans' priorities of national economic development—has produced needless friction with African states. Because it confines American policymakers to myopic political options in their relations with developing nations, the cold war fixation often motivates the chieftains of American foreign policy to decide, or at least to attempt to decide, the ideological order of the nations which are fundamentally concerned with trade and modernization.

Making decisions from the vantage point of two hundred years of American political and economic development, American policymakers have also ignored the gradual and difficult process of change required to transform a society from agrarian to industrial status. They have ignored, for example, the important fact that even in the United States, it took Black Americans until 1965—189 years after independence—to gain the right to vote as a whole. Because they have dismissed such realities, American leaders have been intolerant and unrealistic in demanding that African nations accede to political principles and institutions more appropriate to contemporary practices of Western Europe or the United States. Policymakers ought to formulate policy from an intense knowledge of their own nation as an evolutionary system as well as from a comprehension of such venerated doctrines as the Declaration of Independence.

Moreover, American policy toward Africa, and indeed toward Third World nations generally, must reconcile itself to the irresistible forces of change, including revolution, which affect all societies. "No taxation without representation," after all, was a call to arms that wreaked upheaval in the American colonies. The failure of U.S. decision-makers to accept such forces in contemporary Africa has frequently stiffened their resolve against all change which could not be supervised. It has even caused them to approach human rights, so critical to America's own political system, with abandon or reluctance. This is why Henry Kissinger concluded: "It has some merit for the United States to stand for its principles; the United States should definitely do so. . . . However, I think that making this a vocal objective of our foreign policy involves great dangers: You run the risk of either showing your impotence or producing revolutions in friendly countries, or both."[2]

African states, of course, have been forging their own destinies by ballots as well as bullets. No nation has had a more violent path to independence than Algeria, whose anticolonial revolution spanned seven and a half years. The Angolans, after wresting control from colonial Portugal, then faced an internal opposition supported by the United States. Nevertheless, both of these revolutionary states became significant trade partners with the United States, despite self-chosen ideologies which do not accord with the preferences of Washington. Algeria used its considerable influence to help the United States in obtaining the release of the American hostages in Iran. The independent policies and ideologies of African states, in short, do not prohibit their relations with the United States, even though the ideological predisposition of Americans may cause them to act to the contrary.

Maturity in U.S. relations with Africa has now become essential because of the increasing decline in American national power, as manifested by its economic, military, and strategic capabilities. Already dependent on Africa for such indispensable minerals as oil and cobalt, the United States is likely to become intensely associated with certain African economies in a matrix of exchanges based on mutual dependence, or interdependence. African nations belong to the emergent new international economic order of resource-rich countries which have fastened on to the resource dependency of industrial nations as instruments of national policy. The fundamental principle of this new order was defined by Algeria's late President Houari Boumedienne: "We say to world capitalism that its methods of dealing with us are rejected. A reasonable solution . . . necessitates that we exercise complete national control over our resources. The question here is not one of socialism but rather of national sovereignty."³ The challenge to American power is therefore both political and economic, and it clearly seeks to reverse the old order of two decades ago when Americans, with 6 percent of the world's population, consumed more than 30 percent of its resources, many imported from African and other Third World countries at prices very favorable to the American consumer.

The age of America's international predominance, often characterized as the *pax americana,* generated a complex of nonmilitary institutions reflecting a single consistent and dominant world view in which laissez-faire economics represented the motor force of American material affluence and power. The institutions, such as the United Nations and the World Bank which arose from that era of American hegemony, survive, but with substantially different content and definition. Three African states, for example, joined other Third World members of the Security Council in 1981 to force a vote on economic sanctions against South Africa, polarizing the Third World members and the Western industrial states such as the United States, France, and Britain, which vetoed the motion. The same developing nations, as former victims of colonialism, are also insisting that the world economic system be changed by redrafting global financial and trading policies to permit transfers of capital from the rich nations to the poor.

Charles de Gaulle foresaw the advent of Soviet power after 1957 as the decisive blow to America's predominance in the world, and he shocked Washington by his dramatic decision to terminate France's military commitment to NATO. He believed that this Western defense system under American leadership had ceased to be an invincible bulwark of Western power in the new bipolar era. As he warned his European allies and neighbors: "For Europeans of the West, NATO can no longer guarantee our existence. And from the moment that the effectiveness of the protection becomes doubtful, why should one entrust his destiny to the protector?"⁴

The new economic order emerging from the Arab oil boycott of 1973–1974 thoroughly invalidated the assumptions on which America's cold war fixation was developed by giving rise to the contemporary multipolar system of Western, East European, and Third World forces. In this new order American power will be tested not only by Soviet military rivalry but also by fresh challenges from the Third World's war of economic resources and demonstrations of political will. The American defeat in Vietnam reinforced the conviction that, despite its arsenals of nuclear warheads and space-age devices, the United States lacked the capacity to hold on to the world which once bowed before American power.

American policymakers have preferred to ignore the advent of the new international order. They have been encouraged by economists who even deny the existence of such an order. Few political leaders have had the insight expressed by Senator Gary Hart in 1979: "We have been through a period of shocks over the past five years since the fall of Saigon, the formation of OPEC, and the oil embargo. Our military supremacy seems to have ended. There's increased nationalism abroad, less fear of the United States—not because we're less potent, but because others are more potent."[5]

The United States will become especially vulnerable to pressure resulting from fuel shortages. Although occasional periods of oil glut on the international market will give the United States temporary respite, petroleum imports will remain essential in the long run. A 1981 study by the Rand Corporation confirmed that the prospects of finding more oil and gas within the United States are severely limited; it postulated that domestic oil supplies may be produced for no more than twenty to forty years, and natural gas for seventeen to twenty-six years, because the nation is simply running out of unexplored places where there is any possibility of finding large amounts of oil.[6] Unless alternative fuel sources are developed soon, and in massive quantities, America's oil dependency will become a central target in the oil-rich countries' war of resources.

To some extent, America's declining power in the world may be offset in the future by such economic problems as food scarcity, overpopulation, and stagnation of the rich countries in Africa as in other regions of the Third World. Wassily Leontief, the Nobel Prize winner in economics, has speculated that the Third World nations may not only suffer negative growth in future years, but that many will be in worse economic condition by the year 2000 than they are today.[7] However, such projections based exclusively or primarily on economic factors overlook the paramount role that politics plays in developing nations. Because of the primacy of politics, some leaders of the mineral-rich states are likely to forgo short-term economic advantage in order to press forward their long-term challenges against the Western powers. This means that such nations as Nigeria and Libya will continue to demand changes in the traditional U.S. approach to Africa.

African nations are now in a process of full social and economic mutation that the post-independence era has accelerated. The mutation is evident in the disintegration of traditional ethnic attachments, rampant urbanization, and the widespread adoption of American and European values and practices, especially among the young, who constitute a dominant if not majority group in many African states. Ideology has also become a great factor of the change, and socialism according to Soviet model remains a powerful source of attraction. American policymakers need to produce policies that are responsive to these African developments. They must accept many Africans' perception of the Soviet Union as a consistent supporter of independence movements but not as an aggressor in Africa.[8]

Since 1960 American policymakers' ignorance and neglect of Africa has gradually yielded to political maturity and awareness. Young African affairs specialists have sometimes found employment in the policymaking institutions, where they have attempted to educate decision-makers on African problems and issues. Problems, however, persist. The approach of interventionism as manifested by the Congo syndrome has not died out entirely; it was revived during the 1980 presidential campaign by candidate Reagan's proposition to provide American weapons to UNITA in its die-hard opposition to the Marxist regime governing Angola. It is also clear that the advocates of interventionism have not learned that the "domino" effect could work against the United States—that is, that destabilization by the United States of such pro-Soviet regimes as

Angola could precipitate instability that might lead to the collapse of such American allies as Zaire.

Ignorance too has not disappeared. At his 1981 confirmation hearing Deputy Secretary of State William P. Clark, whose position makes him the second highest ranking official in the State Department, admitted that he did not even know the names of the Prime Ministers of Zimbabwe and South Africa.

White domination of South Africa remains a major concern of independent African states, and the new international system has enhanced the ability of these states to pull the attention of American policymakers to this problem. Apartheid is commonly perceived as an abhorrent and criminal system that cannot be ameliorated through compromise. Violence is the instrument which the Whites used to establish and maintain apartheid, and it seems destined also to be the instrument for the collapse of apartheid. Through their intransigence, the Whites daily foreclose the possibility of peaceful settlement in Namibia as well as racial accommodation in South Africa. Under these circumstances, it is unlikely that the United States will escape involvement in the prospective cataclysm, or manage to preclude Soviet bloc penetration from the region of conflict. Above all, the African war against apartheid guarantees that the United States will not ignore Africa again.

# Notes

## Chapter 1

1. As quoted in Edgar Lockwood, "The Future of the Carter Policy Toward Southern Africa," in *American Policy in Southern Africa*, ed. Rene Lemarchand (Washington, D.C.: University Press of America, 1978), pp. 435–436.
2. As quoted in Ernest W. Lefever, *Spear and Scepter* (Washington, D.C.: The Brookings Institution, 1970), p. 108.
3. Steven R. Weissman, *American Foreign Policy in the Congo* (Ithaca, N.Y.: Cornell University Press, 1974), p. 28.
4. See the account of Catherine Hoskyns, *The Congo Since Independence* (London: Oxford University Press, 1965), p. 100.
5. See Lefever, *Spear and Scepter*, op. cit., p. 91.
6. See Crawford Young, *Politics in the Congo* (Princeton, N.J.: Princeton University Press, 1965), p. 11.
7. Immanuel Wallerstein, "Africa, the United States, and the World Economy: The Historical Bases of American Policy," in *U.S. Policy Toward Africa*, ed. Frederick S. Arkhurst (New York: Praeger, 1975), p. 30.
8. For a discussion of the origins of the containment policy, see "The Sources of Soviet Conduct," *Foreign Affairs*, July 1947, pp. 566–582. George F. Kennan was the anonymous author "X."

9. For a discussion of massive deterrence and retaliation, see John Spanier, *American Foreign Policy Since World War II* (New York: Praeger, 1973).
10. Nzongola-Ntalaja, "The U.S., Zaire and Angola," in Lemarchand, op. cit., p. 155.
11. For a discussion of the Algerian war of independence and the government-in-exile, see Henry F. Jackson, *The FLN in Algeria* (Westport, Conn: Greenwood Press, 1977), Chapters 2–3.
12. Stephen Weissman, "The CIA and U.S. Policy in Zaire and Angola," in Lemarchand, op. cit., p. 385.
13. As quoted in ibid., p. 385.
14. Weissman, op. cit., p. 34.
15. Rupert Emerson, *Africa and United States Policy* (Englewood Cliffs, N.J.: Prentice-Hall, 1967), p. 63.
16. See Ernest W. Lefever, *Uncertain Mandate* (Baltimore: The Johns Hopkins Press, 1967), p. 21.
17. See Robert Cornevin, *Le Zaire* (Paris: Presses Universitaires de France, 1972), p. 19. Also see Hoskyns, op. cit., pp. 5–8.
18. The Senate Intelligence Committee in 1975 confirmed that the CIA delivered poison in an abortive plot to have Lumumba killed in Kinshasa. See Madeleine G. Kalb, "The C.I.A. and Lumumba," *New York Times Magazine,* August 2, 1981.
19. Vernon McKay, ed., *Africa in the United States* (New York: Macfadden-Bartell, 1967), p. 11.
20. See John F. Kennedy, *The Strategy for Peace* (New York: Harper, 1960), pp. 65–81.
21. As cited in Arthur M. Schlesinger, Jr., *A Thousand Days* (Boston: Houghton Mifflin, 1965), p. 575.
22. Lefever, *Spear and Scepter,* op. cit., p. 106.
23. U.S. Government, *U.S. Overseas Loans and Grants* (Washington, D.C.: U.S. Government Printing Office, 1977), p. 87.
24. Nzongola-Ntalaja, op. cit., p. 157.
25. Robert M. Price, *U.S. Foreign Policy in Sub-Saharan Africa: National Interest and Global Strategy* (Berkeley: Institute of International Studies, University of California, Berkeley, 1978), p. 52.
26. *Wall Street Journal,* June 25, 1980.
27. Crawford Young, "Zaire: The Unending Crisis," *Foreign Affairs,* Fall 1978, p. 173.
28. Ibid., pp. 172–173.

29. Interview with Robert Remole, at his retirement home near Mt. Rainier, Washington, December 23, 1979.
30. U.S., Congress, House, Committee on Interior and Insular Affairs, *Sub-Sahara Africa: Its Role in Critical Mineral Needs of the Western World, A Report Prepared by the Subcommittee on Mines and Mining*, 96th Cong., 2d sess., July 1980, p. 6.
31. Young, "Zaire," op. cit., p. 180.
32. The author gathered material for this chapter during a visit to Zaire during February 1976.
33. Emerson, op. cit., p. 61.

**Chapter 2**

1. U.S., Congress, Senate, Committee on Foreign Relations, *The Nomination of Alexander M. Haig, Jr. To Be Secretary of State*, 97th Cong., 1st sess., 1981, p. 147.
2. Ibid., p. 12.
3. Mohamed A. El-Khawas et al., eds., *The Kissinger Study of Southern Africa* (Westport, Conn.: Lawrence Hill, 1976), p. 105.
4. Henry Kissinger, *The White House Years* (Boston: Little, Brown, 1979), p. 119. Emphasis in original.
5. For the best analysis of the Angolan revolution and the various movements promoting it, see John A. Marcum, *The Angolan Revolution: The Anatomy of an Explosion* (Cambridge: M.I.T. Press, 1969), Vol. I; and *The Angolan Revolution: Exile Politics and Guerrilla Warfare* (Cambridge: M.I.T. Press, 1978), Vol. II.
6. Richard Gibson, *African Liberation Movements* (London: Oxford University Press, 1972), p. 201.
7. Ibid.
8. Basil Davidson, "Recent History of Angola," *Africa South of the Sahara 1980–81* (London: Europa Publications, 1980), p. 142.
9. Ibid.
10. Mario de Andrade et al., *The War in Angola: A Socio-Economic Study* (Dar es Salaam: Tanzania Publishing House, 1975), p. 17.
11. Ibid., p. 20.
12. Marcum, *The Angolan Revolution*, Vol I, op. cit., p. 128.
13. As quoted in Gerald Bender, "Kissinger in Angola: Anatomy of Failure," in *American Policy in Southern Africa*, ed. Rene Lemarchand

(Washington, D.C.: University Press of America, 1978), p. 66.
14. Marcum, *The Angolan Revolution,* Vol. I, op. cit., p. 184.
15. Ibid., p. 273.
16. Jennifer Davis et al., *No One Can Stop the Rain: Angola and the MPLA* (New York: Africa Fund, 1976), p. 2.
17. Ibid., p. 2.
18. Interview with Roger Morris, Santa Fe, New Mexico, June 5, 1980. Also see Morris, *Uncertain Greatness: Henry Kissinger and American Foreign Policy* (New York: Harper & Row, 1977), p. 131.
19. See *Los Angeles Times,* June 15, 1980.
20. See El-Khawas et al., op. cit., pp. 101–116.
21. Morris, op. cit., p. 119.
22. El-Khawas et al., op. cit., p. 105.
23. Bender, op. cit., p. 70.
24. U.S., Congress, Senate, Committee on Foreign Relations, *Angola: Hearings before the Subcommittee on African Affairs,* 94th Cong., 2d sess., p. 56.
25. Ibid., p. 9.
26. As cited in John A. Marcum, "Lessons of Angola," *Foreign Affairs,* April 1976, p. 407.
27. Ibid., p. 411.
28. *West Africa,* July 26, 1976, p. 1061.
29. Ibid.
30. Nathaniel Davis, "The Angola Decision of 1975: A Personal Memoir," *Foreign Affairs,* Fall 1978, p. 110.
31. See ibid.
32. John Stockwell, *In Search of Enemies: A CIA Story* (New York: Norton, 1978), p. 54.
33. Ibid., p. 55.
34. Bender, op. cit., p. 75.
35. Marcum, "Lessons of Angola," op. cit., pp. 411–412.
36. Ibid., p. 413.
37. Stockwell, op. cit., p. 170.
38. Bender, op. cit., p. 90.
39. *Washington Post,* January 12, 1977.
40. Marcum, *The Angolan Revolution,* Vol. II, op. cit., p. 268.
41. See *Washington Post,* February 4, 1976. This figure was given by Pieter W. Botha, South Africa's Minister of Defense at the time.

42. Stockwell, op. cit., p. 223. *Christian Science Monitor,* January 5, 1976, reports that there were about three hundred mercenaries.
43. *Washington Post,* December 12, 1975.
44. As quoted in the *Los Angeles Times,* January 3, 1976.
45. *Angola: Hearings before the Subcommittee on African Affairs,* op. cit., p. 13.
46. *Southern Africa,* April 21, 1978.
47. Ibid.
48. See *New York Times,* July 16, 1978.
49. *New York Times,* November 25, 1975.
50. Stockwell, op. cit., p. 235.
51. *Washington Post,* May 15, 1978.
52. U.S., Congress, House, *Congressional Record,* January 27, 1976, p. 334.
53. As quoted in the *Washington Post,* January 12, 1976.
54. Stockwell, op. cit., p. 91.
55. William M. LeoGrande, *Cuba's Policy in Africa, 1959–1980* (Berkeley, Calif.: Institute of International Studies, 1980), p. 18.
56. U.S., Department of State, the Secretary of State, *Press Conference,* December 23, 1975, p. 3.
57. *Angola: Hearings before the Subcommittee on African Affairs,* op. cit., p. 11.
58. This is the amount provided by Stockwell, op. cit., p. 233.
59. Ibid., p. 10.
60. Ibid.
61. See U.S., Department of State, *Department of State Bulletin,* February 2, 1976, p. 126.
62. *New York Times,* March 17, 1976.
63. As cited in *Africa Report,* May-June 1976, p. 19.
64. Transcript of Young's interview with the *Deutsches Allgemeines Sonntagsblatt,* January 17, 1979.
65. *New York Times Magazine,* December 31, 1978.
66. Zbigniew Brzezinski, *Africa and the Communist World* (Palo Alto, Calif.: Stanford University Press, 1963), p. 5.
67. *Playboy,* February 1981, p. 213.
68. See Douglas L. Wheeler, "It's Time to Recognize Angola," *Christian Science Monitor,* March 23, 1979.
69. Paul E. Tsongas, "Of Angola," *New York Times,* March 28, 1979.
70. See *Los Angeles Times,* February 17, 1977.

71. As quoted in *Southern Africa*, December 1978, p. 4.
72. See *Africa Confidential* (London), July 7, 1978.
73. As quoted in *Washington Post*, June 27, 1978.
74. *New York Times*, June 27, 1980.
75. As quoted in *Southern Africa*, July-August 1980, p. 6.
76. As quoted in *Wall Street Journal*, May 6, 1980.
77. *Africa*, May 1979, p. 63.
78. As quoted in *Africa*, May 1979, p. 62.
79. *Washington Post*, June 5, 1980.
80. See *Washington Post*, December 14, 1978.
81. Statement of Richard M. Moose before the House Foreign Affairs Committee, Subcommittee on Africa, September 30, 1980.
82. *Nomination of Alexander M. Haig, Jr.*, op. cit., p. 147.
83. *New York Times*, February 8, 1981.
84. See *New York Times*, February 2, 1981.
85. As cited in U.S., Congress, House, Committee on International Relations, *United States-Angolan Relations, Hearings before the Subcommittee on Africa*, 95th Cong., 2d sess., May 25, 1978, p. 39.
86. As quoted in *Christian Science Monitor*, June 24, 1980.

## Chapter 3

1. For a review of the Free Officers revolution, see P.J. Vatikiotis, *The Egyptian Army in Politics* (Westport, Conn.: Greenwood Press, 1975).
2. An excellent analysis of the Rogers Plan can be found in William B. Quandt, *Decade of Decisions* (Berkeley: University of California Press, 1977), Chapter 3.
3. Gamal Abdul Nasser, *The Philosophy of the Revolution* (Washington, D.C.: Public Affairs Press, 1956), p. 110.
4. For a study on the cultural integration between North Africa and sub-Saharan Africa, see Cheikh Anta Diop, *The African Origin of Civilization* (New York: Lawrence Hill and Co., 1974). A contemporary account of Egypt's Pharaonic past and Africa as a region for the expression of Egyptian foreign policy is offered by Raphael Israeli, "Sadat Between Arabism and Africanism," *Middle East Review*, Spring 1979, pp. 39–48.
5. For a firsthand account of the Czech arms deal by Nasser's close assistant, see Mohamed Heikal *The Sphinx and the Commissar* (New York: Harper & Row, 1978), p. 57 ff.

6. Ibid., pp. 64–65.
7. See Geoffrey Kemp, "Strategy and Arms Levels, 1945–1967" in *Soviet-American Rivalry in the Middle East,* ed. J. C. Hurewitz (New York: Praeger, 1969), pp. 32–33.
8. *New York Times,* July 27, 1980.
9. For an analysis of Soviet-Egyptian ties after the June 1967 war, see Alvin Z. Rubinstein, *Red Star on the Nile* (Princeton, N.J.: Princeton University Press, 1977).
10. John Waterbury, *Egypt: Burdens of the Past, Options for the Future* (Bloomington: Indiana University Press, 1978), p. 3.
11. Ibid.
12. Raymond William Baker, *Egypt's Uncertain Revolution Under Nasser and Sadat* (Cambridge, Mass.: Harvard University Press, 1978), p. 137.
13. Raphael Israeli, *The Public Diary of President Sadat* (Leiden, Holland: E. J. Brill), Part One, p. 109.
14. Ibid., pp. 29–30.
15. Anwar el-Sadat, *In Search of Identity* (New York: Harper & Row, 1978), p. 296.
16. For a detailed analysis of the factors behind Sadat's decision to go to war, see Raymond L. Brown, *Anwar el-Sadat and the October War* (Santa Monica, Calif.: California Seminar on Arms Control and Foreign Policy, March 1980). For an account of the military campaign, see Waterbury, op. cit., pp. 13–32.
17. Heikal, op. cit., p. 261.
18. Roger Morris, *Uncertain Greatness: Henry Kissinger and American Foreign Policy* (New York: Harper & Row, 1977), p. 252.
19. Sadat, op. cit., p. 291. Dean Rusk, appointed as Secretary of State by President Kennedy, was retained in his post by the Johnson Administration.
20. Morris, op. cit., p. 257.
21. Ibid.
22. See Nasser, op. cit., pp. 109–114.
23. See Nasser, op. cit., p. 109. Emphasis in original. For a review of Nasser's policy toward Africa, see Tareq Y. Ismael, *The U.A.R. in Africa* (Evanston, Ill.: Northwestern University Press, 1971).
24. Morris, op. cit., p. 258.
25. *New York Times,* July 28, 1980.
26. Israeli, *The Public Diary of President Sadat,* op. cit., Part Two, p. 896.

27. As quoted in Baker, op. cit., p. 141.
28. Sadat, op. cit., pp. 330–331.
29. See Fouad Ajami, "The End of Pan-Arabism," *Foreign Affairs,* Winter 1978–1979, p. 356.
30. *New York Times,* January 21, 1980.
31. *New York Times,* July 28, 1980.
32. U.S., General Accounting Office, *U.S. Assistance to Egyptian Agriculture: Slow Progress After Five Years* (Washington, D.C.: Government Printing Office, March 16, 1981), p. i.
33. *An-Nahar Arab Report and Memo* (Beirut), September 1, 1980, p. 5.
34. *New York Times,* April 13, 1980.
35. *New York Times,* October 6, 1980.
36. *An-Nahar Arab Report and Memo,* September 1, 1980.
37. Arab Republic of Egypt, Central Agency for Public Mobilisation and Statistics, *Statistical Yearbook* (Cairo), July 1978, pp. 173–174.
38. *Barron's,* April 4, 1977.
39. *An-Nahar Arab Report and Memo,* June 16, 1980, pp. 6–7.
40. *New York Times,* October 6, 1980.
41. For the history of the Muslim Brotherhood, see Christina Phelps Harris, *Nationalism and Revolution in Egypt: The Role of the Muslim Brotherhood* (London: Mouton, 1964), or the case study by Richard P. Mitchell, *The Society of the Muslim Brothers* (London: Oxford University Press, 1969).
42. Sadat, op. cit., pp. 22–26.
43. *Arab World File* (Beirut), "Egypt-Politics: The Religious Extremist Movements," October 25, 1978, No. 1097, I-EGG.
44. Ibid., November 2, 1977, No. 790, I-67.
45. Ibid.
46. Ibid., "Egypt: The Moslem Brotherhood," October 12, No. 771, I-E 64.
47. The basis of such sales is Annex III of the Camp David Accords: "The Treaty of Peace and Annex III thereto provide for establishing normal economic relations between the Parties. In accordance therewith, it is agreed that such relations will include normal commercial sales of oil by Egypt to Israel." Source: U.S., Department of State, *The Egyptian-Israeli Peace Treaty,* Selected Documents No. 11 (Washington, D.C.: Government Printing Office, April 1979), pp. 19–20. The *New York Times,* November 18, 1980, reported sales of $500 million in late 1980.

48. See also Henry F. Jackson, "Sadat's Perils," *Foreign Policy,* Spring 1981.
49. *Middle East and North Africa* (London: Europa Publications, 1979), p. 312.
50. See *Washington Post,* July 27, 1980.
51. See the *New York Times,* May 23, 1980, or *An-Nahar Arab Report and Memo,* May 26, 1980.
52. *Middle East and North Africa,* op. cit., p. 341.
53. *An-Nahar Arab Report and Memo,* September 22, 1980.
54. See the *New York Times,* November 12, 1980.
55. Sadat, op. cit., p. 302.
56. Ibid., July 27, 1980.
57. See Herman Frederick Eilts, "Improve the Framework," *Foreign Policy,* Winter 1980–1981, pp. 3–20.
58. René Dumont, *False Start in Africa* (New York: Praeger, 1969).

**Chapter 4**

1. For a discussion of slavery's relationship to the economic development of the United States, see Eugene D. Genovese, *The Political Economy of Slavery* (New York: Pantheon, 1967). For an analysis of the indispensability of the slave trade to the industrialization of England, see Eric Williams, *Capitalism and Slavery* (New York: Capricorn, 1966).
2. W. E. B. DuBois, *The Souls of Black Folk* (Greenwich, Conn.: Fawcett, 1968), p. 17.
3. The 1980 census showed that Blacks accounted for 11.7 percent of the total American population of 226.5 million, or 26.5 million people. However, certain deficiencies in the Census Bureau's method of counting Black Americans, such as occasional failure or inability to include all ghetto inhabitants in the count, may mean that the Black population is somewhat larger.
4. Ronald W. Walters, "Africa and African America: the Policy Linkage," Howard University, Washington, D.C., June 1978, p. 1. Mimeograph. Emphasis in original.
5. Nathan Glazer, *Affirmative Discrimination* (New York: Basic Books, 1975), p. 201.
6. As quoted in *Southern Africa,* January 1980, p. 5.
7. Randall Robinson, "Message to the President on the Resignation of

Ambassador Andrew Young and on United States Relations with the Middle East and Africa," *TransAfrica News Report,* Summer 1979.

8. Telephone interview with Randall Robinson, New York, N.Y., January 12, 1979.

9. Richard W. Van Alstyne, *The Rising American Empire* (Chicago: Quadrangle, 1965), p. 9.

10. Lawrence A. Marinelli, *The New Liberia* (London: Pall Mall Press, 1964), p. 30.

11. As quoted in ibid.

12. Alphonso Pinkney, *Red, Black, and Green: Black Nationalism in the United States* (New York: Cambridge University Press, 1976), p. 21.

13. Martin Robinson Delany, *The Condition, Elevation, Emigration and Destiny of the Colored People of the United States* (New York: Arno Press, 1968), pp. 31–32.

14. Pinkney, op. cit., p. 22.

15. Marinelli, op. cit., p. 36.

16. J. Gus Liebenow, *Liberia: the Evolution of Privilege* (Ithaca, N.Y.: Cornell University Press, 1969), p. 15.

17. For a case study, see David Apter, *Ghana in Transition* (New York: Atheneum, 1968).

18. Lillie M. Johnson, "Black American Missionaries in Africa" (Ph.D. diss., University of Chicago, 1980). Johnson's study is the source of much of the historical data in this section.

19. Clarence Clendenen et al., *Americans in Africa 1865–1900* (Stanford, Calif.: The Hoover Institution, 1966). p. 114.

20. For a discussion of the Chilembwe rebellion, see Robert I. Rotberg, ed., *Rebellion in Africa* (London: Oxford University Press, 1971), pp. 133–163.

21. As quoted in Johnson, op. cit.

22. William A. Jones, Jr., "A Theological Basis for Armed Struggle" (Address presented at the Summit Conference of Black Religious Leaders Against Apartheid, New York, N.Y., April 18, 1979).

23. *World Almanac: Book of Facts* (New York: Newspaper Enterprise Associates, 1981), p. 335. The number of Muslims in Africa, according to this source, is about 145 million. The rest of Africa's total population of 469.5 million are Christians or belong to various African religions.

24. As quoted in Pinkney, op. cit., p. 43. For biographical studies of Garvey see Edmund D. Cronon, *Black Moses* (Madison: University of

Wisconsin Press, 1964), and Amy Jacques Garvey, *Garvey and Garveyism* (New York: Collier, 1970).

25. For a good analysis of the great migration see Florette Henri, *Black Migration: Movement North 1900–1920* (New York: Anchor Press, 1975).

26. George M. Frederickson, *White Supremacy* (New York: Oxford University Press, 1980), p. 190.

27. Jack D. Foner, *Blacks and the Military in American History* (New York: Praeger, 1974), pp. 124–125. For an interesting account by a contemporary Black, see Hugh Mulzac, *A Star to Steer By* (New York: International Publishers, 1972), Chap. 6.

28. Foner, ibid., p. 126.

29. Willard B. Gatewood, Jr., *Black Americans and the White Man's Burden* (Chicago: University of Illinois Press, 1975), pp. 7–8.

30. For an examination of Harlem's metamorphosis from a White to a Black community, see Gilbert Osofsky, *Harlem: The Making of a Ghetto*, 1890–1930 (New York: Harper & Row, 1966).

31. Tony Martin, *Race First* (Westport, Conn.: Greenwood Press, 1976), pp. 13–14.

32. Robert W. July, *A History of the African People* (New York: Scribner's, 1970), p. 460.

33. See Arnold Rampersad, *The Art and Imagination of W. E. B. DuBois* (Cambridge, Mass.: Harvard University Press, 1976), p. 289.

34. W. E. B. DuBois, *The World and Africa* (New York: International Publishers, 1967), p. 265.

35. As quoted in Rampersad, op. cit., p. 289.

36. For the analysis of Black Americans as a colony, see Stokely Carmichael and Charles V. Hamilton, *Black Power in America* (New York: Vintage, 1967).

37. Controversy around Robeson concerned his militant drive for racial integration and his later involvement with the Communist party.

38. Hollis R. Lynch, *Black American Radicals and the Liberation of Africa: The Council on African Affairs 1937–1955* (Ithaca, N.Y.: Cornell University Africana Studies and Research Center, 1978), p. 23.

39. As quoted in ibid., p. 28.

40. Ibid., p. 30.

41. As quoted in ibid., p. 17.

42. As quoted in ibid., p. 42.

43. As cited in John Henrik Clarke, ed., *Malcolm X* (New York: Collier, 1969), p. 335.

44. As quoted in Adelaide Cromwell Hill and Martin Kilson, eds., *Apropos of Africa* (London: Frank Cass, 1969), p. 211.
45. Interview with Cecil Washington, Director of Africa Program, Operation Crossroads Africa, New York, N.Y., March 16, 1980.
46. See Julius K. Nyerere, *Ujamma—Essays on Socialism* (Dar es Salaam: Oxford University Press, 1968).
47. Interview with C. Payne Lucas, Executive Director of Africare, Inc., Washington, D.C., March 10, 1980.
48. As quoted in Elizabeth Schmidt, *Decoding Corporate Camouflage: U.S. Business Support of Apartheid* (Washington, D.C.: Institute for Policy Studies, 1980), p. 17.
49. Address delivered at the Summit Conference of Black Religious Leaders Against Apartheid, New York, N.Y., April 19, 1979.
50. E. Franklin Frazier, *Black Bourgeoisie* (London: Collier-Macmillan, 1969).
51. See James W. Ivy, "Traditional NAACP Interests in Africa As Reflected in the Pages of *The Crisis,*" in *Africa Seen by American Negro Scholars* (Distributed by the American Society of African Culture, 1963), pp. 229–246.
52. NAACP, *NAACP Task Force on Africa Report and Recommendations,* New York, 1978, pp. 11–13. Significantly, Chapter 27 encourages the U.S. government "to extend diplomatic recognition to Angola, as well as financial assistance to Mozambique and Angola, both of which were denied U.S. foreign aid for fiscal year 1977." Chapter 28 said the NAACP "should work to insure that U.S. policy in Southern Africa and throughout the continent is motivated and based on genuine support of the legitimate aspirations of African people and not solely to counter communist initiatives or influence." (See p. 19.) These positions contrasted tremendously with the NAACP's major position the year before; under the leadership of the Board of Directors Chairman Margaret Bush Wilson, the civil rights organization ceremoniously issued its "Black position" on energy, which incredibly favored profit guarantees for Exxon and the major oil companies through a price deregulation of oil and natural gas. This position, in Wilson's estimation, prepared the way for an alliance among "big government, big minority and big oil." See the *New York Times Magazine,* July 15, 1979, p. 87.
53. *Black Enterprise,* April 1981. This Black magazine conducts an annual nationwide survey of the leading Black businesses. In its June 1980 issue, it ranked Johnson Products Company in fifth place (with 1979

sales of $35.5 million), Afro-International Corporation in sixth place (with 1979 sales of $32 million), and H. F. Henderson Industries in seventy-seventh place (with 1979 sales of $6.5 million).

54. Jake C. Miller, *The Black Presence in American Foreign Affairs* (Washington, D.C.: University Press of America, 1978), p. 107.

55. Ibid., p. 3.

56. Walters, op. cit. The source cites U.S., Department of State, Office of Equal Opportunity, *Personnel Statistics,* June 1978.

57. Interview with Professor C. Clyde Ferguson, Harvard Law School, Cambridge, Mass., March 18, 1980.

58. *New York Times,* May 2, 1979.

59. *New York Times,* August 20, 1979.

60. *New York Amsterdam News,* November 1, 1980.

61. Interview with Donald F. McHenry, U.S. Deputy Representative to the U.N. Security Council, U.S. Mission to the United Nations, New York, N.Y., October 28, 1978.

62. Transcript of Young's interview with the *Deutsches Allgemeines Sonntagsblatt,* January 17, 1979.

63. Interview with Professor Elliott Skinner, Columbia University, New York, November 5, 1978.

64. A 1980 survey of Data Black Public Opinion Polls (New York) revealed that Black Americans were more favorable toward Jews than other White ethnic groups despite the Black-Jewish conflict that arose over Young's resignation. The survey was the first poll of Data Black, whose chairman was sociologist Kenneth B. Clark. The survey polled 1,146 Black adults.

65. Benjamin L. Hooks, "A Declaration of Independence," Black American Leadership Summit, August 22, 1979.

66. Ibid.

67. Preston Greene, "Lessons of Young's Departure," *New York Times,* August 28, 1979.

68. Preston Greene, "Why Only Whisper?" *New York Times,* July 17, 1978.

69. See Joel Dreyfuss and Charles Lawrence III, *The Bakke Case: Politics of Inequality* (New York: Harcourt Brace Jovanovich, 1979).

70. See Nathan Glazer and Daniel P. Moynihan, *Beyond the Melting Pot* (Cambridge, Mass.: M.I.T. Press, 1973), pp. 143–155.

71. *World Almanac,* op. cit., p. 96.

72. George W. Ball, "The Coming Crisis in Israeli-American Relations,"

*Foreign Affairs,* Winter 1979–1980, p. 233. See also *Conversations with Eric Sevareid* (Washington, D.C.: Public Affairs Press, 1976), interview with George Kennan, p. 95.

73. U.S., Agency for International Development, *U.S. Overseas Loans and Grants—Obligations and Loan Authorizations July 1, 1945–September 30, 1979* (Washington: Government Printing Office, 1979), pp. 4 and 19. Also see p. 119.

74. Harold Cruse, *The Crisis of the Negro Intellectual* (New York: William Morrow, 1967), p. 494.

75. U.S., Department of Commerce, Bureau of the Census, *1977 Survey of Minority-Owned Business Enterprises: Black* (Washington, D.C.: Government Printing Office, December 1979), p. 3. There was a total of 231,203 Black firms; in this group were 39,968 firms with paid employees that accounted for as much as $6 billion; the remainder consisted of firms with unpaid employees, such as mom and pop stores.

76. Joint Center for Political Studies, *National Roster of Black Elected Officials* (Washington, D.C.: Joint Center for Political Studies, 1980), p. 1.

77. The District of Columbia and the U.S. Virgin Islands each send a delegate to the House of Representatives, but neither of these Black members has voting rights because they do not represent state congressional districts. Both members belonged to the Congressional Black Caucus.

78. United States, *Report of the National Advisory Commission on Civil Disorders* (New York: New York Times Company, 1968), p. 1.

79. U.S., Department of Commerce, Bureau of the Census, *The Social and Economic Status of the Black Population in the United States: An Historical View, 1790–1978* (Washington, D.C.: Government Printing Office, 1978), p. x.

80. Louis Harris Associates, *Study of Attitudes Toward Racial and Religious Minorities and Toward Women* (Prepared for the National Conference of Christians and Jews, November 1978). The study showed that 49 percent of Whites believe Blacks have less ambition than Whites; 25 percent believe Blacks have less native intelligence; 36 percent believe Blacks want to live from the handout; 29 percent believe Blacks breed crime. The most glaring example of White ignorance was that only 11 percent of the 1,673 White adults in the survey believed unemployment was the biggest problem facing Blacks.

Black Americans, of course, identified unemployment as their top priority. This is not surprising in a period when adult Black unemployment reached 20 percent in such areas as Harlem (in contrast to the national average of about 8 percent), and Black teenage unemployment topped 40 percent (in contrast to about 18 percent for Whites).

81. Robert S. Browne, "Barriers to Black Participation in the U.S. Economy," *Review of Black Political Economy,* August 1970, pp. 57–67.

82. Martin Weil, "Can the Blacks Do for Africa What the Jews Did for Israel?" *Foreign Policy,* Summer 1974, pp. 109–130.

83. Robinson, "Message to the President on the Resignation of Ambassador Andrew Young and on United States Relations with the Middle East and Africa," op. cit.

84. See Thomas Sowell, *Race and Economics* (New York: McKay, 1975), p. 94. Sowell states that "more than 100,000 Japanese-Americans, most of them native-born citizens of the United States, were rounded up and put into internment camps after Pearl Harbor, many losing property they had worked for years to acquire."

85. William J. Foltz, *Elite Opinion on United States Policy Toward Africa: A Survey of Members of the Council on Foreign Relations and Its Affiliated Regional Committees* (New York: Council on Foreign Relations, 1979).

86. Donald F. McHenry, "Captive of No Group," *Foreign Policy,* Summer 1974, p. 146. Emphasis in the original.

87. See, for example, Carl Gershman, "The Black Plight: A Matter of Class," *New York Times Magazine,* October 5, 1980.

88. In his attempt to build an analytical dichotomy between the Black middle class and low-income or indigent Blacks (the so-called underclass), Wilson concludes that "it would be difficult to argue that the plight of the black underclass is solely a consequence of racial oppression, that is, the explicit and overt efforts of whites to keep blacks subjugated in the same way that it would be difficult to explain the rapid economic improvement of the more privileged blacks by arguing that the traditional forms of racial segregation and discrimination still characterize the labor market in American industries. The recent mobility patterns of blacks lend strong support to the view that economic class is clearly more important than race in predetermining job placement and occupational mobility." See William Julius Wilson, *The Declining Significance of Race* (Chicago: University of Chicago Press, 1978), pp. 151–152.

89. See *Journal of Palestine Studies*, Winter 1981, special issue of Black scholarly opinion on the Palestinian issue.

## Chapter 5

1. As quoted in the *Christian Science Monitor*, August 29, 1980.
2. U.S., Congress, House, Committee on Interior and Insular Affairs, Subcommittee on Mines and Mining, *Sub-Sahara Africa: Its Role in Critical Mineral Needs of the Western World*, 96th Cong., 2d sess., July 1980 (Washington, D.C.: Government Printing Office, 1980), p. vii.
3. U.S., Congress, House, Committee on Foreign Affairs, *U.S. Interests in Africa, Hearings before the Subcommittee on Africa*, 96th Cong., 1st sess., 1979, p. 215.
4. *African Business*, May 1980, p. 43.
5. *Chicago Tribune*, June 1, 1980.
6. *New York Times*, December 31, 1980.
7. Sayre P. Schatz, "Nigeria—Moving Up," *Wilson Quarterly*, Winter 1980, p. 64.
8. Henry F. Jackson, "Third-World Power," *New York Times*, December 27, 1980.
9. *New York Times*, July 21, 1980.
10. Olajide Aluko, "Nigeria, the United States and Southern Africa," *African Affairs*, January 1979, p. 96.
11. *Chicago Tribune*, June 1, 1980. Marathon Oil Company, a small American firm, also participated in Nigerian oil development. See also the *Wall Street Journal*, August 1, 1979.
12. A 20 percent interest was divided among Elf, Agip-Phillips, while Shell and BP shared a 10 percent interest each.
13. See *Business Week*, October 1, 1979.
14. *Daily Times* (Nigeria), March 22, 1978. In this report Alfred A. Adewuyi of the Department of Demography and Social Statistics, University of Ife, estimates the population at 100 million on the basis of the number of registered voters in 1978 (forty-eight million).
15. *African Business and Trade*, June 15, 1980, p. 6.
16. See Jean Herskovits, "Democracy in Nigeria," *Foreign Affairs*, Winter 1979–1980, p. 314.
17. Transcript of speech by Alhaji Shehu Shagari, President of Nigeria, before an assembly of the Foreign Policy Association, New York, N.Y., October 5, 1980.

18. *Wall Street Journal*, October 6, 1980.

19. See *International Herald Tribune*, August 1, 1979.

20. *Rand Daily Mail* (Johannesburg), October 20, 1980.

21. Bureau of Mines, U.S. Department of the Interior, "The Mineral Industry of Libya" (preprint from the 1977 *Bureau of Mines Minerals Yearbook*, Washington, D.C.: Government Printing Office, 1980), p. 3.

22. Profits were divided 51–49 percent between Libya and the U.S. companies.

23. Bureau of Mines, U.S. Department of the Interior, op. cit.

24. As quoted in *Newsweek*, June 18, 1979.

25. *New York Times*, May 8, 1981.

26. See the *Washington Post*, August 9, 1980.

27. Ibid., July 27, 1980.

28. *Christian Science Monitor*, August 8, 1980.

29. See *Barron's*, April 4, 1977.

30. See the *Washington Post*, July 27, 1980.

31. U.S., Department of State, American Embassy, Tripoli, *Foreign Economic Trends and Their Implications for the United States—Libya* (Washington, D.C.: Government Printing Office, January 1979), p. 11.

32. For a study on Algeria's early program of socialism, see Henry F. Jackson, *The FLN in Algeria: Party Development in a Revolutionary Society, 1954–1962* (Westport, Conn.: Greenwood Press, 1977), chaps. 7-8.

33. *New York Times*, April 22, 1980.

34. Gerald J. Bender, "U.S. Policy on Angola," *New York Times*, October 23, 1979. See also Table 2 in this chapter.

35. Subcommittee on Mines and Mining, op. cit., p. vii.

36. As quoted in *Time*, January 21, 1980.

37. Ibid., p. 23.

38. Aims Industry/Defence Group, *The Resource War* (London: AIMS, 1980?), p. 3.

39. U.S., Senate, Committee on Foreign Relations, *Imports of Minerals from South Africa by the United States and the OECD Countries*, 96th Cong., 2d sess., September 1980, p. 3.

40. Subcommittee on Mines and Mining, op. cit., p. vii.

41. *U.S. News & World Report*, May 3, 1978. The source erroneously reports that Africa provided only 23 percent of U.S. imports of chromium. This has been corrected to 48 percent.

42. U.S., Department of the Interior, Bureau of Mines, *Mineral Commodity Summaries 1980* (Washington, D.C.: Government Printing Office, January 1980), p. 96.
43. Ibid., p. 18.
44. U.S., Department of the Interior, Bureau of Mines, *Mineral Industries of Africa* (Washington, D.C.: Government Printing Office, 1976), p. 13.
45. *Africa South of the Sahara* (London: Europa Publications, 1980), p. 766.
46. *African Business and Trade,* June 15, 1980.
47. See the *Christian Science Monitor,* August 21, 1980.
48. Jennifer Seymour Whitaker, ed., *Africa and the United States* (New York: New York University Press, 1978), p. 31.
49. *New York Times,* May 9, 1976.
50. Ibid.
51. Ian Mackler, *Pattern for Profit in Southern Africa* (New York: Atheneum, 1975), p. 44.
52. Ibid.
53. See the *New York Times,* February 6, 1980.
54. Ibid.
55. *U.S. Interests in Africa,* op. cit., p. 253. It should be noted that most African coffee beans are mixed with South American beans in the United States, whereas in Europe the African beans are marketed directly.
56. Ibid., p. 252.
57. Ibid., p. 254.
58. There were an estimated four million refugees in Africa in 1980. See *Africa Report,* January–February 1981.
59. National Strategy Information Center, *A White Paper: The Resource War and the U.S. Business Community* (New York, 1980), p. 18.
60. As quoted in James Arnold Miller et al., eds., *The Resource War in 3-D—Dependency, Diplomacy, Defense* (Pittsburgh: World Affairs Council of Pittsburgh, 1980), p. 88.
61. As quoted in the *New York Times,* December 24, 1980.
62. *U.S. Interests in Africa,* op. cit., p. 254.
63. See Robert L. Paarlberg, "Lessons of the Grain Embargo," *Foreign Affairs,* Fall 1980, pp. 150–151.
64. Ibid., p. 157.
65. U.S., Department of State, *Sub-Sahara Africa and the United States*

(Washington, D.C.: Government Printing Office, March 1980), p. 32.

66. U.S., Agency for International Development, *U.S. Overseas Loans and Grants—Obligations and Loan Authorizations July 1, 1945–September 30, 1979* (Washington, D.C.: Government Printing Office, 1980), p. 19.

## Chapter 6

1. Chester A. Crocker, "The American Dimension of Indian Ocean Policy, *Orbis,* Fall 1976, p. 656.
2. Alvin J. Cottrell and Thomas H. Mooner, *U.S. Overseas Bases: Problems of Projecting American Military Power Abroad* (Beverly Hills, Calif.: Sage, 1977), p. 33.
3. *Wall Street Journal,* August 25, 1980.
4. See the *New York Times,* April 22, 1980.
5. *Washington Post,* February 3, 1981.
6. *Africa News,* July 21, 1980.
7. *Washington Post,* March 4, 1981.
8. As quoted in the *New York Times,* July 5, 1980.
9. As quoted in the *Washington Post,* October 1, 1980.
10. U.S., Central Intelligence Agency, National Foreign Assessment Center, *International Energy Statistical Review* (Washington, D.C.: Government Printing Office, February 1981), p. 5.
11. Transcript of televised interview with Secretary of Defense Caspar Weinberger on "Face the Nation," CBS News, March 8, 1981, pp. 4–5.
12. *Los Angeles Times,* September 13, 1980.
13. See Donald B. Easum, "United States Policy toward South Africa," in *Race and Politics in South Africa,* eds. Ian Robertson and Phillip Whitten (New Brunswick, N.J.: Transaction, 1978), p. 226.
14. Elmo R. Zumwalt, Jr., "Heritage of Weakness: An Assessment of the 1970's," in *National Security in the 1980's: From Weakness to Strength,* ed. W. Scott Thompson (San Francisco: Institute for Contemporary Studies, 1980), p. 30 and p. 35. Zumwalt, a retired Admiral of the U.S. Navy, was Chief of Naval Operations.
15. As cited in the *New York Times,* March 19, 1981.
16. William H. Lewis, "How a Defense Planner Looks at Africa," in *Africa: From Mystery to Maze,* ed. Helen Kitchen (Lexington, Mass.: Lexington, 1976), p. 279.

17. Crocker, op. cit.
18. For a review of this history, see Gardner W. Allen, *Our Navy and the Barbary Corsairs* (Boston: Houghton, 1905).
19. John K. Cooley, "The Libyan Menace," *Foreign Policy*, Spring 1981, p. 77. (Also see his article in the *Washington Post*, March 10, 1981.)
20. *New York Times*, March 1, 1981.
21. As quoted in the *Washington Post*, March 10, 1981.
22. See the *New York Times*, March 1, 1981, and also the *Washington Star*, February 13, 1981.
23. Cooley, op. cit., p. 77.
24. Ibid., p. 90.
25. *New York Times*, March 12, 1981.
26. *New York Times*, March 9, 1981.
27. In Algiers the Polisario proclaimed the formation in early 1976 of the Sahara Arab Democratic Republic, its state-in-exile, which thirty-eight nations worldwide recognized by 1980. Among these were twenty-six members of the OAU, or the majority necessary to approve the de facto government's membership.
28. See U.S., Congress, House, Committee on Foreign Affairs, *U.S. Policy and the Conflict in the Western Sahara, Hearings before the Subcommittee on Africa and International Organizations*, 96th Cong., 1st sess., 1979, pp. 108–109.
29. See U.S., Congress, House, Committee on Foreign Affairs, *Arms for Morocco? U.S. Policy Toward the Conflict in the Western Sahara, Report of a Study Mission to Morocco, the Western Sahara, Mauritania, Algeria, Liberia, Spain, and France*, January 1980, p. 10.
30. *New York Times*, March 26, 1981. The equipment here refers to six OV-10 reconnaissance planes and twenty F-5E aircraft.
31. Ibid.
32. *New York Times*, March 12, 1981.
33. David and Marina Ottaway, *Afrocommunism* (New York: Africana, 1981), p. 174.
34. Ibid., pp. 175–176.
35. Ibid., p. 173.
36. National Strategy Information Center, *The Resource War and the U.S. Business Community* (New York, 1980), p. 14.
37. Colin Legum et al., *Africa in the 1980's: A Continent in Crisis* (New York: McGraw-Hill, 1979), pp. 51–52.
38. As quoted in Maxwell J. Mehlman et al., "United States Restrictions on Exports to South Africa," *American Journal of International Law*,

October 1979, p. 582. The legal aspects of the examination here are largely based on this source.

39. Ibid., p. 583.

40. Mohamed A. El-Khawas et al., eds., *The Kissinger Study of Southern Africa* (Westport, Conn.: Lawrence Hill, 1976), p. 107.

41. Michael T. Klare and Eric Prokosch, "Getting Arms to South Africa," *The Nation,* July 8–15, 1978, p. 50–51.

42. Ibid.

43. As quoted in Mehlman, op. cit., p. 589.

44. James Dingeman, "Covert Operations in Central and Southern Africa," in *U.S. Military Involvement in Southern Africa,* ed. Western Massachusetts Association of Concerned African Scholars (Boston: South End Press, 1978), p. 89.

45. John Stockwell, *In Search of Enemies: A CIA Story* (New York: Norton, 1978), pp. 187–188.

46. Interview with Professor C. Clyde Ferguson, Harvard Law School, Cambridge, Mass., March 18, 1980.

47. Mehlman, op. cit., p. 591n.

48. Michael T. Klare, "Memorandum on Recent Reports of Illegal Arms Deliveries to South Africa and Rhodesia/Zimbabwe," Institute of Policy Studies, Washington, D.C. Also see Representative Howard Wolpe's interrogation of Assistant Secretary of State for African Affairs Richard Moose on the Space Research Corporation in U.S., Congress, House, Committee on Foreign Relations, *U.S. Policy Toward South Africa, Hearings before the Subcommittee on International Economic Policy and Trade and on International Organizations,* 96th Cong., 2d sess., 1980, pp. 25–31.

49. Stockholm International Peace Research Institute (SIPRI), *World Armaments and Disarmament: SIPRI Yearbook 1980* (London: Taylor and Francis, 1980), p. 112.

50. Robert I. Rotberg, *Suffer the Future: Policy Choices in Southern Africa* (Cambridge, Mass.: Harvard University Press, 1980), p. 148.

51. Easum, op. cit., p. 228.

52. Rotberg, op. cit., p. 150.

53. Klare and Prokosch, op. cit., p. 51.

54. SIPRI, op. cit., p. 113.

55. Ibid., p. 111.

56. *New York Times,* March 7, 1981. This figure represented existing (post–Camp David) levels of U.S. assistance to Israel. The total

package of $2.2 billion included $1.4 billion in military credits, of which $500 million involved loans that Israel did not have to repay.

57. SIPRI, op. cit., p. 87.

58. See ibid.

59. Transcript of televised interview, "A Conversation with the President," CBS News Special Report with Correspondent Walter Cronkite, March 3, 1981, p. 8.

60. See the *New York Times,* March 26, 1981.

61. See *The Financial Times* (London), August 27, 1980.

62. Ibid.

63. U.S., Central Intelligence Agency, *National Basic Intelligence Factbook* (Washington, D.C.: Government Printing Office, January 1980), p. 180 and p. 149.

64. See U.S., Arms Control and Disarmament Agency, *World Military Expenditures and Arms Transfers 1968–1977* (Washington, D.C.: Government Printing Office, October 1979), p. 8.

65. See *Daedalus,* Fall 1980 and Winter 1981.

66. U.S., Congress, Senate, Committee on Foreign Relations, *The Nomination of Alexander M. Haig Jr. To Be Secretary of State,* 97th Cong., 1st Sess., p. 12.

## Chapter 7

1. U.S., Congress, Senate, Committee on Foreign Relations, *South Africa—U.S. Policy and the Role of U.S. Corporations, Hearings before the Subcommittee on African Affairs,* 94th Cong., 2d Sess., 1976, p. 103.

2. Gwendolen M. Carter, *American Policy and the Search for Justice and Reconciliation in South Africa* (Racine, Wis.: Johnson Foundation, 1976), p. 3.

3. Mohammed A. El-Khawas et al., eds., *The Kissinger Study of Southern Africa* (Westport, Conn: Lawrence Hill, 1976), p. 119.

4. John Blashill, "The Proper Role of U.S. Corporations in South Africa," *Fortune,* July 1972, p. 49.

5. Eric A. Walker, *A History of Southern Africa* (London: Longmans, 1962), p. 770. For an analysis of Afrikaner domination, see T. Dunbar Moody, *The Rise of Afrikanerdom* (Berkeley: University of California Press, 1975). For a contrary viewpoint, see also Jordan K. Ngubane, *An African Explains Apartheid* (London: Pall Mall, 1963).

6. Pierre van der Berghe, *South Africa: a Study in Conflict* (Berkeley: University of California Press, 1970), p. 75.

7. The Nedbank Group, *South Africa: An Appraisal* (Johannesburg: Nedbank Group Economic Unit, 1977), p. 4.

8. Ibid.

9. As quoted in Barbara Rogers, *Divide and Rule: South Africa's Bantustans* (London: International Defence and Aid Fund, 1976), p. 4.

10. Ibid., p. 15. See also Jeffrey Butler et al., *The Black Homelands of South Africa: The Political and Economic Development of Bophuthatswana and KwaZulu* (Berkeley: University of California Press, 1977).

11. "Tribe" has become a word of considerable pejorative connotation. For a discussion, see Mazi Okoro Ojiaku, "European Tribalism and African Nationalism," *Civilisations* 22, no. 3 (1972): 387–404.

12. As quoted in Alex. Hepple, *South Africa: Workers under Apartheid* (London: Christian Action), p. 16.

13. *New York Times,* November 11, 1979.

14. University of South Africa, Bureau of Market Research, *Survey of Race Relations in South Africa* (Johannesburg, March 1979), p. 159.

15. American Committee on Africa, The Africa Fund, *South Africa Fact Sheet* 1979, p. 1.

16. Foreign Policy Study Foundation, *South Africa: Time Running Out* (Berkeley: University of California Press, 1981), p. 113.

17. John Dugard, *Human Rights and the South African Legal Order* (Princeton, N.J.: Princeton University Press, 1978), p. 76.

18. As quoted in William A. Hance, ed., *Southern Africa and the United States* (New York: Columbia University Press, 1968), p. 113.

19. *New York Times,* November 19, 1979. It could not be determined whether the remaining 20 percent consisted of Whites, Coloureds, Asians or some combination of these racial groups.

20. American Assembly, *The United States and Africa* (New York: Columbia University Press, 1958), p. 20.

21. Hance, op. cit., p. 122.

22. Ibid., p. 123.

23. For an examination of the ANC, see A. P. Walshe, *The Rise of African Nationalism in South Africa: The African National Congress, 1912–1952* (Berkeley: University of California Press, 1971).

24. Edward Feit, *Urban Revolt in South Africa 1960–1964* (Evanston, Ill.: Northwestern University Press, 1971), p. 42.

25. As quoted in Clyde Ferguson and William R. Cotter, "South Africa: What Is to Be Done," *Foreign Affairs,* January 1978, p. 259. Italics in original.

26. U.S. Government, National Security Council, *Briefing for NSC Standing Group*, Annex 5. Document released by Lyndon Baines Johnson Library (under Freedom of Information Act), Austin, Texas, 1979.

27. As quoted in Ferguson and Cotter, op. cit., pp. 258–259.

28. U.S. Government, Department of State, confidential telegram from U.N. Ambassador Adlai Stevenson to the Secretary of State, August 21, 1963; document released by Lyndon Baines Johnson Library, Austin, Texas, 1979.

29. Barbara Rogers, *White Wealth and Black Poverty* (Westport, Conn.: Greenwood Press, 1976), p. 102.

30. Ibid., pp. 102–103.

31. "The Engelhard Touch," *Forbes*, August 1, 1969, p. 23.

32. Ibid., p. 20.

33. Ibid., p. 21.

34. As quoted ibid.

35. After Engelhard died in 1971, Oppenheimer's Anglo-American Corporation gave its shares in Hanrovia to Engelhard's heirs; in return his heirs delivered Anglo-American 30 percent of the stock of Engelhard Minerals and Chemicals, a worldwide minerals trading corporation and fabricator that also belonged to Engelhard. Anglo-American thus became the largest owner of the Engelhard company. Source: *Forbes*, December 15, 1972, p. 30.

36. American Committee on South Africa, Africa Fund, *South Africa Fact Sheet*, 1979.

37. As quoted in *Forbes*, August 1, 1965, p. 21.

38. *The Observer Weekly* (South Africa), December 11, 1966.

39. *Forbes*, August 1, 1969, p. 23.

40. U.S., Congress, Senate, Committee on Foreign Relations, *South Africa*, op. cit., p. 2.

41. Lawrence Litvak et al., *South Africa: Foreign Investment and Apartheid* (Washington: Institute of Policy Studies, 1978), p. 44.

42. Council on Economic Priorities, "Fuelling Apartheid," Publication N8-8, December 4, 1978. Also see Desaix Myers III et al., *U.S. Business in South Africa* (Bloomington: University of Indiana Press, 1980), p. 162.

43. As quoted in Martin Bailey and Bernard Rivers, *Oil Sanctions Against South Africa* (United Nations, Centre Against Apartheid, Department of Political and Security Council Affairs, June 1978), p. 19.

44. Ibid., p. 62.

45. American Committee on Africa, Africa Fund, "Fluor: Building Energy Self-Sufficiency in South Africa," 1979, p. 3.
46. Ibid. This source cites *Federal Campaign Reports:* Robert Jepsen, 1978 (Washington, D.C.), p. 6.
47. Karen Rothmeyer, *U.S. Motor Industry in South Africa* (New York: Africa Fund, January 1979), Introduction.
48. *New York Times,* November 24, 1979.
49. U.S., Congress, Senate, *U.S. Corporate Interests in Africa. Report to the Committee on Foreign Relations, Subcommittee on African Affairs,* 95th Cong., 1st Sess., 1978, pp. 33–34.
50. United Nations, Centre Against Apartheid, Department of Political and Security Council Affairs, *Bank Loans to South Africa* (New York: Corporate Data Exchange, 1978), p. 112.
51. Ibid., p. 5.
52. See George M. Houser, *Ending Bank Loans to South Africa* (United Nations, Centre Against Apartheid, Department of Political and Security Council Affairs, June 1979), p. 2.
53. U.S., Congress, Senate, Committee on Foreign Relations, *South Africa-U.S. Policy and the Role of U.S. Corporations,* op. cit., p. 684.
54. *Third Report on the Signatory Companies to the Sullivan Principles* (Cambridge, Mass.: Arthur D. Little, October 15, 1979), p. 21.
55. *Wall Street Journal,* November 23, 1977.
56. U.S., Congress, Senate, *U.S. Corporate Interests in Africa,* op. cit., p. 13.
57. *Third Report on the Signatory Companies to the Sullivan Principles,* op. cit.
58. General Motors Corporation, *Report on the 71st Annual Meeting of Stockholders,* Detroit, Michigan, May 25, 1979, pp. 193–195.
59. *New York Times,* July 13, 1978.
60. Henry A. Kissinger, "United States Policy on Southern Africa," *The Department of State Bulletin* (Washington, D.C.: Government Printing Office, May 31, 1976), p. 673.
61. Ian Mackler, *Pattern for Profit in Southern Africa* (New York: Atheneum, 1975), p. 44.
62. Ibid., p. 49.
63. El-Khawas, op. cit., pp. 108–109.
64. *New York Times,* May 21, 1977.
65. Ibid.
66. *New York Times,* October 18, 1977.
67. *New York Times,* May 22, 1977.

68. *New York Times,* May 23, 1977.

69. Ibid.

70. *New York Times,* October 18, 1977.

71. Ibid.

72. Barbara Rogers, "Sunny South Africa: A Worldwide Propaganda Machine," *Africa Report,* September–October 1977, p. 7.

73. See the *New York Times,* May 30, 1981.

74. *New York Times,* June 28, 1981.

### Conclusion

1. Stanley Macebuh, "Misreading Opportunities in Africa," *Foreign Policy,* Summer 1979, p. 163.

2. *Trialogue,* Fall 1978, p. 3. Transcript of an interview with Kissinger.

3. As cited in John Waterbury and Ragaei El Mallakh, *The Middle East in the Coming Decade* (New York: McGraw-Hill, 1978), p. 111.

4. Charles de Gaulle, *Memoires d'Espoir* (Paris: Plon, 1970), p. 213. Author's translation.

5. As quoted in *New York Times,* December 2, 1979.

6. *New York Times,* April 12, 1981.

7. Interview with Wassily Leontief, New York University, New York City, April 20, 1981.

8. The Nigerian view of the Soviet presence in Africa has been clarified by President Shehu Shagari: "If the U.S. thinks there is [Soviet aggression in Africa] then [the U.S.] does not understand the situation." See *Nigerian Herald,* March 21, 1981.

# Index